THE
GREATEST
THING IN
THE WORLD
& OTHER WRITINGS

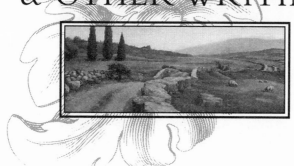

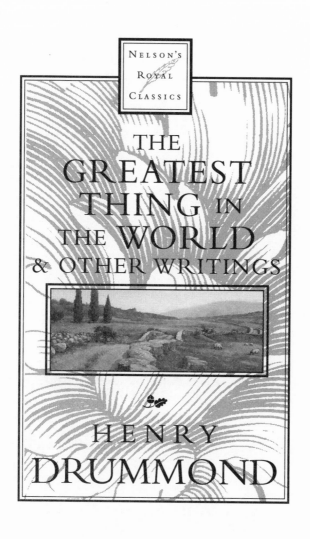

NELSON'S
ROYAL
CLASSICS

THE GREATEST THING IN THE WORLD

& OTHER WRITINGS

HENRY DRUMMOND

THOMAS NELSON PUBLISHERS
Nashville

Library of Congress Cataloging-in-Publication Data

Drummond, Henry, 1851–1897.
   [Selections. 2000]
   The greatest thing in the world and other writings / Henry Drummond.
      p.   cm.—(Nelson's royal classics series)
   ISBN 0-7852-4544-8
   1. Love—Religious aspects—Christianity.   I. Title.   II. Series.
BV4639.D7   2000
241′.1—dc21
                                                     00-056118
                                                     CIP

Printed in the United States of America
1 2 3 4 5 6 7 — 05 04 03 02 01 00

CONTENTS

PUBLISHER'S PREFACE

Since the birth of the Christian church, thousands of writers have examined the teachings of the church and chronicled the experience of faith. Yet only a few of these works stand out as true classics—books that had and continue to have a significant impact on the church and the everyday lives of believers. They describe the core of our beliefs and capture the essence of our Christian experience. They remain an essential part of every Christian's library, and they continue to challenge the way we conceive our faith and our world.

Welcome to Nelson's Royal Classics—our commitment to preserving these treasures and presenting them to a new generation of believers. Every book contains an introduction that will detail the life and faith of the author and define why these works have such an important place in the history of our faith. As you read, you'll find that the timeless wisdom of the writers in this series is not only encouraging and enlightening but also very stimulating. These rich resources will strengthen your spiritual growth and show you ways to grow ever closer to God.

Each volume, such as Sheldon's *In His Steps,* Bunyan's *Pilgrim's Prog-*

ress, or St. Augustine's *Confessions,* is a treasure to be read and cherished. As a series, they become an heirloom library of invaluable worth. Read them now, and share them with others as a way to pass on the heart of Christianity.

HENRY DRUMMOND, 1851–1897

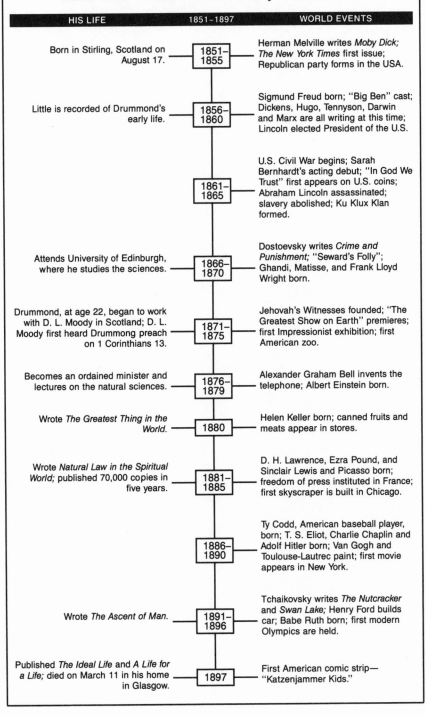

HIS LIFE	1851–1897	WORLD EVENTS
Born in Stirling, Scotland on August 17.	1851–1855	Herman Melville writes *Moby Dick*; *The New York Times* first issue; Republican party forms in the USA.
Little is recorded of Drummond's early life.	1856–1860	Sigmund Freud born; "Big Ben" cast; Dickens, Hugo, Tennyson, Darwin and Marx are all writing at this time; Lincoln elected President of the U.S.
	1861–1865	U.S. Civil War begins; Sarah Bernhardt's acting debut; "In God We Trust" first appears on U.S. coins; Abraham Lincoln assassinated; slavery abolished; Ku Klux Klan formed.
Attends University of Edinburgh, where he studies the sciences.	1866–1870	Dostoevsky writes *Crime and Punishment;* "Seward's Folly"; Ghandi, Matisse, and Frank Lloyd Wright born.
Drummond, at age 22, began to work with D. L. Moody in Scotland; D. L. Moody first heard Drummong preach on 1 Corinthians 13.	1871–1875	Jehovah's Witnesses founded; "The Greatest Show on Earth" premieres; first Impressionist exhibition; first American zoo.
Becomes an ordained minister and lectures on the natural sciences.	1876–1879	Alexander Graham Bell invents the telephone; Albert Einstein born.
Wrote *The Greatest Thing in the World*.	1880	Helen Keller born; canned fruits and meats appear in stores.
Wrote *Natural Law in the Spiritual World;* published 70,000 copies in five years.	1881–1885	D. H. Lawrence, Ezra Pound, and Sinclair Lewis and Picasso born; freedom of press instituted in France; first skyscraper is built in Chicago.
	1886–1890	Ty Codd, American baseball player, born; T. S. Eliot, Charlie Chaplin and Adolf Hitler born; Van Gogh and Toulouse-Lautrec paint; first movie appears in New York.
Wrote *The Ascent of Man*.	1891–1896	Tchaikovsky writes *The Nutcracker* and *Swan Lake;* Henry Ford builds car; Babe Ruth born; first modern Olympics are held.
Published *The Ideal Life* and *A Life for a Life;* died on March 11 in his home in Glasgow.	1897	First American comic strip— "Katzenjammer Kids."

INTRODUCTION

Henry Drummond's influence on his contemporaries is not to be measured by the sale of his books, great as that has been. There was a time when scarcely a week passed in Germany without the publication of a book or pamphlet in which his views were expressed. In Scandinavia, perhaps, no other living Englishman was so widely known. In every part of America his books had an extraordinary circulation. This influence reached all classes. It was strong among scientific men. It penetrated to every section of the Christian Church, and far beyond these limits. Still, when this is said, it remains true that his deepest influence was personal and hidden. In the long series of addresses he delivered all over the world he brought about what may at least be called a crisis in the lives of innumerable hearers.

He received, I venture to say, more of the confidences of people untouched by the ordinary work of the church than any other man of his time. Men and women came to him in their deepest and bitterest perplexities. To such he was accessible, and both by personal interviews and by correspondence, gave such help as he could. He was an ideal confessor. No story of failure daunted or surprised him. For every one he had a message of hope, and, while the warm friend of a chosen circle and acutely responsive to their kindness, he did not seem to lean upon his friends. He himself did not ask for sympathy, and did not seem to need it. The innermost secrets of his life were between himself and his Saviour. While frank and at times even communicative, he had nothing to say about himself or about those who had trusted him. There are multitudes who owed to Henry Drummond all that one man can owe to another, and who felt such a chill pass through them at the news of his death as they can never experience again.

Henry Drummond was born in Stirling, Scotland in 1851. He was surrounded from the first by powerful religious influences of the evangelistic kind. His uncle, Mr. Peter Drummond, was the founder of what is known as the Stirling Tract enterprise, through which many millions of small religious publications have been circulated through the world. As a child he was remarkable for his sunny disposition and his sweet temper, while his religious nature made itself manifest at an early period. In due course he proceeded to the University of Edinburgh, where he distinguished himself in science, but in nothing else. He began to form a library, his first purchase being a volume of extracts from Ruskin's works. Ruskin taught him to see the world as it is, and it soon became a new world to him, full of charm and loveliness. Next to Ruskin he put Emerson, who all his life powerfully affected both his teaching and his style. It was a great secret of his power that he preached nothing except what had personally come home to him and had entered into his heart of hearts.

After completing his University course he went to the New College, Edinburgh, to be trained for the ministry of the Free Church. A crisis was sure to come out of the tensions between the Moderates and the Free Church, and it might very well have been a crisis that would have broken the Church in pieces. That it did not was due largely to the influence of one man—the American Evangelist, Mr. D. L. Moody.

In 1873, Mr. Moody commenced his campaign in the Barclay Free Church, Edinburgh. A few days before, Drummond had read a paper to the Theological Society of his college on Spiritual Diagnosis, in which he maintained that preaching was not the most important thing, but that personal dealing with those in anxiety would yield better results. In other words, he thought that practical religion might be treated as an exact science. Moody at once made a deep impression on Edinburgh, and attracted the ablest students. He missed in this country a sufficient religious provision for young men, and he thought that young men could best be molded by their peers. With his keen American eye he perceived that Drummond was his best instrument, and he immediately associated him in the work.

From the very first Drummond attracted and deeply moved crowds, and for two years he gave himself to this work of evangelism in England, in Scotland, and in Ireland. He made himself a great speaker. He knew how to seize the critical moment, and his modesty, refinement, gentleness, generosity, manliness, and, above all, profound conviction, won for him disciples in every place he visited. When he had completed his studies, after brief intervals of work elsewhere, he found his professional sphere as lecturer on Natural Science in the Free Church College at Glasgow. There he came under the spell of Dr. Marcus Dods, to whom, as he always testified, he owed more than to any other man. He worked in a mission connected with Dr. Dods' congregation, and there preached a series of addresses which were afterwards published as *Natural Law in the Spiritual World*.

His lectureship in Glasgow was constituted into a professor's chair, and he occupied it for the rest of his life. His work gave him considerable freedom. During a few months of the year he lectured on geology and botany, giving also scattered discourses on biological problems and the study of evolution. He gave two examinations each year, the first, which he called the "stupidity" examination, tested the men's knowledge of common things: "Why is grass green?" "Why is the sea salt?" "Why is the heaven blue?" "What is a leaf?" etc. After this Socratic inquiry he began his teaching, and he examined his students at the end.

In his time of leisure he traveled very widely. He paid three visits to America, and one to Australia. He also took a journey to Africa, which he commemorated in a brilliant little book, "Tropical Africa." During these journeys and on other occasions at home he continued his work of evangelism. He addressed himself mainly to students, on whom he had a great influence, and for years went every week to Edinburgh for the purpose of delivering Sunday evening religious addresses to University men. He was invariably followed by crowds, the majority of whom were medical students. He also, on several occasions, delivered addresses in London to social and political leaders, the audience including many of the most eminent men of the time. The substance of these addresses appeared in his famous booklets, beginning with the "Greatest Thing in the World."

Drummond did not begin in the conventional way. He seemed to do without all that is, to most, indispensable. He had, like Emerson, a profound belief in the powers of the human will. His motto might have been: "He who desires to assist other people .... in common conversations will avoid referring to the vices of men, and will take care only sparingly to speak of human impotence, while he will talk largely of human virtue or power, and of the way by which it may be made perfect, so that men being moved, not by fear or aversion, but by the effect of joy, may endeavour, as much as they can, to live under the rule of reason."

Along with this went a passionate devotion to Jesus Christ. Drummond maintained with absolute conviction that Christ could forever and ever meet all the needs of the soul. Drummond asked his hearers to go straight into the presence of Christ, not as He now presents Himself to us bearing in His hand the long roll of His conquests, but as He offered Himself to the Jew by the Sea of Galilee, or in the synagogue of Capernaum, or in the temple of Jerusalem. He denied that the rejection of the nonessential involved parting with the essential, and he strove to go straight to the fountain-head itself. Whatever criticisms may be passed, it will be allowed that few men in the century have done so much to bring their hearers and readers to the feet of Jesus Christ. Drummond believed with his whole heart that men might find power in Christ to change their lives.

He spent very little of his time in his beautiful home at Glasgow. He wandered all over the world and made his way to the hearts of both rich and poor. He had fastidious tastes, was always faultlessly dressed, and could appreciate the surroundings of civilization. But he could at a moment's notice throw them all off and be perfectly happy. He excelled in many sports and was a good shot. Although he refused to quarrel, and had a thoroughly loyal and deeply affectionate nature, he was yet independent of others. He never married. He never undertook any work to which he did not feel himself called. Although he had the most tempting offers from editors nothing would induce him to write unless the subject attracted him, and even then he was unwilling. But everything he published was elaborated with the most scrupulous care. I have never seen manuscripts so carefully revised as his. All he did was apparently done with ease, but there was immense labor behind it.

Although in orders he neither used the title nor the dress that go with them, but preferred to regard himself as a layman. He had a deep sense of the value of the Church and its work, but I think was not himself connected with any Church, and never attended public worship unless he thought the preacher had some message for him. He seemed to be invariably in good spirits, and invariably disengaged. He was always ready for any and every office of friendship. It should be said that, though few men were more criticized or misconceived, he himself never wrote an unkind word about any one, never retaliated, never bore malice, and could do full justice to the abilities and character of his opponents. I have just heard that he exerted himself privately to secure an important appointment for one of his most trenchant critics, and was successful.

With the publication of *The Ascent of Man,* Drummond's career as a public teacher virtually ended. He who had never known an illness, who apparently had been exempted from care and sorrow, was prostrated by a painful and mysterious malady—a chronic affection of the bones. It maimed him greatly. He was laid on his back for more than a year, and had both arms crippled, so that reading was not a pleasure and writing almost impossible. For a long time he suffered acute pain. It was then that some who had greatly misconceived him came to a truer judgement of the man.

Those who had often found the road rough had looked askance at Drummond as a spoiled child of fortune, ignorant of life's real meaning. But when he was struck down in his prime, at the very height of his happiness, it seemed as if his sufferings liberated and revealed the forces of his soul. The spectacle of his long struggle with a mortal disease was something more than impressive. Those who saw him in his illness saw that, as the physical life flickered low, the spiritual energy grew. Always gentle and considerate, he became even more careful, more tender, more thoughtful, more unselfish. He never in any way complained. It was strange and painful, but inspiring, to see his keenness, his mental elasticity, his universal interest. The end came suddenly from a failure of the heart. Those with him received only a few hours' warning of his critical condition. "It was not like death. He lay on his couch in the drawing-room, and passed away in his sleep, with the sun shining in and the birds singing at the open window. There was no sadness nor farewell. It recalled what he himself said of a friend's death—'putting by the well-worn tools without a sigh, and expecting elsewhere better work to do.'"

THE GREATEST THING IN THE WORLD AND OTHER WRITINGS

HENRY DRUMMOND

THE
GREATEST THING
IN THE WORLD

AND OTHER
ADDRESSES

THE GREATEST THING
IN THE WORLD

Though I speak with the tongues of men and of angels, and have not love, I am become as a sounding brass, or a tinkling cymbal. And though I have the gift of prophecy, and understand all mysteries, and all knowledge; and though I have all faith, so that I could remove mountains, and have not Love I am nothing. And though I bestow all my goods to feed the poor, and though I give my body to be burned, and have not Love, it profiteth me nothing.

> *Love suffereth long, and is kind;*
> *Love envieth not;*
> *Love vaunteth not itself, is not puffed up,*
> *Doth not behave itself unseemly,*
> *Seeketh not her own,*
> *Is not easily provoked,*
> *Thinketh no evil;*
> *Rejoiceth not in iniquity, but rejoiceth in the truth;*
> *Beareth all things, believeth all things, hopeth all things,*
> *endureth all things.*

Love never faileth: but whether there be prophecies, they shall fail; whether there be tongues, they shall cease; whether there be knowledge, it shall vanish away. For we know in part, and we prophesy in part. But when that which is perfect is come, then that which is in part shall be done away. When I was a child, I spoke as a child, I understood as a child, I thought as a child: but when I became a man, I put away childish things. For now we see through a glass, darkly; but then face to face: now I know in part; but then shall I know even as also I am known. And now abideth faith, hope, love, these three; but the greatest of these is love.—I Cor. xiii.

CHAPTER ONE

THE CONTRAST

P aul begins by contrasting love with other things that men in those days thought much of. I shall not attempt to go over those things in detail. Their inferiority is already obvious.

He contrasts it with eloquence. And what a noble gift it is, the power of playing upon the souls and wills of men, and rousing them to lofty purposes and holy deeds. Paul says, "If I speak with the tongues of men and of angels, and have not love, I am become as sounding brass, or a tinkling cymbal." And we all know why. We have all felt the brazenness of words without emotion, the hollowness, the unaccountable unpersuasiveness, of eloquence behind which lies no love.

He contrasts it with prophecy. He contrasts it with mysteries. He contrasts with faith. He contrasts it with charity. Why is love greater than faith? Because the end is greater than the means. And why is it greater than charity? Because the whole is greater than the part. love is greater than faith, because the end is greater than the means. What is the use of having faith? It is to connect the soul with God. And what is the object of connecting man with God? That he may become like God. But God is love. Hence Faith, the means, is in order to love, the end. Love, therefore, obviously is greater than faith. It is greater than charity, again, because the whole is greater than a part. Charity is only a little bit of love, one of the innumerable avenues of love, and there may even be, and there is, a great deal of charity without love. It is a very easy thing to toss a copper to a beggar on the street; it is generally an easier thing than not to do it. Yet love is just as often in the withholding. We purchase relief from the sympathetic feelings roused by the spectacle of misery, at the copper's cost. It is too cheap—too cheap for us, and often too dear for the beggar. If we really loved him we would either do more for him, or less.

Then Paul contrasts it with sacrifice and martyrdom. And I beg the little band of would-be missionaries and I have the honor to call some of you by this name for the first time—to remember that though you give your bodies to be burned, and have not love, it profits nothing— nothing! You can take nothing greater to the heathen world than the impress and reflection of the love of God upon your own character. That is the universal language. It will take you years to speak in Chinese, or in the dialects of India. From the day you land, that language of love, understood by all, will be pouring forth its unconscious eloquence. It is the man who is the missionary, it is not his words. His character is his message. In the heart of Africa, among the great lakes, I have come across black men and women who remembered the only white man they ever saw before—David Livingstone; and as you cross his footsteps in that dark continent, men's faces light up as they speak of the kind doctor who passed there years ago. They could not understand him, but they felt the love that beat in his heart. Take into your new sphere of labor, where you also mean to lay down your life, that simple charm, and your lifework must succeed. You can take nothing greater, you need take nothing less. It is not worthwhile going if you take anything less. You may take every accomplishment; you may be braced for every sacrifice; but if you give your body to be burned, and have not love, it will profit you and the cause of Christ nothing.

CHAPTER TWO
THE ANALYSIS

After contrasting love with these things, Paul, in three verses, very short, gives us an amazing analysis of what this supreme thing is. I ask you to look at it. It is a compound thing, he tells us. It is like light. As you have seen a man of science take a beam of light and pass it through a crystal prism, as you have seen it come out on the other side of the prism broken up into its component colors—red, and blue, and yellow, and violet, and orange, and all the colors of the rainbow—so Paul passes this thing, love, through the magnificent prism of his inspired intellect, and it comes out on the other side broken up into its elements. And in these few words we have what one might call the spectrum of love, the analysis of love. Will you observe what its elements are? Will you notice that they have common names; that they are virtues which we hear about every day; that they are things which can be practised by every man in every place in life; and how, by a multitude of small things and ordinary virtues, the supreme thing, the *summum bonum,* is made up?

The spectrum of Love has nine ingredients:—

Patience . . . ."Love suffereth long."
Kindness. . . . ."And is kind."
Generosity . . . ."Love envieth not."
Humility . . . ."Love vaunteth not itself, is not puffed up."
Courtesy . . . ."Doth not behave itself unseemly."
Unselfishness . . . ."Seeketh not her own."
Good Temper . . . ."Is not easily provoked."
Guilelessness . . . ."Thinketh no evil."
Sincerity . . . ."Rejoiceth not in iniquity, but rejoiceth in the truth."

Patience; kindness; generosity; humility; courtesy; unselfishness; good temper; guilelessness; sincerity—these make up the supreme gift, the stature of the perfect man. You will observe that all are in relation to men, in relation to life, in relation to the known today and the near tomorrow, and not to the unknown eternity. We hear much of love to God; Christ spoke much of love to man. We make a great deal of peace with heaven; Christ made much of peace on earth. Religion is not a strange or added thing, but the inspiration of the secular life, the breathing of an eternal spirit through this temporal world. The supreme thing, in short, is not a thing at all, but the giving of a further finish to the multitudinous words and acts which make up the sum of every common day.

There is no time to do more than make a passing note upon each of these ingredients. Love is *patience.* This is the normal attitude of love; love passive, love waiting to begin; not in a hurry; calm; ready to do its work when the summons comes, but meantime wearing the ornament of a meek and quiet spirit. Love suffers long; beareth all things; believeth all things; hopeth all things. For love understands, and therefore waits.

Kindness. Love active. Have you ever noticed how much of Christ's life was spent in doing kind things—in *merely* doing kind things? Run over it with that in view and you will find that He spent a great proportion of His time simply in making people happy, in doing good turns to people. There is only one thing greater than happiness in the world, and that is holiness; and it is not in our keeping; but what God *has* put in our power is the happiness of those about us, and that is largely to be secured by our being kind to them.

"The greatest thing," says someone, "a man can do for his Heavenly Father is to be kind to some of His other children." I wonder why it is that we are not all kinder than we are? How much the world needs it. How easily it is done. How instantaneously it acts. How infallibly it is remembered. How superabundantly it pays itself back—for there is no debtor in the world so honorable, so superbly honorable, as Love. "Love never faileth". Love is success, love is happiness, love is life. "Love, I say," with Browning, "is energy of Life."

> "For life, with all it yields of joy and woe
> And hope and fear,
> Is just our chance o' the prize of learning love—
> How love might be, hath been indeed, and is."

Where love is, God is. He that dwelleth in love dwelleth in God. God is love. Therefore *love*. Without distinction, without calculation, without procrastination, love. Lavish it upon the poor, where it is very easy; especially upon the rich, who often need it most; most of all upon our equals, where it is very difficult, and for whom perhaps we each do least of all. There is a difference between *trying to please* and *giving pleasure*. Give pleasure. Lose no chance of giving pleasure. For that is the ceaseless and anonymous triumph of a truly loving spirit.

"I shall pass through this world but once. Any good thing therefore that I can do, or any kindness that I can show to any human being, let me do it now. Let me not defer it or neglect it, for I shall not pass this way again."

Generosity. "Love envieth not." This is love in competition with others. Whenever you attempt a good work you will find other men doing the same kind of work, and probably doing it better. Envy them not. Envy is a feeling of ill-will to those who are in the same line as ourselves, a spirit of covetousness and detraction. How little Christian work even is a protection against unchristian feeling. That most despicable of all the unworthy moods which cloud a Christian's soul assuredly waits for us on the threshold of every work, unless we are fortified with this grace of magnanimity. Only one thing truly need the Christian envy, the large, rich, generous soul which "envieth not."

And then, after having learned all that, you have to learn this further thing, *Humility*—to put a seal upon your lips and forget what you have done. After you have been kind, after love has stolen forth into the world and done its beautiful work, go back into the shade again and say nothing about it. Love hides even from itself. Love waives even self-satisfaction. "Love vaunteth not itself, is not puffed up."

The fifth ingredient is a somewhat strange one to find in this *summum bonum: courtesy.* This is love in society, love in relation to etiquette. "Love doth not behave itself unseemly." Politeness has been defined as love in trifles. Courtesy is said to be love in little things. And the one secret of politeness is to love. Love cannot behave itself unseemly. You can put the most untutored person into the highest society, and if they have a reservoir of love in their heart, they will not behave themselves unseemly. They simply cannot do it. Carlyle said of Robert Burns that there was no truer gentleman in Europe than the ploughman-poet. It was because he loved everything—the mouse, and the daisy, and all the things, great and small, that God had made. So with this simple passport he could mingle with any society, and enter courts and palaces from his little cottage on the banks of the Ayr. You know the meaning of the word "gentleman." It means a gentle man—a man who does things gently, with love. And that is the whole art and mystery of it. The gentleman cannot in the nature of things do an ungentle, an ungentlemanly thing. The un-gentle soul, the inconsiderate, unsympathetic nature cannot do anything else. "Love doth not behave itself unseemly."

Unselfishness. "Love seeketh not her own." Observe: Seeketh not even that which is her own. In Britain the Englishman is devoted, and rightly, to his rights. But there come times when a man may exercise even the higher right of giving up his rights. Yet Paul does not summon us to give up our rights. Love strikes much deeper. It would have us not seek them at all, ignore them, eliminate the personal element altogether from our calculations. It is not hard to give up our rights. They are often external. The difficult thing is to give up ourselves. The more difficult thing still is not to seek things for ourselves at all. After we have sought them, bought them, won them, deserved them, we have taken the cream off them for ourselves already. Little cross then, perhaps, to give them up. But not to seek them, to look every man not on his own things, but on the things of others—*id opus est.* "Seekest thou great things for thy-self?" said the prophet, *"Seek them not."* Why? Because there is no great-ness in things. Things cannot be great. The only greatness is unselfish love. Even self-denial in itself is nothing, is almost a mistake. Only a great purpose or a mightier love can justify the waste. It is more difficult, I have said, not to seek our own at all, than, having sought it, to give it up. I must take that back. It is only true of a partly selfish heart. Nothing is a hardship to love, and nothing is hard. I believe that Christ's yoke is easy. Christ's "yoke" is just His way of taking life. And I believe it is an easier way than any other. I believe it is a happier way than any other. The most obvious lesson in Christ's teaching is that there is no happiness in having and getting anything, but only in giving. I repeat, *there is no happiness in having or in getting, but only in giving.* And half the world is on the wrong scent in the pursuit of happiness. They think it consists in having and getting, and in being served by others. It consists in giving, and in serving others. He that would be great among you, said Christ, let him serve. He that would be happy, let him remember that there is but one way—it is more blessed, it is more happy, to give than to receive.

The next ingredient is a very remarkable one: *Good Temper.* "Love is not easily provoked." Nothing could be more striking than to find this here. We are inclined to look upon bad temper as a very harmless weakness. We speak of it as a mere infirmity of nature, a family failing, a matter of temperament, not a thing to take into very serious account in estimating a man's character. And yet here, right in the heart of this analysis of love, it finds a place; and the Bible again and again returns to condemn it as one of the most destructive elements in human nature.

The peculiarity of ill temper is that it is the vice of the virtuous. It is often the one blot on an otherwise noble character. You know men who are all but perfect, and women who would be entirely perfect, but for an easily ruffled, quick-tempered, or "touchy" disposition. This compatibility of ill temper with high moral character is one of the strangest and saddest problems of ethics. The truth is there are two great classes of sins—sins of the *body,* and sins of the *disposition.* The prodigal son may be taken as a type of the first, the elder brother of the second. Now society has no doubt whatever as to which of these is the worse. Its brand falls, without a challenge, upon the prodigal. But are we right? We have no balance to weigh one another's sins, and coarser and finer are but human words; but faults in the higher nature may be less venial than those in the lower, and to the eye of Him who is love, a sin against love may seem a hundred times more base. No form of vice—not worldliness, not greed of gold, not drunkenness itself—does more to unchristianize society than evil temper. For embittering life, for breaking up

9

communities, for destroying the most sacred relationships, for devastating homes, for withering up men and women, for taking the bloom off childhood; in short, for sheer gratuitous misery-producing power, this influence stands alone. Look at the elder brother: moral, hard-working, patient, dutiful—let him get all credit for his virtues—look at this man, this baby, sulking outside his own father's door. "He was angry," we read, "and would not go in." Look at the effect upon the father, upon the servants, upon the happiness of the guests. Judge of the effect upon the prodigal—and how many prodigals are kept out of the kingdom of God by the unlovely characters of those who profess to be inside? Analyze, as a study in temper, the thundercloud itself as it gathers upon the elder brother's brow. What is it made of? Jealousy, anger, pride, uncharity, cruelty, self-righteousness, touchiness, doggedness, sullenness—these are the ingredients of this dark and loveless soul. In varying proportions, also, these are the ingredients of all ill temper. Judge if such sins of the disposition are not worse to live in, and for others to live with, than sins of the body. Did Christ indeed not answer the question Himself when He said, "I say unto you, that the publicans and the harlots go into the kingdom of heaven before you." There is really no place in heaven for a disposition like this. A man with such a mood could only make heaven miserable for all the people in it. Except, therefore, such a man be born again, he cannot, he simply cannot, enter the kingdom of heaven. For it is perfectly certain—and you will not misunderstand me—that to enter heaven a man must take it with him.

You will see then why temper is significant. It is not in what it is alone, but in what it reveals. This is why I take the liberty now of speaking of it with such unusual plainness. It is a test for love, a symptom, a revelation of an unloving nature at bottom. It is the intermittent fever which bespeaks unintermittent disease within; the occasional bubble escaping to the surface which betrays some rottenness underneath; a sample of the most hidden products of the soul dropped involuntarily when off one's guard; in a word, the lightning form of a hundred hideous and un-Christian sins. For a want of patience, a want of kindness, a want of generosity, a want of courtesy, a want of unselfishness, are all instantaneously symbolised in one flash of temper.

Hence it is not enough to deal with the temper. We must go to the source, and change the inmost nature, and the angry humors will die away of themselves. Souls are made sweet not by taking the acid fluids out, but by putting something in—a great Love, a new spirit, the Spirit of Christ. Christ, the Spirit of Christ, interpenetrating ours, sweetens, purifies, transforms all. This only can eradicate what is wrong, work a chemical change, renovate and regenerate, and rehabilitate the inner man. Will-power does not change men. Time does not change men. Christ does. Therefore, "Let that mind be in you which was also in Christ Jesus." Some of us have not much time to lose. Remember, once more, that this is a matter of life or death. I cannot help speaking urgently, for myself, for yourselves. "Whoso shall offend one of these little ones, which believe in Me, it were better for him that a millstone were hanged about his neck, and that he were drowned in the depth of the sea." That is to say, it is the deliberate verdict of the Lord Jesus that it is better not to live than not to love. *It is better not to live than not to love.*

Guilelessness and *sincerity* may be dismissed almost with a word. Guilelessness is the grace for suspicious people. And the possession of it is the great secret of personal influence. You will find, if you think for a moment, that the people who influence you are people who believe in you. In an atmosphere of suspicion men shrivel up; but in that atmosphere they expand, and find encouragement and educative fellowship. It is a wonderful thing that here and there in this hard, uncharitable world there should still be left a few rare souls who think no evil. This is the great unworldliness. Love "thinketh no evil," imputes no motive, sees the bright side, puts the best construction on every action. What a delightful state of mind to live in! What a stimulus and benediction even to meet with it for a day! To be trusted is to be saved. And if we try to influence or elevate others, we shall soon see that success is in proportion to their belief of our belief in them. For the respect of another is the first restoration of the self-respect a man has lost; our ideal of what he is becomes to him the hope and pattern of what he may become.

"Love rejoiceth not in iniquity, but rejoiceth in the truth." I have called this *sincerity* from the words rendered in the Authorized Version by "rejoiceth in the truth." And, certainly, were this the real translation, nothing could be more just. For he who loves will love Truth not less than men. He will rejoice in the Truth—rejoice not in what he has been taught to believe; not in this church's doctrine or in that; not in this ism or in that ism; but "in *the Truth*." He will accept only what is real; he will strive to get at facts; he will search for Truth with a humble and unbiased mind, and cherish whatever he finds at any sacrifice. But the more literal translation of the Revised Version calls for just such a sacrifice for truth's sake here. For what Paul really meant is, as we there read,

11

"Rejoiceth not in unrighteousness, but rejoiceth with the truth," a quality which probably no one English word—and certainly not *sincerity*—adequately defines. It includes, perhaps more strictly, the self-restraint which refuses to make capital out of others' faults; the charity which delights not in exposing the weakness of others, but "covereth all things"; the sincerity of purpose which endeavors to see things as they are, and rejoices to find them better than suspicion feared or calumny denounced.

So much for the analysis of love. Now the business of our lives is to have these things fitted into our characters. That is the supreme work to which we need to address ourselves in this world, to learn love. Is life not full of opportunities for learning love? Every man and woman every day has a thousand of them. The world is not a play-ground; it is a schoolroom. Life is not a holiday, but an education. And the one eternal lesson for us all is *how better we can love*. What makes a man a good cricketer? Practice. What makes a man a good artist, a good sculptor, a good musician? Practice. What makes a man a good linguist, a good stenographer? Practice. What makes a man a good man? Practice. Nothing else. There is nothing capricious about religion. We do not get the soul in different ways, under different laws, from those in which we get the body and the mind. If a man does not exercise his arm he develops no biceps, and if a man does not exercise his soul, he acquires no muscle in his soul, no strength of character, no vigor of moral fiber, nor beauty of spiritual growth. Love is not a thing of enthusiastic emotion. It is a rich, strong, manly, vigorous expression of the whole round Christian character—the Christlike nature in its fullest development. And the constituents of this great character are only to be built up by ceaseless practice.

What was Christ doing in the carpenter's shop? Practising. Though perfect, we read that He *learned* obedience, He *increased* in wisdom and in favor with God and man. Do not quarrel therefore with your lot in life. Do not complain of its never-ceasing cares, its petty environment, the vexations you have to stand, the small and sordid souls you have to live and work with. Above all, do not resent temptation; do not be perplexed because it seems to thicken round you more and more, and ceases neither for effort nor for agony nor prayer. That is the practice which God appoints you; and it is having its work in making you patient, and humble, and generous, and unselfish, and kind, and courteous. Do not grudge the hand that is molding the still too shapeless image within you. It is growing more beautiful though you see it not, and every touch of temptation may add to its perfection. Therefore keep in the midst of life. Do not isolate yourself. Be among men, and among things, and among troubles, and difficulties, and obstacles. You remember Goethe's words: *Es bildet ein Talent sich in der Stille, Doch ein Character in dem Strom der Welt.* "Talent develops itself in solitude; character in the stream of life." Talent develops itself in solitude—the talent of prayer, of faith, of meditation, of seeing the unseen; Character grows in the stream of the world's life. That chiefly is where men are to learn love.

How? Now, how? To make it easier, I have named a few of the elements of love. But these are only elements. Love itself can never be defined. Light is a something more than the sum of its ingredients—a glowing, dazzling, tremulous ether. And love is something more than all its elements—a palpitating, quivering, sensitive, living thing. By synthesis of all the colors, men can make whiteness, they cannot make light. By synthesis of all the virtues, men can make virtue, they cannot make love. How then are we to have this transcendent living whole conveyed into our souls? We brace our wills to secure it. We try to copy those who have it. We lay down rules about it. We watch. We pray. But these things alone will not bring Love into our nature. Love is an *effect*. And only as we fulfill the right condition can we have the effect produced. Shall I tell you what the *cause* is?

If you turn to the Revised Version of the First Epistle of John you will find these words: "We love, because He first loved us." "We love," not "We love *Him*." That is the way the old version has it, and it is quite wrong. "We *love*—because He first loved us." Look at that word "because." It is the cause of which I have spoken. "Because He first loved us," the effect follows that we love, we love Him, we love all men. We cannot help it. Because He loved us, we love, we love everybody. Our heart is slowly changed. Contemplate the love of Christ, and you will love. Stand before that mirror, reflect Christ's character, and you will be changed into the same image from tenderness to tenderness. There is no other way. You cannot love to order. You can only look at the lovely object, and fall in love with it, and grow into likeness to it. And so look at this Perfect Character, this Perfect Life. Look at the great sacrifice as He laid down Himself, all through life, and upon the cross of Calvary; and you must love Him. And loving Him, you must become like Him. Love begets love. It is a process of induction. Put a piece of iron in the presence of a magnetized body, and that piece of iron for a time becomes magnetized. It is charged with an attractive force in the mere presence of the original force, and as long as you leave the two side by side, they are both magnets alike. Remain side by side with Him who loved us, and gave Himself for us, and you too will become a centre of power, a permanently attractive force; and like Him you will draw all men unto you, like Him you will be drawn unto all men. That is the inevitable effect of love. Any man who fulfills that cause must have that effect produced in him. Try to give up the idea that religion comes to us by chance, or by mystery, or by caprice. It comes to us by natural law, or by supernatural law, for all law is divine. Edward Irving went to see a dying boy once, and when he entered the room he just put his hand on the sufferer's head, and said, "My boy, God loves you," and went away. And the boy started from his bed, and called out to the people in the house, "God loves me! God loves me!" It changed that boy. The sense that God loved him overpowered him, melted him down, and began the creating of a new heart in him. And that is how the love of God melts down the unlovely heart in man, and begets in him the new creature, who is patient and humble and gentle and unselfish. And there is no other way to get it. There is no mystery about it. We love others, we love everybody, we love our enemies, because He first loved us.

CHAPTER THREE
THE DEFENCE

Now I have a closing sentence or two to add about Paul's reason for singling out love as the supreme possession. It is a very remarkable reason. In a single word it is this: *it lasts*. "Love," urges Paul, "never faileth." Then he begins again one of his marvelous lists of the great things of the day, and exposes them one by one. He runs over the things that men thought were going to last, and shows that they are all fleeting, temporary, passing away.

"Whether there be prophecies, they shall fail." It was the mother's ambition for her boy in those days that he should become a prophet. For hundreds of years God had never spoken by means of any prophet, and at that time the prophet was greater than the king. Men waited wistfully for another messenger to come, and hung upon his lips when he appeared as upon the very voice of God. Paul says, "Whether there be prophecies, they shall fail." This Book is full of prophecies. One by one they have "failed"; that is, having been fulfilled their work is finished; they have nothing more to do now in the world except to feed a devout man's faith.

Then Paul talks about tongues. That was another thing that was greatly coveted. "Whether there be tongues, they shall cease." As we all know, many, many centuries have passed since tongues have been known in this world. They have ceased. Take it in any sense you like. Take it, for illustration merely, as languages in general—a sense which was not in Paul's mind at all, and which though it cannot give us the specific lesson will point the general truth. Consider the words in which these chapters were written—Greek. It has gone. Take the Latin—the other great tongue of those days. It ceased long ago. Look at the Indian language. It is ceasing. The language of Wales, of Ireland, of the Scottish Highlands is dying before our eyes. The most popular book in the English tongue at the present time, except the Bible, is one of Dickens's works, his *Pickwick Papers*. It is largely written in the language of London streetlife; and experts assure us that in fifty years it will be unintelligible to the average English reader.

Then Paul goes farther, and with even greater boldness adds, "Whether there be knowledge, it shall vanish away." The wisdom of the ancients, where is it? It is wholly gone. A schoolboy today knows more than Sir Isaac Newton knew. His knowledge has vanished away. You put yesterday's newspaper in the fire. Its knowledge has vanished away. You buy the old editions of the great encyclopaedias for a few pence. Their knowledge has vanished away. Look how the coach has been superseded by the use of steam. Look how electricity has superseded that, and swept a hundred almost new inventions into oblivion. One of the greatest living authorities, Sir William Thomson, said the other day, "The steam-engine is passing away." "Whether there be knowledge, it shall vanish away." At every workshop you will see, in the back yard, a heap of old iron, a few wheels, a few levers, a few cranks, broken and eaten with rust. Twenty years ago that was the pride of the city. Men flocked in from the country to see the great invention; now it is superseded, its day is done. And all the boasted science and philosophy of this day will soon be old. But yesterday, in the University of Edinburgh, the greatest figure in the faculty was Sir James Simpson, the discoverer of chloroform. The other day his successor and nephew, Professor Simpson, was asked by the librarian of the University to go to the library and pick out the books on his subject that were no longer needed. And his reply to the librarian was this: "Take every textbook that is more than ten years old, and put it down in the cellar." Sir James Simpson was a great authority only a few years ago: men came from all parts of the earth to consult him; and almost the whole teaching of that time is consigned by the science of today to oblivion. And in every branch of science it is the same. "Now we know in part. We see through a glass darkly."

Can you tell me anything that is going to last? Many things Paul did not condescend to name. He did not mention money, fortune, fame; but he picked out the great things of his time, the things the best men thought had something in them, and brushed them peremptorily aside. Paul had no charge against these things in themselves. All he said about them was that they would not last. They were great things, but not supreme things. There were things beyond them. What we are stretches past what we do, beyond what we possess. Many things that men denounce as sins are not sins; but they are temporary. And that is a favorite argument of the New Testament. John says of the world, not that it is wrong, but simply that it "passeth away." There is a great deal in the world that is delightful and beautiful; there is a great deal in it that is great and engrossing; but it will not last. All that is in the world, the lust of the eye, the lust of the flesh, and the pride of life, are but for a little while. Love not the world therefore. Nothing that it contains is worth the life and consecration of an immortal soul. The immortal soul must give itself to something that is immortal. And the only immortal things are these: "Now abideth faith, hope, love, but the greatest of these is love."

Some think the time may come when two of these three things will also pass away—faith into sight, hope into fruition. Paul does not say so. We know but little now about the conditions of the life that is to come. But what is certain is that love must last. God, the Eternal God, is love. Covet therefore that everlasting gift, that one thing which it is certain is going to stand, that one coinage which will be current in the universe when all the other coinages of all the nations of the world shall be useless and dishonored. You will give yourselves to many things; give yourselves first to love. Hold things in their proportion. *Hold things in their proportion.* Let at least the first great object of our lives be to achieve the character defended in these words, the character,—and it is the character of Christ—which is built around love.

I have said this thing is eternal. Did you ever notice how continually John associates love and faith with eternal life? I was not told when I was a boy that "God so loved the world that He gave His only begotten

Son, that whosoever believeth in Him should have everlasting life." What I was told, I remember, was, that God so loved the world that, if I trusted in Him, I was to have a thing called peace, or I was to have rest, or I was to have joy, or I was to have safety. But I had to find out for myself that whosoever trusteth in Him—that is, whosoever loveth Him, for trust is only the avenue to love—hath everlasting *life*. The gospel offers a man life. Never offer men a thimbleful of gospel. Do not offer them merely joy, or merely peace, or merely rest, or merely safety; tell them how Christ came to give men a more abundant life than they have, a life abundant in love, and therefore abundant in salvation for themselves, and large in enterprise for the alleviation and redemption of the world. Then only can the gospel take hold of the whole of a man, body, soul, and spirit, and give to each part of his nature its exercise and reward. Many of the current gospels are addressed only to a part of man's nature. They offer peace, not life; faith, not love; justification, not regeneration. And men slip back again from such religion because it has never really held them. Their nature was not all in it. It offered no deeper and gladder life-current than the life that was lived before. Surely it stands to reason that only a fuller love can compete with the love of the world.

To love abundantly is to live abundantly, and to love forever is to live forever. Hence, eternal life is inextricably bound up with love. We want to live forever for the same reason that we want to live tomorrow. Why do you want to live tomorrow? It is because there is someone who loves you, and whom you want to see tomorrow, and be with, and love back. There is no other reason why we should live on than that we love and are beloved. It is when a man has no one to love him that he commits suicide. So long as he has friends, those who love him and whom he loves, he will live; because to live is to love. Be it but the love of a dog, it will keep him in life; but let that go and he has no contact with life, no reason to live. The "energy of life" has failed. Eternal life also is to know God, and God is love. This is Christ's own definition. Ponder it. "This is life eternal, that they might know Thee the only true God, and Jesus Christ whom Thou hast sent." Love must be eternal. It is what God is. On the last analysis, then, love is life. Love never faileth, and life never faileth, so long as there is love. That is the philosophy of what Paul is showing us; the reason why in the nature of things love should be the supreme thing—because it is going to last; because in the nature of things it is an eternal life. That life is a thing that we are living now, not that we get when we die. We shall have a poor chance of getting it when we die unless we are living now. No worse fate can befall a man in this world than to live and grow old alone, unloving, and unloved. To be lost is to live in an unregenerate condition, loveless and unloved; and to be saved is to love; and he that dwelleth in love dwelleth already in God. For God is love.

Now I have all but finished. How many of you will join me in reading this chapter once a week for the next three months? A man did that once and it changed his whole life. Will you do it? It is for the greatest thing in the world. You might begin by reading it every day, especially the verses which describe the perfect character. "Love suffereth long, and is kind; love envieth not; love vaunteth not itself." Get these ingredients into your life. Then everything that you do is eternal. It is worth doing. It is worth giving time to. No man can become a saint in his sleep. To fulfill the condition required demands a certain amount of prayer and meditation and time, just as improvement in any direction, bodily or mental, requires preparation and care. Address yourselves to that one thing; at any cost have this transcendent character exchanged for yours. You will find as you look back upon your life that the moments that stand out, the moments when you have really lived, are the moments when you have done things in a spirit of love. As memory scans the past, above and beyond all the transitory pleasures of life, there leap forward those supreme hours when you have been enabled to do unnoticed kindnesses to those round about you, things too trifling to speak about, but which you feel have entered into your eternal life. I have seen almost all the beautiful things God has made; I have enjoyed almost every pleasure that He has planned for man; yet as I look back I see standing out above all the life that has gone four or five short experiences when the love of God reflected itself in some poor imitation, some small act of love of mine, and these seem to be the things which alone of all one's life abide. Everything else in all our lives is transitory. Every other good is visionary. But the acts of love which no man knows about, or can ever know about—they never fail.

In the Book of Matthew, where the Judgment Day is depicted for us in the imagery of One seated upon a throne and dividing the sheep from the goats, the test of a man then is not, "How have I believed?" but "How have I loved?" The test of religion, the final test of religion, is not religiousness, but love. I say the final test of religion at that great Day is not religiousness, but love; not what I have done, not what I have believed, not what I have achieved, but how I have discharged the common charities of life. Sins of commission in that awful indictment are not even referred to. By what we have not done, *by sins of omission,* we are judged. It could not be otherwise. For the withholding of love is the negation of the Spirit of Christ, the proof that we never knew Him, that for us He lived in vain. It means that He suggested nothing in all our thoughts, that He inspired nothing in all our lives, that we were not once near enough to Him to be seized with the spell of His compassion for the world. It means that—

"I lived for myself, I thought for myself,
For myself, and none beside—
Just as if Jesus had never lived,
As if He had never died."

It is the Son of *Man* before whom the nations of the world shall be gathered. It is in the presence of *humanity* that we shall be charged. And the spectacle itself, the mere sight of it, will silently judge each one. Those will be there whom we have met and helped; or there, the unpitied multitude whom we neglected or despised. No other witness need be summoned. No other charge than lovelessness shall be preferred. Be not deceived. The words which all of us shall one day hear, sound not of theology but of life, not of churches and saints but of the hungry and the poor, not of creeds and doctrines but of shelter and clothing, not of Bibles and prayer-books but of cups of cold water in the name of Christ. Thank God the Christianity of today is coming nearer the world's need. Live to help that on. Thank God men know better, by a hairsbreadth, what religion is, what God is, who Christ is, where Christ is. Who is Christ? He who fed the hungry, clothed the naked, visited the sick. And where is Christ? Where?—whosoever shall receive a little child in My name receiveth Me. And who are Christ's? Everyone that loveth is born of God.

I CORINTHIANS 13

A Modern NKJV *Translation*

Though I speak with the tongues of men and of angels, but have not love, I have become sounding brass or a clanging cymbal. And though I have the gift of prophecy, and understand all mysteries and all knowledge, and though I have all faith, so that I could remove mountains, but have not love, I am nothing. And though I bestow all my goods to feed the poor, and though I give my body to be burned, but have not love, it profits me nothing.

Love suffers long and is kind; love does not envy; love does not parade itself, is not puffed up; does not behave rudely, does not seek its own, is not provoked, thinks no evil; does not rejoice in iniquity, but rejoices in truth; bears all things, believes all things, hopes all things, endures all things. Love never fails.

But whether there are prophecies, they will fail; whether there are tongues, they will cease; whether there is knowledge, it will vanish away. For we know in part and prophecy in part. But when that which is perfect has come, then that which is in part will be done away.

When I was a child, I spoke as a child, I understood as a child, I thought as a child; but when I became a man, I put away childish things.

For now we see in a mirror, dimly, but then face to face. Now I know in part, but then I shall know just as I also am known.

And now abide faith, hope, love, these three; but the greatest of these is love.

THE PROGRAM OF CHRISTIANITY

To Preach Good Tidings unto the Meek:
To Bind up the Broken-hearted:
To proclaim Liberty to the Captives and the Opening of the Prison to
*   Them that are Bound:*
To Proclaim the Acceptable Year of the Lord, and the Day of Vengeance
*   of our God:*
To Comfort all that Mourn:
To Appoint unto them that Mourn in Zion:
To Give unto them—
Beauty for Ashes,
The Oil of Joy for Mourning,
The Garment of Praise for the Spirit of Heaviness.

CHAPTER ONE
THE FOUNDING OF THE SOCIETY

I t is a somewhat startling thought—it will not be misunderstood—
that Christ probably did not save many people while He was here.
Many an evangelist, in that direction, has done much more. He
never intended to finish the world single-handed, but announced from
the first that others would not only take part, but do "greater things"
than He. For amazing as the attention was that He was able to give to
individuals, this was not the whole aim He had in view. His immediate

work was to enlist men in His enterprise, to rally them into a great company or society for the carrying out of His plans.

The name by which this society was known was *The Kingdom of God*. Christ did not coin this name; it was an old expression, and good men had always hoped and prayed that some such society would be born in their midst. But it was never either defined or set going in earnest until Christ made its realization the passion of His life.

How keenly He felt regarding His task, how enthusiastically He set about it—every page of His life bears witness. All reformers have one or two great words which they use incessantly, and by mere reiteration imbibed indelibly in the thought and history of their time. Christ's great word was the kingdom of God. Of all the words of His that have come down to us this is by far the commonest. One hundred times it occurs in the Gospels. When He preached He had almost always this for a text. His sermons were explanations of the aims of His society, of the different things it was like, of whom its membership consisted, what they were to do or to be, or not do or not be. And even when He does not actually use the word, it is easy to see that all He said and did had reference to this. Philosophers talk about thinking in categories—the mind living, as it were, in a particular room with its own special furniture, pictures, and viewpoints, these giving a consistent direction and color to all that is there thought or expressed. It was in the category of the kingdom that Christ's thought moved. Though one time He said He came to save the lost, or at another time to give men life, or to do His Father's will, these were all included among the objects of His society.

No one can ever know what Christianity is till he has grasped this leading thought in the mind of Christ. Peter and Paul have many wonderful and necessary things to tell us about what Christ was and did, but we are looking now at what Christ's own thought was. Do not think this is a mere modern theory. These are His own life-plans taken from His own lips. Do not allow any isolated text, even though it seems to sum up for you the Christian life, to keep you from trying to understand Christ's program as a whole. The perspective of Christ's teaching is not everything, but without it everything will be distorted and untrue. There is much good in a verse, but often much evil. To see some small soul pirouetting throughout life on a single text, and judging all the world because it cannot find a partner, is not a Christian sight. Christianity does not grudge such souls their comfort. What it grudges is that they make Christ's kingdom uninhabitable to thoughtful minds. Be sure that whenever the religion of Christ appears small, or forbidding, or narrow, or inhuman, you are dealing not with the whole—which is a matchless moral symmetry—nor even with an arch or column—for every detail is perfect—but with some cold stone removed from its place and suggesting nothing of the glorious structure from which it came.

Tens of thousands of persons who are familiar with religious truths have not noticed yet that Christ ever founded a society at all. The reason is partly that people have read texts instead of reading their Bible, partly that they have studied theology instead of studying Christianity, and partly because of the noiselessness and invisibility of the kingdom of God itself. Nothing truer was ever said of this kingdom than that "It cometh without observation." Its first discovery, therefore, comes to the Christian with all the force of a revelation. The sense of belonging to such a society transforms life. It is the difference between being a solitary knight tilting single-handed, and often defeated, at whatever enemy one chances to meet on one's little acre of life, and the *feel* of belonging to a mighty army marching throughout all time to a certain victory. This note of universality given to even the humblest work we do, this sense of comradeship, this link with history, this thought of a definite campaign, this promise of success, is the possession of every obscurest unit in the kingdom of God.

CHAPTER TWO
THE PROGRAM OF THE SOCIETY

Hundreds of years before Christ's Society was formed, its Programme had been issued to the world. I cannot think of any scene in history more dramatic than when Jesus entered the church in Nazareth and read it to the people. Not that when He appropriated to Himself that venerable fragment from Isaiah He was uttering a manifesto or announcing His formal program. Christ never did things formally. We think of the words, as He probably thought of them, not in their old-world historical significance, nor as a full expression of His future aims, but as a summary of great moral facts now and always to be realized in the world since he appeared.

Remember as you read the words to what grim reality they refer. Recall what Christ's problem really was, what His society was founded for. This program deals with a real world. Think of it as you read—not of the surface-world, but of the world as it is, as it sins and weeps, and curses and suffers and sends up its long cry to God. Limit it if you like to the world around your door, but think of it—of the city and the hospital and the dungeon and the graveyard, of the sweating-shop and the pawn-shop and the drink-shop; think of the cold, the cruelty, the fever, the famine, the ugliness, the loneliness, the pain. And then try to keep down the lump in your throat as you take up His program and read—

TO BIND UP THE BROKEN-HEARTED:
TO PROCLAIM LIBERTY TO THE CAPTIVES:
TO COMFORT ALL THAT MOURN:
TO GIVE UNTO THEM—
BEAUTY FOR ASHES,
THE OIL OF JOY FOR MOURNING,
THE GARMENT OF PRAISE FOR THE SPIRIT OF HEAVINESS.

What an exchange—beauty for ashes, joy for mourning, liberty for chains! No marvel "the eyes of all them that were in the synagogue were fastened on Him" as He read; or that they "wondered at the gracious words which proceeded out of His lips." Only one man in that congregation, only one man in the world today could hear these accents with dismay—the man, the culprit, who has said hard words of Christ.

We are all familiar with the protest "Of course"—as if there were no other alternative to a person of culture—"Of course I am not a Christian, but I always speak *respectfully* of Christianity." Respectfully of Christianity! No remark fills one's soul with such sadness. One can understand a man as he reads these words being stricken speechless; one can see the soul within him rise to a white heat as each fresh benediction falls upon his ear and drives him, a half-mad enthusiast, to bear them to the world. But in what school has he learned of Christ who offers the Savior of the world his respect?

Men repudiate Christ's religion because they think it a small and limited thing, a scheme with no large human interests to commend it to this great social age. I ask you to note that there is not one burning interest of the human race which is not represented here. What are the great words of Christianity according to this program? Take as specimens these:

LIBERTY,
COMFORT,
BEAUTY,
JOY.

These are among the greatest words of life. Give them their due extension, the significance which Christ undoubtedly saw in them and which Christianity undoubtedly yields, and there is almost no great want or interest of mankind which they do not cover.

These are not only the greatest words of life but they are the best. This program, to those who have misread Christianity, is a series of surprises. Observe the most prominent note in it. It is *gladness*. Its first word is "good-tidings," its last is "joy." The saddest words of life are also there—but there as the diseases which Christianity comes to cure. No life that is occupied with such an enterprise could be other than radiant. The contribution of Christianity to the joy of living, perhaps even more to the joy of *thinking*, is unspeakable. The joyful life is the life of the larger mission, the disinterested life, the life of the overflow from self, the "more abundant life" which comes from following Christ. And the joy of thinking is the larger thinking, the thinking of the man who holds in his hand some program for humanity. The Christian is the only man who has any program at all—any program either for the world or for himself. Goethe, Byron, Carlyle taught humanity much, but they had no program for it. Byron's thinking was suffering; Carlyle's despair. Christianity alone exults. The belief in the universe as moral, the inter- pretation of history as progress, the faith in good as eternal, in evil as self-consuming, in humanity as evolving—these Christian ideas have transformed the malady of thought into a bounding hope. It was no sentiment but a conviction matured amid calamity and submitted to the tests of life that inspired the great modern poet of optimism to proclaim:—

"Gladness be with Thee, Helper of the world!
I think this is the authentic sign and seal
Of Godship, that it ever waxes glad,
And more glad, until gladness blossoms, bursts

Into a rage to suffer for mankind
And recommence at sorrow."

But that is not all. Man's greatest needs are often very homely. And it is almost as much in its fearless recognition of the commonplace woes of life, and its deliberate offerings to minor needs, that the claims of Christianity to be a religion for humanity stand. Look, for instance, at the closing sentence of this program. Who would have expected to find among the special objects of Christ's solicitude the *spirit of heaviness?* Supreme needs, many and varied, had been already dealt with on this program; many applicants had been met; the list is about to close. Suddenly the writer remembers the nameless malady of the poor—that mysterious disease which the rich share but cannot alleviate, which is too subtle for doctors, too incurable for parliaments, too unpicturesque for philanthropy, too common even for sympathy. Can Christ meet that?

If Christianity could even deal with the world's depression, could cure mere dull spirits, it would be the Physician of humanity. But it can. It has the secret, a hundred secrets, for the lifting of the world's gloom. It cannot immediately remove the physiological causes of dullness— though obedience to its principles can do an infinity to prevent them, and its inspirations can do even more to lift the mind above them. But where the causes are moral or mental or social the remedy is in every Christian's hand. Think of anyone at this moment whom the spirit of heaviness haunts. You think of a certain old woman. But you know for a fact that you can cure her. You did so, perfectly, only a week ago. A mere visit, and a little present, or the visit without any present, set her up for seven long days, and seven long nights. The machinery of the kingdom is very simple and very silent, and the most silent parts do most, and we all believe so little in the medicines of Christ that we do not know what ripples of healing are set in motion when we simply smile on one another. Christianity wants nothing so much in the world as sunny people, and the old are hungrier for love than for bread, and the Oil of Joy is very cheap, and if you can help the poor on with a garment of praise, it will be better for them than blankets.

Or perhaps you know someone else who is dull—not an old woman this time, but a very rich and important man. But you also know perfectly what makes him dull. It is either his riches or his importance. Christianity can cure either of these though you may not be the person to apply the cure—at a single hearing. Or here is a third case, one of your own servants. It is a case of *monotony.* Prescribe more variety, leisure, recreation—anything to relieve the wearing strain. A fourth case—your most honored guest: condition—leisure, health, accomplishments, means; disease—spiritual obesity; treatment—talent to be put out to usury. And so on down the whole range of life's dejection and *ennui.*

Perhaps you tell me this is not Christianity at all; that everybody could do that. The curious thing is that everybody does not. Good-will to men came into the world with Christ, and wherever that is found, in Christian or heathen land, there Christ is, and there His Spirit works. And if you say that the chief end of Christianity is not the world's happiness, I agree; it was never meant to be; but the strange fact is that, without making it its chief end, it wholly and infallibly, and quite universally, leads to it. Hence the note of joy, though not the highest on Christ's program, is a loud and ringing note, and none who serve in His Society can be long without its music. Time was when a Christian used to apologize for being happy. But the day has always been when he ought to apologize for being miserable.

Christianity, you will observe, really works. And it succeeds not only because it is divine, but because it is so very human—because it is common-sense. Why should the garment of praise destroy the spirit of heaviness? Because an old woman cannot sing and cry at the same moment.

The society of Christ is a sane society. Its methods are rational. The principle in the old woman's case is simply that one emotion destroys another. Christianity works, as a railway man would say, with points. It switches souls from valley lines to mountain lines, not stemming the currents of life but diverting them. In the rich man's case the principle of cure is different, but it is again principle, not necromancy. His spirit of heaviness is caused, like any other heaviness, by the earth's attraction. Take away the earth and you take away the attraction. But if Christianity can do anything it can take away the earth. By the wider extension of horizon which it gives, by the new standard of values, by the mere setting of life's small pomps and interests and admirations in the light of the eternal, it dissipates the world with a breath. All that tends to abolish worldliness tends to abolish unrest, and hence, in the rush of modern life, one far-reaching good of all even commonplace Christian preaching, all Christian literature, all which holds the world doggedly to the idea of a God and a future life, and reminds mankind of infinity and eternity.

Side by side with these influences, yet taking the world at a wholly different angle, works another great Christian force. How many opponents of religion are aware that one of the specific objects of Christ's society is beauty? The charge of vulgarity against Christianity is an old one. If it means that Christianity deals with the ruder elements in human nature, it is true, and that is its glory. But if it means that it has no respect for the finer qualities, the charge is baseless. For Christianity not only encourages whatsoever things are lovely, but wars against that whole theory of life which would exclude them. It prescribes aestheticism. It proscribes asceticism. And for those who preach to Christians that in these enlightened days they must raise the masses by giving them noble sculptures and beautiful paintings and music and public parks, the answer is that these things are all already being given, and given daily, and with an increasing sense of their importance, by the society of Christ. Take away from the world the beautiful things which have not come from Christ and you will make it poorer scarcely at all. Take away from modern cities the paintings, the monuments, the music for the people, the museums and the parks which are not the gifts of Christian men and Christian municipalities, and in ninety cases out of a hundred you will leave them unbereft of so much as a well-shaped lamp-post.

It is impossible to doubt that the Decorator of the World shall not continue to serve to His later children, and in ever finer forms, the inspirations of beautiful things. More fearlessly than he has ever done, the Christian of modern life will use the noble spiritual leverages of art. That this world, the people's world, is a bleak and ugly world, we do not forget; it is ever with us. But we esteem too little the mission of beautiful things in haunting the mind with higher thoughts and begetting the mood which leads to God. Physical beauty makes moral beauty. Loveliness does more than destroy ugliness; it destroys matter. A mere touch of it in a room, in a street, even on a door knocker, is a spiritual force. Ask the working-man's wife, and she will tell you there is a moral effect even in a clean tablecloth. If a barrel-organ in a slum can but drown a curse, let no Christian silence it. The mere light and color of the wall-advertisements are a gift of God to the poor man's somber world.

One Christmastime a poor drunkard told me that he had gone out the night before to take his usual chance of the temptations of the street. Close to his door, at a shop window, an angel—so he said—arrested him. It was a large Christmas card, a glorious white thing with tinsel wings, and as it glittered in the gas-light it flashed into his soul a sudden thought of heaven. It recalled the earlier heaven of his infancy, and he thought of his mother in the distant glen, and how it would please her if she got this Christmas angel from her prodigal. With money already pledged to the devil he bought the angel, and with it a new soul and future for himself. That was a real angel. For that day as I saw its tinsel pinions shine in his squalid room, I knew what Christ's angels were. They are all beautiful things, which daily in common homes are bearing up heavy souls to God.

But do not misunderstand me. This angel was made of pasteboard: a pasteboard angel can never save a soul. Tinsel reflects the sun, but warms nothing. Our program must go deeper. Beauty may arrest the drunkard, but it cannot cure him.

It is here that Christianity asserts itself with a supreme individuality. It is here that it parts company with civilization, with politics, with all secular schemes of social reform. In its diagnosis of human nature, it finds that which most other systems ignore; which, if they see, they cannot cure; which, left undestroyed, makes every reform futile, and every inspiration vain. That thing is *sin*. Christianity, of all other philanthropies, recognizes that man's devouring need is *liberty*—liberty to stop sinning; to leave the prison of his passions, and shake off the fetters of his past. To surround *captives* with statues and pictures, to offer *Them-that-are-Bound* a higher wage or a cleaner street or a few more cubic feet of air per head, is solemn trifling. It is a cleaner soul they want; a purer air, or any air at all, for their higher selves.

And where the cleaner soul is to come from apart from Christ I cannot tell. "By no political alchemy," Herbert Spencer tells us, "can you get golden conduct out of leaden instincts." The power to set the heart right, to renew the springs of action, comes from Christ. The sense of the infinite worth of the single soul, and the recoverableness of man at his worst, are the gifts of Christ. The freedom from guilt, the forgiveness of sins, come from Christ's cross; the hope of immortality springs from Christ's grave. We believe in the gospel of better laws and an improved environment; we hold the religion of Christ to be a social religion; we magnify and call Christian the work of reformers, statesmen, philanthropists, educators, inventors, sanitary officers, and all who directly or remotely aid, abet, or further the higher progress of mankind; but in Him alone, in the fullness of that word, do we see the Saviour of the world.

30

There are earnest and gifted lives today at work among the poor whose lips at least will not name the name of Christ. I speak of them with respect; their shoe-latchets many of us are not worthy to unloose. But because the creed of the neighboring mission-hall is a travesty of religion they refuse to acknowledge the power of the living Christ to stop man's sin, of the dying Christ to forgive it. O, narrowness of breadth! Because there are ignorant doctors, do I yet rail at medicine or start a hospital of my own? Because the poor raw evangelist, or the narrow ecclesiastic, offer their little all to the poor, shall I repudiate all they do not know of Christ because of the little that they do know? Of gospels for the poor which have not some theory, state it how you will, of personal conversion one cannot have much hope. Personal conversion means for life a personal religion, a personal trust in God, a personal debt to Christ, a personal dedication to His cause. These, brought about how you will, are supreme things to aim at, supreme losses if they are missed. Sanctification will come to masses only as it comes to individual men; to work with Christ's program and ignore Christ is to utilize the sun's light without its energy.

But this is not the only point at which the uniqueness of this society appears. There is yet another depth in humanity which no other system even attempts to sound. We live in a world not only of sin but of sorrow—

> "There is no flock, however watched and tended,
> But one dead lamb is there;
> There is no home, howe'er defended,
> But has one vacant chair."

When the flock thins, and the chair empties, who is to be near to heal? At that moment the gospels of the world are on trial. In the presence of death how will they act? Act! They are blotted out of existence. Philosophy, politics, reforms are no more. The picture galleries close. The sculptures hide. The committees disperse. There is crape on the door; the world withdraws. Observe, *it withdraws*. It has no mission.

So awful in its loneliness was this hour that the Romans paid a professional class to step in with its mummeries and try to fill it. But that is Christ's own hour. Next to righteousness the greatest word of Christianity is Comfort. Christianity has almost a monopoly of Comfort. Renan was never nearer the mark than when he spoke of the Bible as "the great Book of the consolation of humanity." Christ's program is full of comfort, studded with comfort: "to bind up the broken-hearted, to comfort all that mourn, to give unto them that mourn in Zion." Even the "good tidings" to the "meek" are, in the Hebrew, a message to the "afflicted" or "the poor." The word gospel itself comes down through the Greek from this very passage, so that whatever else Christ's gospel means, it is first an evangel for suffering men.

One note in this program jars with all the rest. When Christ read from Isaiah that day He never finished the passage. A terrible word, Vengeance, yawned like a precipice across His path; and in the middle of a sentence "He closed the Book, and gave it again to the minister, and sat down". A day of vengeance from our God—these were the words before which Christ paused. When the prophet proclaimed it some great historical fulfilment was in his mind. Had the people to whom Christ read been able to understand its ethical equivalents He would probably have read on. For, so understood, instead of filling the mind with fear, the thought of this dread day inspires it with a solemn gratitude. The work of the Avenger is a necessity. It is part of God's philanthropy.

For I have but touched the surface in speaking of the sorrow of the world as if it came from people dying. It comes from people living. Before ever the Broken-Hearted can be healed a hundred greater causes of suffering than death must be destroyed. Before the Captive can be free a vaster prison than his own sins must be demolished. There are hells on earth into which no breath of heaven can ever come; these must be swept away. There are social soils in which only unrighteousness can flourish; these must be broken up.

And that is the work of the day of vengeance. When is that day? It is now. Who is the avenger? Law. What law? Criminal law, sanitary law, social law, natural law. Wherever the poor are trodden upon or tread upon one another; wherever the air is poison and the water foul; wherever want stares, and vice reigns, and rags rot—there the Avenger takes his stand. Whatever makes it more difficult for the drunkard to reform, for the children to be pure, for the widow to earn a wage, for any of the wheels of progress to revolve—with these he deals. Delay him not. He is the messenger of Christ. Despair of him not, distrust him not. His day dawns slowly, but his work is sure. Though evil stalks the world, it is on the way to execution; though wrong reigns, it must end in self-combustion. The very nature of things is God's avenger; the very story of civilization is the history of Christ's throne.

Anything that prepares the way for a better social state is the fit work of the followers of Christ. Those who work on the more spiritual levels leave too much unhonored the slow toil of multitudes of un-churched souls who prepare the material or moral environments without which these higher labors are in vain. Prevention is Christian as well as cure; and Christianity travels sometimes by the most circuitous paths. It is given to some to work for immediate results, and from year to year they are privileged to reckon up a balance of success. But these are not always the greatest in the kingdom of God. The men who get no stimulus from any visible reward, whose lives pass while the objects for which they toil are still too far away to comfort them; the men who hold aloof from dazzling schemes and earn the misunderstanding of the crowd because they foresee remoter issues, who even oppose a seeming good because a deeper evil lurks beyond—these are the *statesmen* of the king-dom of God.

CHAPTER THREE
THE MACHINERY OF THE SOCIETY

Such in dimmest outline is the program of Christ's society. Did you know that all this was going on in the world? Did you know that Christianity was such a living and purpose-like thing? Look back to the day when that program was given, and you will see that it was not merely written on paper. Watch the drama of the moral order rise up, scene after scene, in history. Study the social evolution of humanity, the spread of righteousness, the amelioration of life, the freeing of slaves, the elevation of woman, the purification of religion, and ask what these can be if not the coming of the kingdom of God on earth. For it is precisely through the movements of nations and the lives of men that this kingdom comes. Christ might have done all this work Himself, with His own hands. But He did not. The crowning wonder of His scheme is that He entrusted it to men. It is the supreme glory of humanity that the machinery for its redemption should have been placed within itself. I think the saddest thing in Christ's life was that after founding a society with aims so glorious He had to go away and leave it.

But in reality He did not leave it. The old theory that God made the world, made it as an inventor would make a machine, and then stood looking on to see it work, has passed away. God is no longer a remote spectator of the natural world, but immanent in it, pervading matter by His present Spirit, and ordering it by His will. So Christ is immanent in men. His work is to move the hearts and inspire the lives of men, and through such hearts to move and reach the world. Men, only men, can carry out this work. This humanness, this inwardness, of the kingdom is one reason why some scarcely see that it exists at all. We measure great movements by the loudness of their advertisement, or the place their externals fill in the public eye. This kingdom has no externals. The usual methods of propagating a great cause were entirely discarded by Christ. The sword He declined; money He had none; literature He never used; the church disowned Him; the state crucified Him. Planting His ideals in the hearts of a few poor men, He started them out unheralded to revolutionize the world. They did it by making friends and by making enemies; they went about, did good, sowed seed, died, and lived again in the lives of those they helped. These in turn, a fraction of them, did the same. They met, they prayed, they talked of Christ, they loved, they went among other men, and by act and word passed on their secret. The machinery of the kingdom of God is purely social. It acts, not by commandment, but by contagion; not by fiat, but by friendship. "The kingdom of God is like unto leaven, which a woman took and hid in three measures of meal till the whole was leavened."

After all, like all great discoveries once they are made, this seems absolutely the most feasible method that could have been devised. Men *must* live among men. Men *must* influence men. Organizations, institutions, churches, have too much rigidity for a thing that is to flood the world. The only fluid in the world is man. War might have won for Christ's cause a passing victory; wealth might have purchased a superficial triumph; political power might have gained a temporary success. But in these, there is no note of universality, of solidarity, of immortality. To live through the centuries and pervade the uttermost ends of the earth, to stand while kingdoms tottered and civilizations changed, to survive fallen churches and crumbling creeds—there was no soil for the kingdom of God like the hearts of common men. Some who have written about this kingdom have emphasized its moral grandeur, others its universality, others its adaptation to man's needs. One great writer speaks of its prodigious originality, another chiefly notices its success. I confess what almost strikes me most is the miracle of its simplicity.

Men, then, are the only means God's Spirit has of accomplishing His purpose. What men? You. Is it worth doing, or is it not? Is it worthwhile joining Christ's society or is it not? What do *you* do all day? What is your personal stake in the coming of the kingdom of Christ on earth? You are not interested in religion, you tell me; you do not care for your "soul". It was not about your religion I ventured to ask, still less about your soul. That you have no religion, that you do not care for your soul, does not absolve you from caring for the world in which you live. But you do not believe in this church, you reply, or accept this doctrine, or that. Christ does not, in the first instance, ask your thoughts, but your work. No man has a right to postpone his *life* for the sake of his thoughts. Why? Because this is a real world, not a *think* world. Treat it as a real world—act. Think by all means, but think also of what is actual, of what the stern world is like, of how much even you, creedless and churchless, could do to make it better. The thing to be anxious about is not to be right with man, but with mankind. And, so far as I know, there is nothing so much on all fours with mankind as Christianity.

There are versions of Christianity, it is true, which no self-respecting mind can do other than disown—versions so hard, so narrow, so unreal, so super-theological, that practical men can find in them neither outlet for their lives nor resting-place for their thoughts. With these we have nothing to do. With these Christ had nothing to do—except to oppose them with every word and act of His life. It too seldom occurs to those who repudiate Christianity because of its narrowness or its unpracticalness, its sanctimoniousness or its dulness, that these were the very things which Christ strove against and unweariedly condemned. It was the one risk of His religion being given to the common people—an inevitable risk which He took without reserve—that its infinite lustre should be tarnished in the fingering of the crowd or have its great truths narrowed into mean and unworthy moulds as they passed from lip to lip. But though the crowd is the object of Christianity, it is not its custodian. Deal with the founder of this great commonwealth Himself. Any man of honest purpose who will take the trouble to inquire at firsthand what Christianity really is, will find it a thing he cannot get away from. Without either argument or pressure, by the mere practicalness of its aims and the pathos of its compassions, it forces its august claim upon every serious life.

He who joins this society finds himself in a large place. The kingdom of God is a society of the best men, working for the best ends, according to the best methods. Its membership is a multitude whom no man can number; its methods are as various as human nature; its field is the world. It is a commonwealth, yet it honors a King; it is a social brotherhood, but it acknowledges the Fatherhood of God. Though not a philosophy the world turns to it for light; though not political it is the incubator of all great laws. It is more human than the state, for it deals with deeper needs; more catholic than the church, for it includes whom the church rejects. It is a propaganda, yet it works not by agitation but by ideals. It is a religion, yet it holds the worship of God to be mainly the service of man. Though not a scientific society its watchword is evolution; though not an ethic, it possesses the Sermon on the Mount. This mysterious society owns no wealth but distributes fortunes. It has no minutes for history keeps them; no member's roll for no one could make it. Its entry-money is nothing; its subscription, all you have. The society never meets and it never adjourns. Its law is one word—loyalty; its gospel one message—love. Verily "Whosoever will lose his life for My sake shall find it."

The program for the other life is not out yet. For this world, for these faculties, for his one short life, I know nothing that is offered to man to compare with membership in the kingdom of God. Among the mysteries which compass the world beyond, none is greater than how there can be in store for man a work more wonderful, a life more God-like than this. If you know anything better, live for it; if not, in the name of God and of humanity, carry out Christ's plan.

THE CITY WITHOUT A CHURCH

I, John,
Saw the Holy City,
New Jerusalem,
Coming down from God out of Heaven.

★   ★   ★

And I saw no Temple therein.

★   ★   ★

And His servants shall serve Him;
And they shall see His Face;
And His Name shall be written on their foreheads.

CHAPTER ONE
I SAW THE CITY

Two very startling things arrest us in John's vision of the future. The first is that the likest thing to heaven he could think of was a city; the second, that there was no church in that city. Almost nothing more revolutionary could be said, even to the modern world, in the name of religion. *No church*—that is the defiance of religion; a *city*—that is the antipodes of heaven. Yet John combines

37

these contradictions in one daring image, and holds up to the world the picture of a city without a church as his ideal of the heavenly life.

By far the most original thing here is the simple conception of heaven as a city. The idea of religion without a church—"I saw no Temple therein"—is anomalous enough; but the association of the blessed life with a city—the one place in the world from which heaven seems most far away—is something wholly new in religious thought. No other religion which has a heaven ever had a heaven like this. The Greek, if he looked forward at all, awaited the Elysian Fields; the Eastern sought Nirvana. All other heavens have been gardens, dreamlands—passivities more-or-less aimless. Even to the majority among ourselves heaven is a siesta and not a city. It remained for John to go straight to the other extreme and select the citadel of the world's fever, the ganglion of its unrest, the heart and focus of its most strenuous toil, as the framework for his ideal of the blessed life.

The heaven of Christianity is different from all other heavens, because the religion of Christianity is different from all other religions. Christianity is the religion of cities. It moves among real things. Its sphere is the street, the market-place, the working-life of the world.

And what interests one for the present in John's vision is not so much what it reveals of a heaven beyond, but what it suggests of the nature of the heavenly life in this present world. Find out what a man's heaven is—no matter whether it be a dream or a reality, no matter whether it refers to an actual heaven or to a kingdom of God to be realized on earth—and you pass by an easy discovery to what his religion is; herein lies one value at least of this allegory. It is a touchstone for Christianity, a test for the solidity or the insipidity of one's religion, for the wholesomeness or the fatuousness of one's faith, for the usefulness or the futility of one's life. For this vision of the city marks off in lines, which no eye can mistake, the true area which the religion of Christ is meant to inhabit, and announces for all time the real nature of the saintly life.

City life is human life at its most intense, man in his most real relations. And the nearer one draws to reality, the nearer one draws to the working sphere of religion. Wherever real life is, there Christ goes. And He goes there, not only because the great need lies there, but because there is found, so to speak, the raw material with which Christianity works—the life of man. To do something with this, to infuse something into this, to save and inspire and sanctify this, the actual working life of the world, is what He came for. Without human life to act upon, without the relations of men with one another, of master with servant, husband with wife, buyer with seller, creditor with debtor, there is no such thing as Christianity. With actual things, with humanity in its everyday dress, with the traffic of the streets, with gates and houses, with work and wages, with sin and poverty, with these *things,* and all the things and all the relations and all the people of the city, Christianity has to do and has more to do than with anything else. To conceive of the Christian religion as itself a thing—a something which can exist apart from life; to think of it as something added on to being, something kept in a separate compartment called the soul, as an extra accomplishment like music, or a special talent like art, is totally to misapprehend its nature. It is that which fills all compartments. It is that which makes the whole life music and every separate action a work of art. Take away action and it is not. Take away people, houses, streets, character, and it ceases to be. Without these there may be sentiment, or rapture, or adoration, or superstition; there may even be religion, but there can never be the religion of the Son of Man.

If heaven were a siesta, religion might be conceived of as a reverie. If the future life were to be mainly spent in a temple, the present life might be mainly spent in church. But if heaven be a city, the life of those who are going there must be a real life. The man who would enter John's heaven, no matter what piety or what faith he may profess, must be a real man. Christ's gift to men was life, a rich and abundant life. And life is meant for living. An abundant life does not show itself in abundant dreaming, but in abundant living—in abundant living among real and tangible objects and to actual and practical purposes. "His servants," John tells us, "shall serve." In this vision of the city, he confronts us with a new definition of a Christian man—the perfect saint is the perfect citizen.

To make cities—that is what we are here for. To make good cities—that is for the present hour the main work of Christianity. For the city is strategic. It makes the towns; the towns make the villages; the villages make the country. He who makes the city makes the world. After all, though men make cities, it is cities which make men. Whether our national life is great or mean, whether our social virtues are mature or stunted, whether our sons are moral or vicious, whether religion is possible or impossible, depends upon the city. When Christianity shall take upon itself in full responsibility the burden and care of cities, the kingdom of God will openly come on earth. What Christianity waits for also, as its final apologetic and justification to the world, is the founding of a city which shall be in visible reality a city of God. People do not dispute that religion is in the church. What is now wanted is to let them see it in the city. One Christian city, one city in any part of the earth, whose citizens from the greatest to the humblest lived in the Spirit of Christ, where religion had overflowed the churches and passed into the streets, inundating every house and workshop, and permeating the whole social and commercial life—one such Christian city would seal the redemption of the world.

Some such city, surely, was what John saw in his dream. Whatever reference we may find there to a world to come, is it not equally lawful to seek the scene upon this present world? John saw his city *descending out of heaven.* It was, moreover, no strange apparition, but a city which he knew. It was Jerusalem, a new *Jerusalem.* The significance of that name has been altered for most of us by religious poetry; we spell it with a capital and speak of the New Jerusalem as a synonym for heaven. Yet why not take it simply as it stands, as a new Jerusalem? Try to restore the natural force of the expression—suppose John to have lived today and to have said London? "I saw a new London?" Jerusalem was John's London. All the grave and sad suggestion that the word London brings up today to the modern reformer, the word Jerusalem recalled to him. What in his deepest hours he longed and prayed for was a new Jerusalem, a reformed Jerusalem. And just as it is given to the man in modern England who is a prophet, to the man who believes in God and in the moral order of the world, to discern a new London shaping itself through all the sin and chaos of the city, so was it given to John to see a new Jerusalem rise from the ruins of the old.

We have no concern—it were contrary to critical method—to press the allegory in detail. What we take from it, looked at in this light, is the broad conception of a transformed city, the great Christian thought that the very cities where we live, with all their suffering and sin, shall one day, by the gradual action of the forces of Christianity, be turned into heavens on earth. This is a spectacle which profoundly concerns the world. To the reformer, the philanthropist, the economist, the politician, this vision of the city is the great classic of social literature. What John saw, we may fairly take it, was the future of all cities. It was the dawn of a new social order, a regenerate humanity, a purified society, an actual transformation of the cities of the world into cities of God.

This city, then, which John saw is none other than your city, the place where you live—as it might be, and as you are to help to make it. It is London, Berlin, New York, Paris, Melbourne, Calcutta—these as they might be, and in some infinitesimal degree as they have already begun to be. In each of these, and in every city throughout the world today, there is a city descending out of heaven from God. Each one of us is daily building up this city or helping to keep it back. Its walls rise slowly, but, as we believe in God, the building can never cease. For the might of those who build, be they few or many, is so surely greater than the might of those who retard, that no day's sun sets over any city in the land that does not see some stone of the invisible city laid. To believe this is faith. To live for this is Christianity.

The project is delirious? Yes—to atheism. To John it was the most obvious thing in the world. Nay, knowing all he knew, its realization was inevitable. We forget, when the thing strikes us as strange, that John knew Christ. Christ was the Light of the World—the Light of the *World*. This is all that he meant by his vision, that Christ is the Light of the World. This Light, John saw, would fall everywhere—especially upon cities. It was irresistible and inextinguishable. No darkness could stand before it. One by one the cities of the world would give up their night. Room by room, house by house, street by street, they would be changed. Whatsoever worketh abomination or maketh a lie would disappear. Sin, pain, sorrow, would silently pass away. One day the walls of the city would be jasper; the very streets would be paved with gold. Then the kings of the earth would bring their glory and honor into it. In the midst of the streets there should be a tree of life. And its leaves would go forth for the healing of the nations.

Survey the cities of the world today, survey your own city—town, village, home—and prophesy. God's kingdom is surely to come in this world. God's will is surely to be done on earth as it is done in heaven. Is not this one practicable way of realizing it? When a prophet speaks of something that is to be, that coming event is usually brought about by no unrelated cause or sudden shock, but in the ordered course of the world's drama. With Christianity as the supreme actor in the world's drama, the future of its cities is even now quite clear. Project the lines of Christian and social progress to their still far-off goal, and see even now that heaven must come to earth.

CHAPTER TWO
HIS SERVANTS SHALL SERVE

If anyone wishes to know what he can do to help on the work of God in the world let him make a city, or a street, or a house of a city. Men complain of the indefiniteness of religion. There are thousands ready in their humble measure to offer some personal service for the good of men, but they do not know where to begin. Let me tell you where to begin—where Christ told His disciples to begin, at the nearest city. I promise you that before one week's work is over you will never again be haunted by the problem of the indefiniteness of Christianity. You will see so much to do, so many actual things to be set right, so many merely material conditions to alter, so much striving with employers of labor, and city councils, and trade agitators, and boards, and vestries, and committees; so much pure unrelieved uninspiring hard work, that you will begin to wonder whether in all this naked realism you are on holy ground at all. Do not be afraid of missing heaven in seeking a better earth. The distinction between secular and sacred is a confusion and not a contrast; and it is only because the secular is so intensely sacred that so many eyes are blind before it. The really secular thing in life is the spirit which despises under that name what is but part of the everywhere present work and will of God. Be sure that, down to the last and pettiest detail, all that concerns a better world is the direct concern of Christ.

I make this, then, in all seriousness as a definite practical proposal. You wish, you say, to be a religious man. Well, be one. There is your city; begin. But what are you to believe? Believe in your city. What else? In Jesus Christ. What about Him? That He wants to make your city better; that that is what He would be doing if He lived there. What else? Believe in yourself—that you, even you, can do some of the work which He would like done, and that unless you do it, it will remain undone. How are you to begin? As Christ did. First He looked at the city; then He wept over it; then He died for it.

Where are you to begin? Begin where you are. Make that one corner, room, house, office as like heaven as you can. Begin? Begin with the paper on the walls, make that beautiful; with the air, keep it fresh; with the very drains, make them sweet; with the furniture, see that it be honest. Abolish whatsoever worketh abomination—in food, in drink, in luxury, in books, in art; whatsoever maketh a lie—in conversation, in social intercourse, in correspondence, in domestic life. This done, you have arranged for a heaven, but you have not got it. Heaven lies within, in kindness, in humbleness, in unselfishness, in faith, in love, in service. To get these in, get Christ in. Teach all in the house about Christ—what He did, and what He said, and how He lived, and how He died, and how He dwells in them, and how He makes all one. Teach it not as a doctrine, but as a discovery, as your own discovery. Live your own discovery.

Then pass out into the city. Do all to it that you have done at home. Beautify it, ventilate it, drain it. Let nothing enter it that can defile the streets, the stage, the newspaper offices, the booksellers' counters; nothing that maketh a lie in its warehouses, its manufactures, its shops, its art galleries, its advertisements. Educate it, amuse it, church it. Christianize capital; dignify labor. Join councils and committees. Provide for the poor, the sick, and the widow. So will you serve the city.

If you ask me which of all these things is the most important, I reply that among them there is only one thing of superlative importance and that *is yourself.* By far the greatest thing a man can do for his city is to be a good man. Simply to live there as a good man, as a Christian man of action and practical citizen, is the first and highest contribution any one can make to its salvation. Let a city be a Sodom or a Gomorrah, and if there be but ten righteous men in it, it will be saved.

It is here that the older, the more individual, conception of Christianity, did such mighty work for the world—it produced good men. It is goodness that tells, goodness first and goodness last. Good men even with small views are immeasurably more important to the world than small men with great views. But given good men, such men as were produced even by the self-centered theology of an older generation, and add that wider outlook and social ideal which are coming to be the characteristics of the religion of this age, and Christianity has an equipment for the reconstruction of the world, before which nothing can stand. Such good men will not merely content themselves with being good men. They will be forces—according to their measure, public forces. They will take the city in hand, some a house, some a street, and some the whole. Of set purpose they will serve. Not ostentatiously, but silently, in ways varied as human nature, and many as life's opportunities, they will minister to its good.

To help the people, also, to be good people, good fathers, and mothers, and sons, and citizens—is worth all else rolled into one. Arrange the government of the city as you may, perfect all its philanthropic machinery, make righteous its relations great and small, equip it with galleries and parks, and libraries and music, and carry out the whole programme of social reform, and the one thing needful is still without the gates. The gospel of material blessedness is part of a gospel—a great and Christian part—but when held up as the whole gospel for the people it is as hollow as the void of life whose circumference even it fails to touch.

There are countries in the world—new countries—where the people, rising to the rights of government, have already secured almost all that reformers cry for. The lot of the working man there is all but perfect. His wages are high, his leisure great, his home worthy. Yet in tens of thousands of cases the secret of life is unknown.

It is idle to talk of Christ as a social reformer if by that is meant that His first concern was to improve the organization of society, or provide the world with better laws. These were among His objects, but His first was to provide the world with better men. The one need of every cause and every community still is for better men. If every workshop held a workman like Him who worked in the carpenter's shop at Nazareth, the labor problem and all other workman's problems would soon be solved. If every street had a home or two like Mary's home in Bethany, the domestic life of the city would be transformed in three generations.

External reforms—education, civilization, public schemes, and public charities—have each their part to play. Any experiment that can benefit by one hairbreadth any single human life is a thousand times worth trying. There is no effort in any single one of these directions but must, as Christianity advances, be pressed by Christian men to ever further and fuller issues. But those whose hands have tried the ways, and the slow work of leavening men one by one with the spirit of Jesus Christ.

The thought that the future, that any day, may see some new and mighty enterprise of redemption, some new departure in religion, which shall change everything with a breath and make all that is crooked straight, is not at all likely to be realized. There is nothing wrong with the lines on which redemption runs at present except the want of faith to believe in them, and the want of men to use them. The kingdom of God is like leaven, and the leaven is with us now. The quantity at work in the world may increase, but that is all. For nothing can ever be higher than the Spirit of Christ or more potent as a regenerating power on the lives of men.

Do not charge me with throwing away my brief because I return to this old, old plea for the individual soul. I do not forget that my plea is for the city. But I plead for good men, because good men are good leaven. If their goodness stop short of that, if the leaven does not mix with that which is unleavened, if it does not do the work of leaven— that is, to *raise something*—it is not the leaven of Christ. The question for good men to ask themselves is: Is my goodness helping others? Is it a private luxury, or is it telling upon the city? Is it bringing any single human soul nearer happiness or righteousness?

If you ask what particular scheme you shall take up, I cannot answer. Christianity has no set schemes. It makes no choice between conflicting philanthropies, decides nothing between competing churches, favors no particular public policy, organizes no one line of private charity. It is not essential even for all of us to take any public or formal line. Christianity is not all carried on by committees, and the kingdom of God has other ways of coming than through municipal reforms. Most of the stones for the building of the city of God, and all the best of them, are made by *mothers.* But whether or not you shall work through public channels, or only serve Christ along the quieter paths of home, no man can determine but yourself.

There is an almost awful freedom about Christ's religion. "I do not call you servants." He said, "for the servant knoweth not what his lord doeth. I have called you friends." As Christ's friends, His followers are supposed to know what He wants done, and for the same reason they will try to do it—this is the whole working basis of Christianity. Surely next to its love for the chief of sinners, the most touching thing about the religion of Christ is its amazing trust in the least of saints. Here is the mightiest enterprise ever launched upon this earth, mightier even than its creation, for it is its re-creation, and the carrying of it out is left, so to speak, to haphazard—to individual loyalty, to free enthusiasms, to uncoerced activities, to an uncompelled response to the pressures of God's Spirit. Christ sets His followers no tasks. He appoints no hours. He allots no sphere. He Himself simply went about and did good. He did not stop life to do some special thing which should be called religious. His life was His religion. Each day as it came brought round in the ordinary course its natural ministry. Each village along the highway had someone waiting to be helped. His pulpit was the hillside; His congregation a woman at a well. The poor, wherever He met them, were His clients; the sick, as often as He found them, His opportunity. His work was everywhere; His workshop was the world. One's associations of Christ are all of the wayside. We never think of Him in connection with a church. We cannot picture Him in the garb of a priest or belonging to any of the classes who specialize religion. His service was of a universal human order. He was the Son of Man, the citizen.

This, remember, was the highest life ever lived, this informal citizen-life. So simple a thing it was, so natural, so human, that those who saw it first did not know it was religion, and Christ did not pass among them as a very religious man. Nay, it is certain, and it is an infinitely significant thought, that the religious people of His time not only refused to accept this type of religion as any kind of religion at all, but repudiated and denounced Him as its bitter enemy.

Inability to discern what true religion is, is not confined to the Pharisees. Multitudes still who profess to belong to the religion of Christ, scarcely know it when they see it. The truth is, men will hold to almost anything in the name of Christianity, believe anything, do anything—except its common and obvious tasks. Great is the mystery of what has passed in this world for religion.

CHAPTER THREE
I SAW NO TEMPLE THERE

"I saw no church there," said John. Nor is there any note of surprise as he marks the omission of what one half of Christendom would have considered the first essential. For beside the type of religion he had learned from Christ, the church type—the merely church type—is an elaborate evasion. What have the pomp and circumstance, the fashion and the form, the vestures and the postures, to do with Jesus of Nazareth? At a stage in personal development and for a certain type of mind, such things may have a place. But when mistaken for Christianity, no matter how they aid it, or in what measure they conserve it, they defraud the souls of men, and rob humanity of its dues. It is because to large masses of people Christianity has become synonymous with a temple service that other large masses of people decline to touch it. It is a mistake to suppose that the working classes of this country are opposed to Christianity. No man can ever be opposed to Christianity who knows what it *really* is. The working men would still follow Christ if He came among them. As a matter of fact they do follow anyone, preacher or layman, in pulpit or on platform, who is the least like Him. But what they cannot follow, and must evermore live outside of, is a worship which ends with the worshipper, a religion expressed only in ceremony, and a faith unrelated to life.

Perhaps the most dismal fact of history is the failure of the great organized bodies of ecclesiasticism to understand the simple genius of Christ's religion. Whatever the best in the churches of all time may have thought of the life and religion of Christ, taken as a whole they have succeeded in leaving upon the mind of a large portion of the world an impression of Christianity which is the direct opposite of the reality. Down to the present hour almost whole nations in Europe live, worship, and die under the belief that Christ is an ecclesiastical Christ, religion the sum of all the churches' observances, and faith an adhesion to the churches' creeds. I do not apportion blame; I simply record the fact. Everything that the spiritual and temporal authority of man could do has been done—done in ignorance of the true nature of Christianity— to dislodge the religion of Christ from its natural home in the heart of humanity. In many lands the churches have literally stolen Christ from the people; they have made the Son of Man the priest of an order; they have taken Christianity from the city and imprisoned it behind altar rails; they have withdrawn it from the national life and doled it out to the few who pay to keep the unconscious deception up.

Do not do the church, the true church at least, the injustice to think that she does not know all this. Nowhere, not even in the fiercest secular press, is there more exposure of this danger, more indignation at its continuance, than in many of the churches of today. The protest against the confusion of Christianity with the church is the most threadbare of pulpit themes. Before the University of Oxford, from the pulpit of St. Mary's, these words were lately spoken: "If it is strange that the church of the darker ages should have needed so bitter a lesson (the actual demolition of their churches), is it not ten times stranger still that the church of the days of greater enlightenment should be found again making the chief part of its business the organizing of the modes of worship; that the largest efforts which are owned as the efforts of the churches are made for the establishment and maintenance of worship; that our chief controversies relate to the teaching and the ministry of a system designed primarily, if not exclusively, for worship; that even the fancies and the refinements of such a system divide us; that the breach between things secular and things religious grows wider instead of their being made to blend into one; and that the vast and fruitful spaces of the actual

47

life of mankind lie still so largely without the gates? The old Jerusalem was all temple. The medieval church was all temple. But the ideal of the new Jerusalem was—no temple, but a God-inhabited society. Are we not reversing this ideal in an age when the church still means in so many mouths the clergy, instead of meaning the Christian society, and when nine men are striving to get men to go to church for one who is striving to make men realize that they themselves are the church?"

Yet even with words so strong as these echoing daily from Protestant pulpits, the superstition reigns in all but unbroken power. And everywhere still men are found confounding the spectacular services of a church, the vicarious religion of a priest, and the traditional belief in a creed, with the living religion of the Son of Man.

"I saw no Temple there"—the future city will be a city without a church. Ponder that fact, realize the temporariness of the church, then—go and build one. Do not imagine, because all this has been said, that I mean to depreciate the church. On the contrary, if it were mine to build a city, a city where all life should be religious, and all men destined to become members of the body of Christ, the first stone I should lay there would be the foundation-stone of a church. Why? Because, among other reasons, the product which the church on the whole best helps to develop, and in the largest quantity, is that which is most needed by the city.

For the present, and for a long time to come, the manufactory of good men, the nursery of the forces which are to redeem the city, will in the main be found to be some more or less formal, more-or-less imperfect, Christian church. Here and there an unchurched soul may stir the multitudes to lofty deeds; isolated men; strong enough to preserve their souls apart from the church, but shortsighted enough perhaps to fail to see that others cannot, may set high examples and stimulate to national reforms. But for the rank and file of us, made of such stuff as we are made of, the steady pressures of fixed institutions, the regular diets of a common worship, and the education of public Christian teaching are too obvious safeguards of spiritual culture to be set aside. Even Renan declares his conviction that "Beyond the family and outside the state, man has need of the church . . . Civil society, whether it calls itself a commune, a canton, a province, a state, or fatherland, has many duties towards the improvement of the individual; but what it does is necessarily limited. The family ought to do much more, but often it is insufficient; sometimes it is wanting altogether. The association created in the name of moral principle can alone give to every man coming into this world a bond which unites him with the past, duties as to the future, examples to follow, a heritage to receive and to transmit, and a tradition of devotion to continue." Apart altogether from the quality of its contribution to society, in the mere quantity of the work it turns out it stands alone. Even for social purposes the church is by far the greatest employment bureau in the world. And the man who, seeing where it falls short, withholds on that account his witness to its usefulness, is a traitor to history and to fact.

"The church," as the preacher whom I have already quoted, most truly adds, "is a society which tends to embrace the whole life of man-kind, to bind all their relations together by a Divine sanction. As such, it blends naturally with the institutions of common life—those institutions which, because they are natural and necessary, are therefore Divine. What it aims at is not the recognition by the nation of a worshipping body, governed by the ministers of public worship, which calls itself the church, but that the nation and all classes in it should act upon Christian principle, that laws should be made in Christ's spirit of justice, that the relations of the powers of the state should be maintained on a basis of Christian equity, that all public acts should be done in Christ's Spirit, and with mutual forbearance, that the spirit of Christian charity should be spread through all ranks and orders of the people. The church will maintain public worship as one of the greatest supports of a Christian public life but it will always remember that the true service is a life of devotion to God and man far more than the common utterance of prayer." I have said that were it mine to build a city, the first stone I should lay there would be the foundation-stone of a church. But if it were mine to preach the first sermon in that church, I should choose as the text, "I saw no church therein." I should tell the people that the great use of the church is to help men to do without it As the old ecclesiastical term has it, church services are "diets" of worship. They are meals. All who are hungry will take them, and, if they are wise, regularly. But no workman is paid for his meals. He is paid for the work he does in the strength of them. No Christian is paid for going to church. He goes there for a meal, for strength from God and from his fellow-worshippers to do the work of life—which is the work of Christ. The church is a Divine institution because it is so very human an institution. As a channel of nourishment, as a stimulus to holy deeds, as a link with all holy lives, let all men use it, and to the utmost of their opportunity. But by all that they know of Christ or care for man, let them beware of mistaking its services for Christianity. What church services really express is the *want* of Christianity. And when that which is perfect in Christianity is come, all this, as the mere passing stay and scaffolding of struggling souls, must vanish away.

If the masses who never go to church only knew that the churches were the mute expression of a Christian's *wants* and not the self-advertisement of his sanctity, they would have more respectful words for churches. But they have never learned this. And the result in their case of confounding religion with the church is even more serious than in the case of the professing Christian. When they break with the church, it means to them a break with all religion. As things are it could scarce be otherwise. With the church in ceaseless evidence before their eyes as the acknowledged custodian of Christianity; with actual stone and lime in every street representing the place where religion dwells; with a professional class moving out and in among them, holding in their hands the souls of men, and almost the keys of heaven—how is it possible that those who turn their backs on all this should not feel outcast from the church's God? It is not possible. Without a murmur, yet with results to themselves most disastrous and pathetic, multitudes accept this false dividing-line and number themselves as excommunicate from all good. The masses will never return to the church till its true relation to the city is more defined. And they can never have that most real life of theirs made religious so long as they rule themselves out of court on the ground that they have broken with ecclesiastical forms. The life of the masses is the most real of all lives. It is full of religious possibilities. Every movement of it and every moment of it might become of supreme religious value, might hold a continuous spiritual discipline, might perpetuate, and that in most natural ways, a moral influence which should pervade all cities and all states. But they must first be taught what Christianity really is, and learn to distinguish between religion and the church. After that, if they be taught their lesson well, they will return to honor both.

Our fathers made much of "meetness" for heaven. By prayer and fasting, by self-examination and meditation, they sought to fit themselves "for the inheritance of the saints in light." Important beyond measure in their fitting place are these exercises of the soul. But whether alone they fit men for the inheritance of the saints depends on what a saint is. If a saint is a devotee and not a citizen, if heaven is a cathedral and not a city, then these things do fit for heaven. But if life means action, and heaven service; if spiritual graces are acquired for use and not for ornament, then devotional forms have a deeper function. The Puritan preachers were wont to tell their people to "practice dying." Yes; but what is dying? It is going to a city. And what is required of those who would go to a city? The practice of citizenship—the due employment of the unselfish talents, the development of public spirit, the payment of the full tax to the great brotherhood, the subordination of personal aims to the common good. And where are these to be learned? Here; in cities here. There is no other way to learn them. There is no heaven to those who have not learned them.

No church however holy, no priest however earnest, no book however sacred, can transfer to any human character the capacities of citizenship—those capacities which in the very nature of things are *necessities* to those who would live in the kingdom of God. The only preparation which multitudes seem to make for heaven is for its judgment bar. What will they do in its streets? What have they learned of citizenship? What have they practiced of love? How like are they to its Lord? To "practice dying" is to practice living. Earth is the rehearsal for heaven. The eternal beyond is the eternal here. The street-life, the home-life, the business-life, the city-life in all the varied range of its activity, are an apprenticeship for the city of God. There is no other apprenticeship for it. To know how to serve Christ in these is to "practice dying."

To move among the people on the common street; to meet them in the market-place on equal terms; to live among them not as saint or monk, but as brother-man with brother-man; to serve God not with form or ritual, but in the free impulse of a soul; to bear the burdens of society and relieve its needs; to carry on the multitudinous activities of the city—social, commercial, political, philanthropic—in Christ's Spirit and for His ends: this is the religion of the Son of Man, and the only meetness for heaven which has much reality in it.

No; the church with all its splendid equipment, the cloister with all its holy opportunity, are not the final instruments for fitting men for heaven. The city, in many of its functions, is a greater church than the church. It is amid the whirr of its machinery and in the discipline of its life that the souls of men are really made. How great its opportunity is few of us are aware. It is such slow work getting better, the daily round is so very common, our ideas of a heavenly life are so unreal and mystical that even when the highest heaven lies all around us, when we might touch it, and dwell in it every day we live, we almost fail to see that it is there. The heaven of our childhood, the spectacular heaven, the heaven which is a *place,* so dominates thought even in our maturer years, that we are slow to learn the fuller truth that heaven is a *state.* But John, who is responsible before all other teachers for the dramatic view of heaven, has not failed in this very allegory to proclaim the further lesson. Having brought all his scenery upon the stage and pictured a material heaven of almost unimaginable splendor, the seer turns aside before he closes for a revelation of a profounder kind. Within the heavenly city, he opens the gate of an inner heaven. It is the spiritual heaven—the heaven of those who serve. With two flashes of his pen he tells the citizens of God all that they will ever need or care to know as to what heaven really means. "His servants shall serve Him; and *they shall see His face; and His character shall be written on their characters."*

They shall see His face. Where? In the city. When? In eternity? No; tomorrow. Those who serve in any city cannot help continually seeing Christ. He is there with them. He is there before them. They cannot but meet. No gentle word is ever spoken that Christ's voice does not also speak; no meek deed is ever done that the unsummoned vision does not there and then appear. Whoso, in whatsoever place, receiveth a little child in My name receiveth Me.

This is how men get to know God—by doing His will. And there is no other way. And this is how men become like God; how God's character becomes written upon men's characters. Acts react upon souls. Good acts make good men; just acts, just men; kind acts, kind men; divine acts, divine men. And there is no other way of becoming good, just, kind, divine. And there is no heaven for those who have not become these. For these are heaven.

When John's heaven faded from his sight, and the prophet woke to the desert waste of Patmos, did he grudge to exchange the heaven of his dream for the common tasks around him? Was he not glad to be alive, and there? And would he not straightway go to the city, to whatever struggling multitude his prison-rock held, if so be that he might prove his dream and among them see His face? Traveller to God's last city, be glad that you are alive. Be thankful for the city at your door and for the chance to build its walls a little nearer heaven before you go. Pray for yet a little while to redeem the wasted years. And week by week as you go forth from worship, and day by day as you awake to face this great and needy world, learn to "seek a city" there, and in the service of its neediest citizen find heaven.

THE CHANGED LIFE

We All
With unveiled face
Reflecting
As a Mirror
The Glory of the Lord
Are transformed
Into the same image
From Glory to Glory
Even as from the Lord
The Spirit

CHAPTER ONE
THE CHANGED LIFE

I protest that if some great power would agree to make me always think what is true and do what is right, on condition of being turned into a sort of clock and wound up every morning, I should instantly close with the offer."

These are the words of Mr. Huxley. The infinite desirability, the infinite difficulty of being good—the theme is as old as humanity. The man does not live from whose deeper being the same confession has not risen, or who would not give his all tomorrow, if he could "close with the offer" of becoming a better man.

I propose to make that offer now. In all seriousness, without being "turned into a sort of clock," the end can be attained. Under the right conditions it is as natural for character to become beautiful as it is for a flower; and if on God's earth, there is not some machinery for effecting it, the supreme gift to the world has been forgotten. This is simply what man was made for. With Browning: "I say that man was made to grow, not stop." Or in the deeper words of an older Book: "Whom He did foreknow, He also did predestine . . . to be conformed to the image of His Son."

Let me begin by naming, and in part discarding, some processes in vogue already, for producing better lives. These processes are far from wrong; in their place they may even be essential. One ventures to disparage them only because they do not turn out the most perfect possible work.

The first imperfect method is to rely on resolution. In will-power, in mere spasms of earnestness there is no salvation. Struggle, effort, even agony, have their place in Christianity as we shall see; but this is not where they come in. In mid-Atlantic the other day, the Etruria in which I was sailing, suddenly stopped. Something had gone wrong with the engines. There were five hundred able-bodied men on board the ship. Do you think if we had gathered together and pushed against the masts we could have pushed it on? When one attempts to sanctify himself by effort, he is trying to make his boat go by pushing against the mast. He is like a drowning man trying to lift himself out of the water by pulling at the hair of his own head. Christ held up this method almost to ridicule when He said, "Which of you by taking thought can add a cubit to his stature?" The one redeeming feature of the self-sufficient method is this—that those who try it find out almost at once that it will not gain the goal.

Another experimenter says:—"But that is not my method. I have seen the folly of a mere wild struggle in the dark. I work on a principle. My plan is not to waste power on random effort, but to concentrate on a single sin. By taking one at a time and crucifying it steadily, I hope in the end to extirpate all." To this, unfortunately, there are four objections. For one thing life is too short; the name of sin is Legion. For another thing, to deal with individual sins is to leave the rest of the nature for the time untouched. In the third place, a single combat with a special sin does not affect the root and spring of the disease. If only one of the channels of sin be obstructed, experience points to an almost certain overflow through some other part of the nature. Partial conversion is almost always accompanied by such moral leakage, for the pent-up energies accumulate to the bursting point, and the last state of that soul may be worse than the first. In the last place, religion does not consist in negatives, in stopping this sin and stopping that. The perfect character can never be produced with a pruning knife.

But a third protests:—"So be it I make no attempt to stop sins one by one. My method is just the opposite. I copy the virtues one by one." The difficulty about the copying method is that it is apt to be mechanical. One can always tell an engraving from a picture, an artificial flower from a real flower. To copy virtues one by one has somewhat the same effect as eradicating the vices one by one; the temporary result is an overbalanced and incongruous character. Someone defines a prig as "a creature that is over-fed for its size." One sometimes finds Christians of this species—over-fed on one side of their nature, but dismally thin and starved-looking on the other. The result, for instance, of copying humility, and adding it on to an otherwise worldly life, is simply grotesque. A rabid temperance advocate, for the same reason, is often the poorest of creatures, flourishing on a single virtue, and quite oblivious that his temperance is making a worse man of him and not a better. These are examples of fine virtues spoiled by association with mean companions. Character is a unity, and all the virtues must advance together to make the perfect man. This method of sanctification, nevertheless, is in the true direction. It is only in the details of execution that it fails.

A fourth method I need scarcely mention, for it is a variation on those already named. It is the very young man's method; and the pure earnestness of it makes it almost desecration to touch it. It is to keep a private note-book with columns for the days of the week, and a list of virtues with spaces against each for marks. This, with many stern rules for preface, is stored away in a secret place, and from time to time, at nightfall, the soul is arraigned before it as before a private judgment bar. This living by code was Franklin's method. I suppose thousands more could tell how they had hung up in their bed-rooms, or hid in lock-fast drawers, the rules which one solemn day they drew up to shape their lives. This method is not erroneous, only somehow its success is poor. You bear me witness that it fails? And it fails generally for very matter-of-fact reasons—most likely because one day we forget the rules.

All these methods that have been named—the self-sufficient method, the self-crucifixion method, the mimetic method, and the diary method—are perfectly human, perfectly natural, perfectly ignorant, and, as they stand, perfectly inadequate. It is not argued, I repeat, that they must be abandoned. Their harm is rather that they distract attention from the true working method, and secure a fair result at the expense of the perfect one. What that perfect method is we shall now go on to ask.

Chapter Two
THE FORMULA OF SANCTIFICATION

A formula, a recipe, for sanctification—can one seriously speak of this mighty change as if the process were as definite as for the production of so many volts of electricity? It is impossible to doubt it. Shall a mechanical experiment succeed infallibly, and the one vital experiment of humanity remain a chance? Is corn to grow by method, and character by caprice? If we cannot calculate to a certainty that the forces of religion will do their work, then is religion vain? And if we cannot express the law of these forces in simple words, then is Christianity not the world's religion but the world's conundrum?

Where, then, shall one look for such a formula? Where one would look for any formula—among the textbooks. And if we turn to the textbooks of Christianity we shall find a formula for this problem as clear and precise as any in the mechanical sciences. If this simple rule, moreover, be but followed fearlessly, it will yield the result of a perfect character as surely as any result that is guaranteed by the laws of nature. The finest expression of this rule in Scripture, or indeed in any literature, is probably one drawn up and condensed into a single verse by Paul. You will find it in a letter—the second to the Corinthians—written by him to some Christian people who, in a city which was a byword for depravity and licentiousness, were seeking the higher life. To see the point of the words we must take them from the immensely improved rendering of the Revised translation, for the older version in this case greatly obscures the sense. They are these: "We all, with unveiled face reflecting as a mirror the glory of the Lord, are transformed into the same image from glory to glory, even as from the Lord the Spirit."

Now observe at the outset the entire contradiction of all our previous efforts, in the simple passive "we *are* transformed." We *are changed,* as the old version has it—we do not change ourselves. No man can change himself. Throughout the New Testament you will find that wherever these moral and spiritual transformations are described the verbs are in the passive. Presently it will be pointed out that there is a *rationale* in this, but meantime do not toss these words aside as if this passivity denied all human effort or ignored intelligible law. What is implied for the soul here is no more than is everywhere claimed for the body. In physiology the verbs describing the processes of growth are in the passive. Growth is not voluntary; it takes place, it happens, it is wrought upon matter. So here. "Ye must be born again"—we cannot *born* ourselves. "Be not conformed to this world but *be ye transformed*"—we are subjects to a transforming influence, we do not transform ourselves. Not more certain is it that it is something outside the thermometer that produces a change in the thermometer, than it is something outside the soul of man that produces a moral change upon him. That he must be susceptible to that change, that he must be a party to it, goes without saying; but that neither his aptitude nor his will can produce it, is equally certain.

Obvious as it ought to seem, this may be to some an almost startling revelation. The change we have been striving after is not to be produced by any more striving after. It is to be wrought upon us by the molding of hands beyond our own. As the branch ascends, and the bud bursts, and the fruit reddens under the cooperation of influences from the outside air, so man rises to the higher stature under invisible pressures from without. The radical defect of all our former methods of sanctification was the attempt to generate from within that which can only be wrought upon us from without. According to the first law of motion: Every body continues in its state of rest, or of uniform motion in a straight line, except in so far as it may be compelled *by impressed forces* to change that state. This is also a first law of Christianity. Every man's character remains as it is, or continues in the direction in which it is going, until it is compelled *by impressed forces* to change that state. Our failure has been the failure to put ourselves in the way of the impressed forces. There is a clay, and there is a Potter; we have tried to get the clay to mold the clay.

Whence, then, these pressures, and where this Potter? The answer of the formula is "By reflecting as a mirror the glory of the Lord we are changed." But this is not very clear. What is the "glory" of the Lord, and how can mortal man reflect it, and how can that act as an "impressed force" in molding him to a nobler form? The word "glory"—the word which has to bear the weight of holding those "impressed forces"—is a stranger in current speech, and our first duty is to seek out its equivalent in working English. It suggests at first a radiance of some kind, something dazzling or glittering, some halo such as the old masters loved to paint round the heads of their Ecce Homos. But that is paint, mere matter, the visible symbol of some unseen thing. What is that unseen thing? It is that of all unseen things, the most radiant, the most beautiful, the most Divine, and that is *character*. On earth, in heaven, there is nothing so great, so glorious as this. The word has many meanings; in ethics it can have but one. Glory is character and nothing less, and it can be nothing more. The earth is "full of the glory of the Lord," because it is full of His character. The "beauty of the Lord" is character. "The effulgence of His glory" is character. "The glory of the Only Begotten" is character, the character which is "fullness of grace and truth." And when God told His people *His name,* He simply gave them His character, His character which was Himself. "And the Lord proclaimed the Name of the Lord . . . the Lord, the Lord God, merciful and gracious, long-suffering and abundant in goodness and truth." Glory then is not something intangible, or ghostly, or transcendental. If it were this, how could Paul ask men to reflect it? Stripped of its physical enswathement, it is beauty, moral and spiritual beauty, beauty infinitely real, infinitely exalted, yet infinitely near and infinitely communicable.

With this explanation read over the sentence once more in paraphrase: We all reflecting as a mirror the character of Christ are transformed into the same Image from character to character—from a poor character to a better one, from a better one to one a little better still, from that to one still more complete, until by slow degrees the Perfect Image is attained. Here the solution of the problem of sanctification is compressed into a sentence: Reflect the character of Christ and you will become like Christ.

All men are mirrors—that is the first law on which this formula is based. One of the aptest descriptions of a human being is that he is a mirror. As we sat at table to-night, the world in which each of us lived and moved throughout this day was focussed in the room. What we saw as we looked at one another was not one another, but one another's world. We were an arrangement of mirrors. The scenes we saw were all reproduced; the people we met walked to and fro; they spoke, they bowed, they passed us by, did everything over again as if it had been real. When we talked, we were but looking at our own mirror and describing what flitted across it; our listening was not hearing, but seeing—we but looked on our neighbor's mirror. All human intercourse is a seeing of reflections. I meet a stranger in a railway carriage. The cadence of his first word tells me he is English, and comes from Yorkshire. Without knowing it he has reflected his birthplace, his parents, and the long history of their race. Even physiologically he is a mirror. His second sentence records that he is a politician, and a faint inflexion in the way he pronounces *The Times* reveals his party. In his next remarks I see reflected a whole world of experiences. The books he has read, the people he has met, the influences that have played upon him and made him the man he is—these are all registered there by a pen which lets nothing pass, and whose writing can never be blotted out. What I am reading in him meantime he also is reading in me; and before the journey is over we could half write each other's lives. Whether we like it or not, we live in glass houses. The mind, the memory, the soul, is simply a vast chamber panelled with looking-glass. And upon this miraculous arrangement and endowment depends the capacity of mortal souls to "reflect the character of the Lord."

But this is not all. If all these varied reflections from our so-called secret life are patent to the world, how close the writing, how complete the record, within the soul itself? For the influences we meet are not simply held for a moment on the polished surface and thrown off again into space. Each is retained where first it fell, and stored up in the soul forever.

This law of assimilation is the second, and by far the most impressive truth which underlies the formula of sanctification—the truth that men are not only mirrors, but that these mirrors so far from being mere reflectors of the fleeting things they see, transfer into their own inmost substance, and hold in permanent preservation the things that they reflect. No one knows how the soul can hold these things. No one knows how the miracle is done. No phenomenon in nature, no process in chemistry, no chapter in necromancy can even help us to begin to understand this amazing operation. For, think of it, the past is not only focused there, in a man's soul; it is there. How could it be reflected from there if it were not there? All things that he has ever seen, known, felt, believed of the surrounding world are now within him, have become part of him, in part are him—he has been changed into their image. He may deny it, he may resent it, but they are there. They do not adhere to him, they are transfused through him. He cannot alter or rub them out. They are not in his memory, they are in him. His soul is as they have filled it, made it, left it. These things, these books, these events, these influences are his makers. In their hands are life and death, beauty and deformity. When once the image or likeness of any of these is fairly presented to the soul, no power on earth can hinder two things happening—it must be absorbed into the soul, and forever reflected back again from character.

Upon these astounding yet perfectly obvious psychological facts, Paul bases his doctrine of sanctification. He sees that character is a thing built up by slow degrees, that it is hourly changing for better or for worse according to the images which flit across it. One step further and the whole length and breadth of the application of these ideas to the central problem of religion will stand before us.

CHAPTER THREE
THE ALCHEMY OF INFLUENCE

If events change men, much more persons. No man can meet another on the street without making some mark upon him. We say we exchange words when we meet; what we exchange is souls. And when intercourse is very close and very frequent, so complete is this exchange that recognizable bits of the one soul begin to show in the other's nature, and the second is conscious of a similar and growing debt to the first. This mysterious approximating of two souls who has not witnessed? Who has not watched some old couple come down life's pilgrimage hand in hand with such gentle trust and joy in one another that their very faces wore the self-same look? These were not two souls; it was a composite soul. It did not matter to which of the two you spoke, you would have said the same words to either. It was quite indifferent which replied, each would have said the same. Half a century's *reflecting* had told upon them: they were changed into the same image. It is the law of influence that *we become like those whom we habitually admire:* these had become like because they habitually admired. Through all the range of literature, of history, and biography this law presides. Men are all mosaics of other men. There was a savor of David about Jonathan and a savor of Jonathan about David. Jean Valjean, in the masterpiece of Victor Hugo, is Bishop Bienvenu risen from the dead. Metempsychosis is a fact. George Eliot's message to the world was that men and women make men and women.

The family, the cradle of mankind, has no meaning apart from this. Society itself is nothing but a rallying point for these omnipotent forces to do their work. On the doctrine of influence, in short, the whole vast pyramid of humanity is built.

But it was reserved for Paul to make the supreme application of the law of influence. It was a tremendous inference to make, but he never hesitated. He himself was a changed man: he knew exactly what had done it; it was Christ on the Damascus road they met, and from that hour his life was absorbed in His. The effect could not but follow—on words, on deeds, on career, on creed. The "impressed forces" did their vital work. He became like Him whom he habitually loved. "So we all," he writes, "reflecting as a mirror the glory of Christ are changed into the same image."

Nothing could be more simple, more intelligible, more natural, more supernatural. It is an analogy from an everyday fact. Since we are what we are by the impacts of those who surround us, those who surround themselves with the highest will be those who change into the highest. There are some men and some women in whose company we are always at our best. While with them we cannot think mean thoughts or speak ungenerous words. Their mere presence is elevation, purification, sanctity. All the best stops in our nature are drawn out by their intercourse, and we find a music in our souls that was never there before. Suppose even *that* influence prolonged through a month, a year, a lifetime, and what could not life become? Here, even on the common plane of life, talking our language, walking our streets, working side by side, are sanctifiers of souls; here, breathing through common play, is heaven; here, energies charged even through a temporal medium with a virtue of regeneration. If to live with men, diluted to the millionth degree with the virtue of the Highest, can exalt and purify the nature, what bounds can be set to the influence of Christ? To live with Socrates—with unveiled face—must have made one wise; with Aristides, just. Francis of Assisi must have made one gentle; Savonarola, strong. But to have lived with Christ? To have lived with Christ must have made one like Christ; that is to say, *A Christian.*

As a matter of fact, to live with Christ did produce this effect. It produced it in the case of Paul. And during Christ's lifetime the experiment was tried in an even more startling form. A few raw, unspiritual, uninspiring men, were admitted to the inner circle of His friendship. The change began at once. Day by day we can almost see the first disciples grow. First there steals over them the faintest possible adumbration of His character, and occasionally, very occasionally, they do a thing, or say a thing that they could not have done or said had they not been living there. Slowly the spell of His life deepens. Reach after reach of their nature is overtaken, thawed, subjugated, sanctified. Their manners soften, their words become more gentle, their conduct more unselfish. As swallows who have found a summer, as frozen buds the spring, their starved humanity bursts into a fuller life. They do not know how it is, but they are different men. One day they find themselves like their Master, going about and doing good. To themselves it is unaccountable, but they cannot do otherwise. They were not told to do it, it came to them to do it. But the people who watch them know well how to account for it—"They have been," they whisper, "with Jesus." Already even, the mark and seal of His character is upon them—"They have been with Jesus." Unparalleled phenomenon, that these poor fishermen should remind other men of Christ! Stupendous victory and mystery of regeneration that mortal men should suggest to the world, *God!*

There is something almost melting in the way His contemporaries, and John especially, speak of the influence of Christ. John lived himself in daily wonder at Him; he was overpowered, overawed, entranced, transfigured. To his mind it was impossible for anyone to come under this influence and ever be the same again. "Whosoever abideth in Him sinneth not," he said. It was inconceivable that he should sin, as inconceivable as that ice should live in a burning sun, or darkness co-exist with noon. If anyone did sin, it was to John the simple proof that he could never have met Christ. "Whosoever sinneth," he exclaims, "hath not seen *Him,* neither known *Him.*" Sin was abashed in this Presence. Its roots withered. Its sway and victory were forever at an end.

But these were His contemporaries. It was easy for *them* to be influenced by Him, for they were every day and all the day together. But how can we mirror that which we have never seen? How can all this stupendous result be produced by a memory, by the scantiest of all biographies, by One who lived and left this earth eighteen hundred years ago? How can modern men today make Christ, the absent Christ, their most constant companion still? The answer is that friendship is a spiritual thing. It is independent of matter, or space, or time. That which I love in my friend is not that which I see. What influences me in my friend is not his body but his spirit. It would have been an ineffable experience truly to have lived at that time—

"I think when I read the sweet story of old,
How when Jesus was here among men,
He took little children like lambs to His fold,
I should like to have been with him then.

"I wish that His hand had been laid on my head,
That His arms had been thrown around me,
And that I had seen His kind look when He said,
Let the little ones come unto Me."

And yet, if Christ were to come into the world again, few of us probably would ever have a chance of seeing Him. Millions of her subjects, in this little country, have never seen their own queen. And there would be millions of the subjects of Christ who could never get within speaking distance of Him if He were here. Our companionship with Him, like all true companionship, is a spiritual communion. All friendship, all love, human and divine, is purely spiritual. It was after He was risen that He influenced even the disciples most. Hence in reflecting the character of Christ it is no real obstacle that we may never have been in visible contact with Himself.

There lived once a young girl whose perfect grace of character was the wonder of those who knew her. She wore on her neck a gold locket which no one was ever allowed to open. One day, in a moment of unusual confidence, one of her companions was allowed to touch its spring and learn its secret. She saw written these words—*"Whom having not seen, I love."* That was the secret of her beautiful life. She had been changed into the same image.

Now this is not imitation, but a much deeper thing. Mark this distinction. For the difference in the process, as well as in the result, may be as great as that between a photograph secured by the infallible pencil of the sun, and the rude outline from a schoolboy's chalk. Imitation is mechanical, reflection organic. The one is occasional, the other habitual. In the one case, man comes to God and imitates Him; in the other, God comes to man and imprints Himself upon him. It is quite true that there is an imitation of Christ which amounts to reflection. But Paul's term includes all that the other holds, and is open to no mistake.

"Make Christ your most constant companion"—this is what it practically means for us. Be more under His influence than under any other influence. Ten minutes spent in His society every day, ay, two minutes if it be face to face, and heart to heart, will make the whole day different.

Every character has an inward spring, let Christ be it. Every action has a key-note, let Christ set it. Yesterday you got a certain letter. You sat down and wrote a reply which almost scorched the paper. You picked the cruellest adjectives you knew and sent it forth, without a pang, to do its ruthless work. You did that because your life was set in the wrong key. You began the day with the mirror placed at the wrong angle. Tomorrow, at daybreak, turn it towards Him, and even to your enemy the fashion of your countenance will be changed. Whatever you then do, one thing you will find you could not do—you could not write that letter. Your first impulse may be the same, your judgment may be unchanged, but if you try it the ink will dry on your pen, and you will rise from your desk an unavenged but a greater and more Christian man. Throughout the whole day your actions, down to the last detail, will do homage to that early vision. Yesterday you thought mostly about your-self. To-day the poor will meet you, and you will feed them. The helpless, the tempted, the sad, will throng about you, and each you will befriend. Where were all these people yesterday? Where they are today, but you did not see them. It is in reflected light that the poor are seen. But your soul today is not at the ordinary angle. "Things which are not seen" are visible. For a few short hours you live the eternal life. The eternal life, the life of faith, is simply the life of the higher vision. Faith is an attitude—a mirror set at the right angle.

When tomorrow is over, and in the evening you review it, you will wonder how you did it. You will not be conscious that you strove for anything, or imitated anything, or crucified anything. You will be conscious of Christ; that He was with you, that without compulsion you were yet compelled, that without force, or noise, or proclamation, the revolution was accomplished. You do not congratulate yourself as one who has done a mighty deed, or achieved a personal success, or stored up a fund of "Christian experience" to ensure the same result again. What you are conscious of is "the glory of the Lord." And what the world is conscious of, if the result be a true one, is also "the glory of the Lord." In looking at a mirror one does not see the mirror, or think of it, but only of what it reflects. For a mirror never calls attention to itself except when there are flaws in it.

That this is a real experience and not a vision, that this life is possible to men, is being lived by men today, is simple biographical fact. From a thousand witnesses I cannot forbear to summon one. The following are the words of one of the highest intellects this age has known, a man who shared the burdens of his country as few have done, and who, not in the shadows of old age, but in the high noon of his success, gave this confession—I quote it with only a few abridgments—to the world:—

"I want to speak tonight only a little, but that little I desire to speak of the sacred name of Christ, who is my life, my inspiration, my hope, and my surety. I cannot help stopping and looking back upon the past. And I wish, as if I had never done it before, to bear witness, not only that it is by the grace of God, but that it is by the grace of God as manifested in Christ Jesus, that I am what I am. I recognize the sublimity and grandeur of the revelation of God in His eternal fatherhood as one that made the heavens, that founded the earth, and that regards all the tribes of the earth, comprehending them in one universal mercy; but it is the God that is manifested in Jesus Christ, revealed by His life, made known by the inflections of His feelings, by His discourse, and by His deeds—it is that God that I desire to confess tonight, and of whom I desire to say, "By the love of God in Christ Jesus I am what I am.""

"If you ask me precisely what I mean by that, I say, frankly, that more than any recognized influence of my father or my mother upon me; more than the social influence of all the members of my father's household; more, so far as I can trace it, or so far as I am made aware of it, than all the social influences of every kind, Christ has had the formation of my mind and my disposition. My hidden ideals of what is beautiful I have drawn from Christ. My thoughts of what is manly, and noble, and pure, have almost all of them arisen from the Lord Jesus Christ. Many men have educated themselves by reading Plutarch's *Lives of the Ancient Worthies,* and by setting before themselves one and another of these that in different ages have achieved celebrity, and they have recognized the great power of these men on themselves. Now I do not perceive that poet, or philosopher, or reformer, or general, or any other great man, ever has dwelt in my imagination and in my thought as the simple Jesus has. For more than twenty-five years I instinctively have gone to Christ to draw a measure and a rule for everything. Whenever there has been a necessity for it, I have sought—and at last almost spontaneously—to throw myself into the companionship of Christ; and early, by my imagination, I could see Him standing and looking quietly and lovingly upon me. There seemed almost to drop from His face an influence upon me that suggested what was the right thing in the controlling of passion, in the subduing of pride, in the overcoming of selfishness; and it is from Christ, manifested to my inward eye, that I have con-

65

sciously derived more ideals, more models, more influences, than from any human character whatever.

"That is not all. I feel conscious that I have derived from the Lord Jesus Christ every thought that makes heaven a reality to me, and every thought that paves the road that lies between me and heaven. All my conceptions of the progress of grace in the soul; all the steps by which divine life is evolved; all the ideals that overhang the blessed sphere which awaits us beyond this world—these are derived from the Savior. The life that I now live in the flesh I live by the faith of the Son of God.

"That is not all. Much as my future includes all these elements which go to make the blessed fabric of earthly life, yet, after all, what the summer is compared with all its earthly products—flowers, and leaves, and grass—that is Christ compared with all the products of Christ in my mind and in my soul. All the flowers and leaves of sympathy; all the twining joys that come from my heart as a Christian—these I take and hold in the future, but they are to me what the flowers and leaves of summer are compared with the sun that makes the summer. Christ is the Alpha and Omega, the beginning and the end of my better life.

"When I read the Bible, I gather a great deal from the Old Testament, and from the Pauline portions of the New Testament; but after all, I am conscious that the fruit of the Bible is Christ. That is what I read it for, and that is what I find that is worth reading. I have had a hunger to be loved of Christ. You all know, in some relations, what it is to be hungry for love. Your heart seems unsatisfied till you can draw something more toward you from those that are dearest to you. There have been times when I have had an unspeakable heart-hunger for Christ's love. My sense of sin is never strong when I think of the law; my sense of sin is strong when I think of love—if there is any difference between law and love. It is when drawing near the Lord Jesus Christ, and longing to be loved, that I have the most vivid sense of unsymmetry, of imperfection, of absolute unworthiness, and of my sinfulness. Character and conduct are never so vividly set before me as when in silence I bend in the presence of Christ, revealed not in wrath, but in love to me. I never so much long to be lovely, that I may be loved, as when I have this revelation of Christ before my mind.

"In looking back upon my experience, that part of my life which stands out, and which I remember most vividly, is just that part that has had some conscious association with Christ. All the rest is pale, and thin, and lies like clouds on the horizon. Doctrines, systems, measures, methods—what may be called the necessary mechanical and external part of worship; the part which the senses would recognize—this seems to have withered and fallen off like leaves of last summer; but that part which has taken hold of Christ abides."

Can anyone hear this life-music, with its throbbing refrain of Christ, and remain unmoved by envy or desire? Yet till we have lived like this we have never lived at all.

CHAPTER FOUR
THE FIRST EXPERIMENT

Then you reduce religion to a common friendship? A common friendship—Who talks of a *common* friendship? There is no such thing in the world. On earth no word is more sublime. Friendship is the nearest thing we know to what religion is. God is love. And to make religion akin to friendship is simply to give it the highest expression conceivable by man. But if by demurring to "a common friendship" is meant a protest against the greatest and the holiest in religion being spoken of in intelligible terms, then I am afraid the objection is all too real. Men always look for a mystery when one talks of sanctification; some mystery apart from that which must ever be mysterious wherever the Spirit works. It is thought some peculiar secret lies behind it, some occult experience which only the initiated know. Thousands of persons go to church every Sunday hoping to solve this mystery. At meetings, at conferences, many a time they have reached what they thought was the very brink of it, but somehow no further revelation came. Poring over religious books, how often were they not within a paragraph of it; the next page, the next sentence, would discover all, and they would be borne on a flowing tide forever. But nothing happened. The next sentence and the next page were read, and still it eluded them; and though the promise of its coming kept faithfully up to the end, the last chapter found them still pursuing. Why did nothing happen? Because there was nothing to happen—nothing of the kind they were looking for. Why did it elude them? Because there was no "it." When shall we learn that the pursuit of holiness is simply the pursuit of Christ? When shall we substitute for the "it" of a fictitious aspiration, the approach to a Living Friend? Sanctity is in character and not in moods; Divinity in our own plain calm humanity, and in no mystic rapture of the soul.

And yet there are others who, for exactly a contrary reason, will find scant satisfaction here. Their complaint is not that a religion expressed in terms of friendship is too homely, but that it is still too mystical. To "abide" in Christ, to "make Christ our most constant companion" is to them the purest mysticism. They want something absolutely tangible and absolutely direct. These are not the poetical souls who seek a sign, a mysticism in excess; but the prosaic natures whose want is mathematical definition in details. Yet it is perhaps not possible to reduce this problem to much more rigid elements. The beauty of friendship is its infinity, One can never evacuate life of mysticism. Home is full of it, love is full of it, religion is full of it. Why stumble at that in the relation of man to Christ which is natural in the relation of man to man?

If anyone cannot conceive or realize a mystical relation with Christ, perhaps all that can be done is to help him to step on to it by still plainer analogies from common life. How do I know Shakespeare or Dante? By communing with their words and thoughts. Many men know Dante better than their own fathers. He influences them more. As a spiritual presence he is more near to them, as a spiritual force more real. Is there any reason why a man greater than Shakespeare or Dante, who also walked this earth, who left great words behind Him, who has great works everywhere in the world now, should not also instruct, inspire, and mold the characters of men? I do not limit Christ's influence to this. It is this, and it is more. But Christ, so far from resenting or discouraging this relation of friendship, Himself proposed it. "Abide in Me" was almost His last word to the world. And He partly met the difficulty of those who feel its intangibleness by adding the practical clause, "If ye abide in Me *and My words abide in you.*"

Begin with His words. Words can scarcely ever be long impersonal. Christ Himself was a Word, a word made flesh. Make His words flesh; do them, live them, and you must live Christ. *"He that keepeth My commandments,* he it is that loveth Me." Obey Him and you must love Him. Abide in Him and you must obey Him. *Cultivate* His friendship. Live after Christ, in His Spirit, as in His presence, and it is difficult to think what more you can do. Take this at least as a first lesson, as introduction. If you cannot at once and always feel the play of His life upon yours, watch for it also indirectly. "The whole earth is full of the character of the Lord." Christ is the Light of the world, and much of His Light is reflected from things in the world—even from clouds. Sunlight is stored in every leaf, from leaf through coal, and it comforts us thence when days are dark and we cannot see the sun. Christ shines through men, through books, through history, through nature, music, art. Look for Him there. "Every day one should either look at a beautiful picture, or hear beautiful music, or read a beautiful poem." The real danger of mysticism is not making it broad enough.

Do not think that nothing is happening because you do not see yourself grow, or hear the whirr of the machinery. All great things grow noiselessly. You can see a mushroom grow, but never a child. Mr. Darwin tells us that evolution proceeds by "numerous, successive, and slight modifications." Paul knew that, and put it, only in more beautiful words, into the heart of his formula. He said for the comforting of all slowly perfecting souls that they grew "from character to character." "The inward man" he says elsewhere, "is renewed from day to day." All thorough work is slow; all true development by minute slight and insensible metamorphoses. The higher the structure, moreover, the slower the progress. As the biologist runs his eye over the long ascent of life, he sees the lowest forms of animals develop in an hour; the next above these reach maturity in a day; those higher still take weeks or months to perfect; but the few at the top demand the long experiment of years. If a child and an ape are born on the same day, the last will be in full possession of its faculties and doing the active work of life before the child has left its cradle. Life is the cradle of eternity. As the man is to the animal in the slowness of his evolution, so is the spiritual man to the natural man. Foundations which have to bear the weight of an eternal life must be surely laid. Character is to wear forever; who will wonder or grudge that it cannot be developed in a day?

To await the growing of a soul, nevertheless, is an almost divine act of faith. How pardonable, surely, the impatience of deformity with itself, of a consciously despicable character standing before Christ, wondering, yearning, hungering to be like that? Yet must one trust the process fearlessly, and without misgiving. "The Lord the Spirit" will do His part. The tempting expedient is, in haste for abrupt or visible progress, to try some method less spiritual, or to defeat the end by watching for effects instead of keeping the eye on the cause. A photograph prints from the negative only while exposed to the sun. While the artist is looking to see how it is getting on, he simply stops the getting on. Whatever of wise supervision the soul may need, it is certain it can never be overexposed, or, that, being exposed, anything else in the world can improve the result or quicken it. The creation of a new heart, the renewing of a right spirit is an omnipotent work of God. Leave it to the Creator. "He which hath begun a good work in you will perfect it unto that day."

No man, nevertheless, who feels the worth and solemnity of what is at stake will be careless as to his progress. To become like Christ is the only thing in the world worth caring for, the thing before which every ambition of man is folly, and all lower achievement vain. Those only who make this quest the supreme desire and passion of their lives can even begin to hope to reach it. If, therefore, it has seemed up to this point as if all depended on passivity, let me now assert, with conviction more intense, that all depends on activity. A religion of effortless adoration may be a religion for an angel but never for a man. Not in the contemplative, but in the active lies true hope; not in rapture, but in reality lies true life; not in the realm of ideals but among tangible things is man's sanctification wrought. Resolution, effort, pain, self-crucifixion, agony—all the things already dismissed as futile in themselves must now be restored to office, and a tenfold responsibility laid upon them. For what is their office? Nothing less than to move the vast inertia of the soul, and place it, and keep it where the spiritual forces will act upon it. It is to rally the forces of the will, and keep the surface of the mirror bright, and ever in position. It is to uncover the face which is to look at Christ, and draw down the veil when unhallowed sights are near. You have, perhaps, gone with an astronomer to watch him photograph the spectrum of a star. As you entered the dark vault of the observatory you saw him begin by lighting a candle. To see the star with? No; but to see to adjust the instrument to see the star with. It was the star that was going to take the photograph; it was, also, the astronomer. For a long time he worked in the dimness, screwing tubes and polishing lenses and adjusting reflectors, and only after much labor the finely focused instrument was brought to bear. Then he blew out the light, and left the star to do its work upon the plate alone. The day's task for the Christian is to bring his instrument to bear. Having done that he may blow out his candle. All the evidences of Christianity which have brought him there, all aids to faith, all acts of worship, all the leverages of the Church, all prayer and meditation, all girding of the will—these lesser processes, these candle-light activities for that supreme hour may be set aside. But, remember, it is but for an hour. The wise man will be he who quickest lights his candle; the wisest he who never lets it out. Tomorrow, the next moment, he, a poor, darkened, slurred soul, may need it again to focus the Image better, to take a mote off the lens, to clear the mirror from a breath with which the world has dulled it.

No readjustment is ever required on behalf of the Star. That is one great fixed point in this shifting universe. But *the world moves.* And each day, each hour, demands a further motion and re-adjustment for the soul. A telescope in an observatory follows a star by clockwork, but the clockwork of the soul is called the *will.* Hence, while the soul in passivity reflects the Image of the Lord, the will in intense activity holds the mirror in position lest the drifting motion of the world bear it beyond the line of vision. To "follow Christ" is largely to keep the soul in such position as will allow for the motion of the earth. And this calculated counteracting of the movements of a world, this holding of the mirror exactly opposite to the mirrored, this steadying of the faculties unerringly, through cloud and earthquake, fire and sword, is the stupendous cooperating labor of the will. It is all man's work. It is all Christ's work. In practice, it is both; in theory it is both. But the wise man will say in practice, "It depends upon myself."

In the Galerie des Beaux Arts in Paris there stands a famous statue. It was the last work of a great genius, who, like many a genius, was very poor and lived in a garret which served as studio and sleeping-room alike. When the statue was all but finished, one midnight a sudden frost fell upon Paris. The sculptor lay awake in the fireless room and thought of the still moist clay, thought how the water would freeze in the pores and destroy in an hour the dream of his life. So the old man rose from his couch and heaped the bed-clothes reverently round his work. In the morning when the neighbors entered the room the sculptor was dead. But the statue lived.

The image of Christ that is forming within us—that is life's one charge. Let every project stand aside for that. "Till Christ be formed" no man's work is finished, no religion crowned, no life has fulfilled its end. Is the infinite task begun? When, how, are we to be different? Time cannot change men. Death cannot change men. Christ can. Wherefore, *put on Christ.*

PAX VOBISCUM

Come unto Me all ye that are weary and heavy-laden and I will give you rest. Take My Yoke upon you and learn of Me, for I am Meek and Lowly in heart, and ye shall find Rest unto your souls. For My Yoke is easy and My Burden Light.

INTRODUCTORY

I heard the other morning a sermon by a distinguished preacher upon "rest." It was full of delightful thoughts; but when I came to ask myself, "How does he say I can yet rest?" there was no answer. The sermon was sincerely meant to be practical, yet it contained no experience that seemed to me to be tangible, nor any advice which could help me to find the thing itself as I went about the world that afternoon. Yet this omission of the only important problem was not the fault of the preacher. The whole popular religion is in the twilight here. And when pressed for really working specifics for the experiences with which it deals, it falters, and seems to lose itself in mist.

This want of connection between the great words of religion and everyday life has bewildered and discouraged all of us. Christianity possesses the noblest words in the language; its literature overflows with terms expressive of the greatest and happiest moods which can fill the soul of man. Rest, joy, peace, faith, love, light—these words occur with such persistency in hymns and prayers that an observer might think they formed the staple of Christian experience. But on coming to close quarters with the actual life of most of us, how surely would he be disenchanted. I do not think we ourselves are aware how much our religious life is made up of phrases; how much of what we call Christian experience is only a dialect of the churches, a mere religious phraseology with almost nothing behind it in what we really feel and know.

For some of us, indeed, the Christian experiences seem further away than when we took the first steps in the Christian life. That life has not opened out as we had hoped; we do not regret our religion, but we are disappointed with it. There are times, perhaps, when wandering notes from diviner music stray into our spirits; but these experiences come at few and fitful moments. We have no sense of possession in them. When they visit us, it is a surprise. When they leave us, it is without explanation. When we wish their return, we do not know how to secure it.

All which points to a religion without solid base, and a poor and flickering life. It means a great bankruptcy in those experiences which give Christianity its personal solace and make it attractive to the world, and a great uncertainty as to any remedy. It is as if we knew everything about health—except the way to get it.

I am quite sure that the difficulty does not lie in the fact that men are not in earnest. This is simply not the fact. All around us Christians are wearing themselves out in trying to be better. The amount of spiritual longing in the world—in the hearts of unnumbered thousands of men and women in whom we should never suspect it; among the wise and thoughtful; among the young and gay, who seldom assuage and never betray their thirst—this is one of the most wonderful and touching facts of life. It is not more heat that is needed, but more light; not more force, but a wiser direction to be given to very real energies already there.

What Christian experience wants is *thread,* a vertebral column, method. It is impossible to believe that there is no remedy for its unevenness and dishevelment, or that the remedy is a secret. The idea, also, that some few men, by happy chance or happier temperament, have acquired the secret—as if there were some sort of knack or trick of it—is wholly incredible. Religion must ripen its fruit for men of every temperament; and the way even into its highest heights must be by a gateway through which the peoples of the world may pass.

I shall try to lead up to this gateway by a very familiar path. But as that path is strangely unfrequented, and even unknown where it passes into the religious sphere, I must dwell for a moment on the commonest of commonplaces.

Chapter One
EFFECTS REQUIRE CAUSES

Nothing that happens in the world happens by chance. God is a God of order. Everything is arranged upon definite principles, and never at random. The world, even the religious world, is governed by law. Character is governed by law. Happiness is governed by law. The Christian experiences are governed by law. Men, forgetting this, expect rest, joy, peace, faith, to drop into their souls from the air like snow or rain. But in point of fact they do not do so; if they did they would no less have their origin in previous activities and be controlled by natural laws. Rain and snow do drop from the air, but not without a long previous history. They are the mature effects of former causes. Equally so are rest, and peace, and joy. They, too, have each a previous history. Storms and winds and calms are not accidents, but are brought about by antecedent circumstances. Rest and peace are but calms in man's inward nature, and arise through causes as definite and as inevitable.

Realize it thoroughly: it is a methodical not an accidental world. If a housewife turns out a good cake, it is the result of a sound recipe, carefully applied. She cannot mix the assigned ingredients and fire them for the appropriate time without producing the result. It is not she who has made the cake; it is nature. She brings related things together; sets causes at work; these causes bring about the result. She is not a creator, but an intermediary. She does not expect random causes to produce specific effects—random ingredients would only produce random cakes. So it is in the making of Christian experiences. Certain lines are followed; certain effects are the result. These effects cannot but be the result. But the result can never take place without the previous cause. To expect results without antecedents is to expect cakes without ingredients. That impossibility is precisely the almost universal expectation.

Now what I mainly wish to do is to help you to firmly grasp this simple principle of cause and effect in the spiritual world. And instead of applying the principle generally to each of the Christian experiences in turn, I shall examine its application to one in some little detail. The one I shall select is rest. And I think anyone who follows the application in this single instance will be able to apply it for himself to all the others.

Take such a sentence as this: African explorers are subject to fevers which cause restlessness and delirium. Note the expression, "cause restlessness." *Restlessness has a cause.* Clearly, then, any one who wished to get rid of restlessness would proceed at once to deal with the cause. If that were not removed, a doctor might prescribe a hundred things, and all might be taken in turn, without producing the least effect. Things are so arranged in the original planning of the world that certain effects must follow certain causes, and certain causes must be abolished before certain effects can be removed. Certain parts of Africa are inseparably linked with the physical experience called fever; this fever is in turn infallibly linked with a mental experience called restlessness and delirium. To abolish the mental experience, the radical method would be to abolish the physical experience, and the way of abolishing the physical experience would be to abolish Africa, or to cease to go there. Now this holds good for all other forms of Restlessness. Every other form and kind of Restlessness in the world has a definite cause, and the particular kind of Restlessness can only be removed by removing the allotted cause.

All this is also true of rest. Restlessness has a cause. Must not *rest* have a cause? Necessarily. If it were a chance world we would not expect this; but, being a methodical world, it cannot be otherwise. Rest, physical rest, moral rest, spiritual rest, every kind of rest has a cause, as certainly as restlessness. Now causes are discriminating. There is one kind of cause for every particular effect, and no other; and if one particular effect is desired, the corresponding cause must be set in motion. It is no use proposing finely devised schemes, or going through general pious exercises in the hope that somehow rest will come. The Christian life is not casual but causal. All nature is a standing protest against the absurdity of expecting to secure spiritual effects, or any effects, without the employment of appropriate causes. The Great Teacher dealt what ought to have been the final blow to this infinite irrelevancy by a single question, "Do men gather grapes of thorns or figs of thistles?"

Why, then, did the Great Teacher not educate His followers fully? Why did He not tell us, for example, how such a thing as rest might be obtained? The answer is, that *He did.* But plainly, explicitly, in so many words? Yes, plainly, explicitly, in so many words. He assigned rest to its cause, in words with which each of us has been familiar from our earliest childhood.

He begins, you remember—for you at once know the passage I refer to—almost as if rest could be had without any cause: "Come unto Me" He says, "and I will *give* you rest."

Rest, apparently, was a favor to be bestowed; men had but to come to Him; He would give it to every applicant. But the next sentence takes that all back. The qualification, indeed, is added instantaneously. For what the first sentence seemed to give was next thing to an impossibility. For how, in a literal sense, can rest be *given?* One could no more give away rest than he could give away laughter. We speak of "causing" laughter, which we can do; but we cannot give it away. When we speak of giving pain, we know perfectly well we cannot give pain away. And when we aim at giving pleasure, all that we do is to arrange a set of circumstances in such a way as that these shall cause pleasure. Of course there is a sense, and a very wonderful sense, in which a Great Personality breathes upon all who come within its influence an abiding peace and trust. Men can be to other men as the shadow of a great rock in a thirsty land. Much more Christ; much more Christ as Perfect Man; much more still as Savior of the world. But it is not this of which I speak. When Christ said He would give men rest, He meant simply that He would put them in the way of it. By no act of conveyance would, or could, He make over His own rest to them. He could give them His recipe for it. That was all. But He would not make it for them; for one thing, it was not in His plan to make it for them; for another thing, men were not so planned that it could be made for them; and for yet another thing, it was a thousand times better that they should make it for themselves.

That this is the meaning becomes obvious from the wording of the second sentence: "Learn of Me and ye shall *find* rest." Rest, that is to say, is not a thing that can be given, but a thing to be *acquired.* It comes not by an act, but by a process. It is not to be found in a happy hour, as one finds a treasure; but slowly, as one finds knowledge. It could indeed be no more found in a moment than could knowledge. A soil has to be prepared for it. Like a fine fruit, it will grow in one climate and not in another; at one altitude and not at another. Like all growths, it will have an orderly development and mature by slow degrees.

The nature of this slow process Christ clearly defines when He says we are to achieve rest by *learning*. "Learn of Me," He says, "and ye shall find rest to your souls." Now consider the extraordinary originality of this utterance. How novel the connection between these two words, "learn" and "rest"? How few of us have ever associated them—ever thought that rest was a thing to be learned; ever laid ourselves out for it as we would to learn a language; ever practiced it as we would practice the violin. Does it not show how entirely new Christ's teaching still is to the world, that so old and threadbare an aphorism should still be so little applied? The last thing most of us would have thought of would have been to associate *rest* with *work*.

What must one work at? What is that which if duly learned will find the soul of man in rest? Christ answers without the least hesitation. He specifies two things—meekness and lowliness. "Learn of Me," He says, "for I am *meek* and *lowly* in heart." Now these two things are not chosen at random. To these accomplishments, in a special way, rest is attached. Learn these, in short, and you have already found rest. These as they stand are direct causes of rest; will produce it at once; cannot but produce it at once. And if you think for a single moment, you will see how this is necessarily so, for causes are never arbitrary, and the connection between antecedent and consequence here and everywhere lies deep in the nature of things.

What is the connection, then? I answer by a further question. What are the chief causes of *unrest*? If you know yourself, you will answer pride, selfishness, ambition. As you look back upon the past years of your life, is it not true that its unhappiness has chiefly come from the succession of personal mortifications and almost trivial disappointments which the intercourse of life has brought you? Great trials come at lengthened intervals, and we rise to breast them; but it is the petty friction of our everyday life with one another, the jar of business or of work, the discord of the domestic circle, the collapse of our ambition, the crossing of our will, the taking down of our conceit, which make inward peace impossible. Wounded vanity, then, disappointed hopes, unsatisfied selfishness—these are the old, vulgar, universal sources of man's unrest.

Now it is obvious why Christ pointed out as the two chief objects for attainment the exact opposites of these. To meekness and lowliness these things simply do not exist. They cure unrest by making it impossible. These remedies do not trifle with surface symptoms; they strike at once at removing causes. The ceaseless chagrin of a self-centered life can be removed at once by learning meekness and lowliness of heart. He who learns them is forever proof against it. He lives henceforth a charmed life.

Christianity is a fine inoculation, a transfusion of healthy blood into an anemic or poisoned soul. No fever can attack a perfectly sound body; no fever of unrest can disturb a soul which has breathed the air or learned the ways of Christ. Men sigh for the wings of a dove that they may fly away and be at rest. But flying away will not help us. "The kingdom of God is *within you.*" We aspire to the top to look for rest; it lies at the bottom. Water rests only when it gets to the lowest place. So do men. Hence, be lowly. The man who has no opinion of himself at all can never be hurt if others do not acknowledge him. Hence, be meek. He who is without expectation cannot fret if nothing comes to him. It is self-evident that these things are so. The lowly man and the meek man are really above all other men, above all other things. They dominate the world because they do not care for it. The miser does not possess gold, gold possesses him. But the meek possess it. "The meek" said Christ, "inherit the earth." They do not buy it; they do not conquer it; but they inherit it.

There are people who go about the world looking out for slights, and they are necessarily miserable, for they find them at every turn—especially the imaginary ones. One has the same pity for such men as for the very poor. They are the morally illiterate. They have had no real education, for they have never learned how to live. Few men know how to live. We grow up at random, carrying into mature life the merely animal methods and motives which we had as little children. And it does not occur to us that all this must be changed; that much of it must be reversed; that life is the finest of the fine arts; that it has to be learned with lifelong patience, and that the years of our pilgrimage are all too short to master it triumphantly.

Yet this is what Christianity is for—to teach men the art of life. And its whole curriculum lies in one word—"Learn of Me." Unlike most education, this is almost purely personal, it is not to be had from books or lectures or creeds or doctrines. It is a study from the life. Christ never said much in mere words about the Christian graces. He lived them, He was them. Yet we do not merely copy Him. We learn His art by living with Him, like the old apprentices with their masters.

Now we understand it all? Christ's invitation to the weary and heavy-laden is a call to begin life over again upon a new principle upon His own principle. "Watch My way of doing things," He says. "Follow Me. Take life as I take it. Be meek and lowly and you will find rest."

I do not say, remember, that the Christian life to every man, or to any man, can be a bed of roses. No educational process can be this. And perhaps if some men knew how much was involved in the simple "learn" of Christ, they would not enter His school with so irresponsible a heart. For there is not only much to learn, but much to unlearn. Many men never go to this school at all till their disposition is already half ruined and character has taken on its fatal set. To learn arithmetic is difficult at fifty—much more to learn Christianity. To learn simply what it is to be meek and lowly, in the case of one who has had no lessons in that in childhood, may cost him half of what he values most on earth. Do we realize, for instance, that the way of teaching humility is generally *by humiliation?* There is probably no other school for it. When a man enters himself as a pupil in such a school, it means a very great thing. There is much rest there, but there is also much work.

I should be wrong, even though my theme is the brighter side, to ignore the cross and minimize the cost. Only it gives to the cross a more definite meaning, and a rarer value, to connect it thus directly and *causally* with the growth of the inner life. Our platitudes on the "benefits of affliction" are usually about as vague as our theories of Christian experience. "Somehow," we believe affliction does us good. But it is not a question of "Somehow." The result is definite, calculable, necessary. It is under the strictest law of cause and effect. The first effect of losing one's fortune, for instance, is humiliation; and the effect of humiliation, as we have just seen, is to make one humble; and the effect of being humble is to produce rest. It is a round-about way, apparently, of producing rest; but nature generally works by circular processes; and it is not certain that there is any other way of becoming humble, or of finding rest. If a man could make himself humble to order, it might simplify matters, but we do not find that this happens. Hence we must all go through the mill. Hence death, death to the lower self, is the nearest gate, and the quickest road to life.

Yet this is only half the truth. Christ's life outwardly was one of the most troubled lives that was ever lived: Tempest and tumult, tumult and tempest, the waves breaking over it all the time till the worn body was laid in the grave. But the inner life was a sea of glass. The great calm was always there. At any moment you might have gone to Him and found rest. And even when the blood-hounds were dogging Him in the streets of Jerusalem, He turned to His disciples and offered them, as a last legacy, "My peace." Nothing ever for a moment broke the serenity of Christ's life on earth. Misfortune could not reach Him; He had no fortune. Food, raiment, money-fountain-heads of half the world's weariness—He simply did not care for; they played no part in His life; He "took no thought" for them. It was impossible to affect Him by lowering His reputation; He had already made Himself of no reputation. He was dumb before insult. When He was reviled He reviled not again. In fact, there was nothing that the world could do to Him that could ruffle the surface of His spirit.

Such living, as mere living, is altogether unique. It is only when we see what it was in Him that we can know what the word rest means. It lies not in emotions, nor in the absence of emotions. It is not a hallowed feeling that comes over us in church. It is not something that the preacher has in his voice. It is not in nature, nor in poetry, nor in music—though in all these there is soothing. It is the mind at leisure from itself. It is the perfect poise of the soul; the absolute adjustment of the inward man to the stress of all outward things; the preparedness against every emergency; the stability of assured convictions; the eternal calm of an invulnerable faith; the repose of a heart set deep in God. It is the mood of the man who says, with Browning, "God's in His heaven, all's well with the world."

Two painters each painted a picture to illustrate his conception of rest. The first chose for his scene a still, lone lake among the far-off mountains. The second threw on his canvas a thundering waterfall, with a fragile birch-tree bending over the foam; at the fork of a branch, almost wet with the cataract's spray, a robin sat on its nest. The first was only *Stagnation;* the last was *rest.* For in rest there are always two elements—tranquillity and energy; silence and turbulence; creation and destruction; fearlessness and fearfulness. This it was in Christ.

It is quite plain from all this that whatever else He claimed to be or to do, He at least knew how to live. All this is the perfection of living, of living in the mere sense of passing through the world in the best way. Hence His anxiety to communicate His idea of life to others. He came, He said, to give men life, true life, a more abundant life than they were living; "the life," as the fine phrase in the Revised Version has it, "that is life indeed." This is what He Himself possessed, and it was this which He offers to all mankind. And hence His direct appeal for all to come to Him who had not made much of life, who were weary and heavy-laden. These He would teach His secret. They, also, should know "the life that is life indeed."

CHAPTER TWO
WHAT YOKES ARE FOR

There is still one doubt to clear up. After the statement, "Learn of Me," Christ throws in the disconcerting qualification, "*Take My yoke upon you and learn of Me.*" Why, if all this be true, does He call it a *yoke?* Why, while professing to give rest, does He with the next breath whisper "burden"? Is the Christian life after all, what its enemies take it for—an additional weight to the already great woe of life, some extra punctiliousness about duty, some painful devotion to observances, some heavy restriction and trammelling of all that is joyous and free in the world? Is life not hard and sorrowful enough without being fettered with yet another yoke?

It is astounding how so glaring a misunderstanding of this plain sentence should ever have passed into currency. Did you ever stop to ask what a yoke is really for? Is it to be a burden to the animal which wears it? It is just the opposite. It is to make its burden light. Attached to the oxen in any other way than by a yoke, the plough would be intolerable. Worked by means of a yoke, it is light. A yoke is not an instrument of torture; it is an instrument of mercy. It is not a malicious contrivance for making work hard; it is a gentle device to make hard labor light. It is not meant to give pain, but to save pain. And yet men speak of the yoke of Christ as if it were a slavery, and look upon those who wear it as objects of compassion. For generations we have had homilies on "The Yoke of Christ," some delighting in portraying its narrow exactions; some seeking in these exactions the marks of its divinity; others apologizing for it, and toning it down; still others assuring us that, although it be very bad, it is not to be compared with the positive blessings of Christianity. How many, especially among the young, has this one mistaken phrase driven forever away from the kingdom of God? Instead of making Christ attractive, it makes Him out a taskmaster, narrowing life by petty restrictions, calling for self-denial where none is necessary, making misery a virtue under the plea that it is the yoke of Christ, and happiness criminal because it now and then evades it. According to this conception, Christians are at best the victims of a depressing fate; their life is a penance; their hope for the next world purchased by a slow martyrdom in this.

The mistake has arisen from taking the word "yoke" here in the same sense as in the expressions "under the yoke," or "wear the yoke in

81

his youth." But in Christ's illustration it is not the *jugum* of the Roman soldier, but the simple "harness" or "ox-collar" of the Eastern peasant. It is the literal wooden yoke which He, with His own hands in the carpenter's shop, had probably often made. He knew the difference between a smooth yoke and a rough one, a bad fit and a good fit; the difference also it made to the patient animal which had to wear it. The rough yoke galled, and the burden was heavy; the smooth yoke caused no pain, and the load was lightly drawn. The badly fitted harness was a misery; the well fitted collar was "easy."

And what was the "burden"? It was not some special burden laid upon the Christian, some unique infliction that he alone must bear. It was what all men bear. It was simply life, human life itself, the general burden of life which all must carry with them from the cradle to the grave. Christ saw that men took life painfully. To some it was a weariness, to others a failure, to many a tragedy, to all a struggle and a pain. How to carry this burden of life had been the whole world's problem. It is still the whole world's problem. And here is Christ's solution: "Carry it as I do. Take life as I take it. Look at it from My point of view. Interpret it upon My principles. Take My yoke and learn of Me, and you will find it easy. For My yoke is easy, works easily, sits right upon the shoulders, and *therefore* my burden is light."

There is no suggestion here that religion will absolve any man from bearing burdens. That would be to absolve him from living, since it is life itself that is the burden. What Christianity does propose is to make it tolerable. Christ's yoke is simply His secret for the alleviation of human life, His prescription for the best and happiest method of living. Men harness themselves to the work and stress of the world in clumsy and unnatural ways. The harness they put on is antiquated. A rough, ill-fitted collar at the best, they make its strain and friction past enduring, by placing it where the neck is most sensitive; and by mere continuous irritation this sensitiveness increases until the whole nature is quick and sore.

This is the origin, among other things, of a disease called "touchiness"—a disease which, in spite of its innocent name, is one of the gravest sources of restlessness in the world. Touchiness, when it becomes chronic, is a morbid condition of the inward disposition. It is self-love inflamed to the acute point; conceit, *with a hair-trigger.* The cure is to shift the yoke to some other place; to let men and things touch us through some new and perhaps as yet unused part of our nature; to become meek and lowly in heart while the old nature is becoming numb from want of use. It is the beautiful work of Christianity everywhere to adjust the burden of life to those who bear it, and them to it. It has a perfectly miraculous gift of healing. Without doing any violence to human nature, it sets it right with life, harmonizing it with all surrounding things, and restoring those who are jaded with the fatigue and dust of the world to a new grace of living. In the mere matter of altering the perspective of life and changing the proportions of things, its function in lightening the care of man is altogether its own. The weight of a load depends upon the attraction of the earth. But suppose the attraction of the earth were removed? A ton on some other planet, where the attraction of gravity is less, does not weigh half a ton. Now Christianity removes the attraction of the earth, and this is one way in which it diminishes men's burden. It makes them citizens of another world. What was a ton yesterday is not half a ton today. So, without changing one's circumstances, merely by offering a wider horizon and a different standard, it alters the whole aspect of the world.

Christianity as Christ taught it is the truest philosophy of life ever spoken. But let us be quite sure when we speak of Christianity that we mean Christ's Christianity. Other versions are either caricatures, or exaggerations, or misunderstandings, or shortsighted and surface readings. For the most part their attainment is hopeless and the results wretched. But I care not who the person is, or through what vale of tears he has passed, or is about to pass, there is a new life for him along this path.

CHAPTER THREE

HOW FRUITS GROW

Were rest my subject, there are other things I should wish to say about it, and other kinds of rest of which I should like to speak. But that is not my subject. My theme is that the Christian experiences are not the work of magic, but come under the law of cause and effect. And I have chosen rest only as a single illustration of the working of that principle. If there were time I might next run over all the Christian experiences in turn, and show how the same wide law applies to each. But I think it may serve the better purpose if I leave this further exercise to yourselves. I know no Bible study that you will find more full of fruit, or which will take you nearer to the ways of God, or make the Christian life itself more solid or more sure. I shall add only a single other illustration of what I mean, before I close.

Where does joy come from? I knew a Sunday scholar whose conception of joy was that it was a thing made in lumps and kept somewhere in Heaven, and that when people prayed for it, pieces were somehow let down and fitted into their souls. I am not sure that views as gross and material are not often held by people who ought to be wiser. In reality, joy is as much a matter of cause and effect as pain. No one can get joy by merely asking for it. It is one of the ripest fruits of the Christian life, and, like all fruits, must be grown. There is a very clever trick in India called the mango-trick. A seed is put in the ground and covered up, and after diverse incantations a full-blown mango-bush appears within five minutes. I never met anyone who knew how the thing was done, but I never met anyone who believed it to be anything else than a conjuring-trick. The world is pretty unanimous now in its belief in the orderliness of nature. Men may not know how fruits grow, but they do know that they cannot grow in five minutes. Some lives have not even a stalk on which fruits could hang, even if they did grow in five minutes. Some have never planted one sound seed of joy in all their lives; and others who may have planted a germ or two have lived so little in sunshine that they never could come to maturity.

Whence, then, is joy? Christ put His teaching upon this subject into one of the most exquisite of His parables. I should in any instance have appealed to His teaching here, as in the case of rest, for I do not wish you to think I am speaking words of my own. But it so happens that He has dealt with it in a passage of unusual fullness.

I need not recall the whole illustration. It is the parable of the vine. Did you ever think why Christ spoke that parable? He did not merely throw it into space as a fine illustration of general truths. It was not simply a statement of the mystical union, and the doctrine of an indwelling Christ. It was that, but it was more. After He had said it, He did what was not an unusual thing when He was teaching His greatest lessons. He turned to the disciples and said He would tell them why He had spoken it. It was to tell them how to get joy. "These things have I spoken unto you," He said, "that My joy might remain in you and that your joy might be full." It was a purposed and deliberate communication of His secret of happiness.

Go back over these verses, then, and you will find the causes of this effect, the spring, and the only spring, out of which true Happiness comes. I am not going to analyze them in detail. I ask you to enter into the words for yourselves. Remember, in the first place, that the vine was the Eastern symbol of joy. It was its fruit that made glad the heart of man. Yet, however innocent that gladness—for the expressed juice of the grape was the common drink at every peasant's board—the gladness was only a gross and passing thing. This was not true happiness, and the vine of the Palestine vineyards was not the true vine. *Christ* was "the *true* Vine." Here, then, is the ultimate source of joy. Through whatever media it reaches us, all true joy and gladness find their source in Christ. By this, of course, is not meant that the actual joy experienced is transferred from Christ's nature, or is something passed on from Him to us. What is passed on is His method of getting it. There is, indeed, a sense in which we can share another's joy or another's sorrow. But that is another matter. Christ is the source of joy to men in the sense in which He is the source of rest. His people share His life, and therefore share its consequences, and one of these is joy. His method of living is one that in the nature of things produces joy. When He spoke of His joy remaining with us He meant in part that the causes which produced it should continue to act. His followers, that is to say, by *repeating* His life would experience its accompaniments. His joy, His kind of joy, would remain with them.

The medium through which this joy comes is next explained: "He that abideth in Me, the same bringeth forth much fruit." Fruit first, joy next; the one the cause or medium of the other. Fruit-bearing is the necessary antecedent; joy both the necessary consequent and the necessary accompaniment. It lies partly in the bearing fruit, partly in the fellowship which makes that possible. Partly that is to say, joy lies in mere constant living in Christ's presence, with all that that implies of peace, of shelter, and of love; partly in the influence of that life upon mind and character and will; and partly in the inspiration to live and work for others, with all that that brings of self-riddance and joy in other's gain. All these, in different ways and at different times, are sources of pure happiness. Even the simplest of them—to do good to other people—is an instant and infallible specific. There is no mystery about happiness whatever. Put in the right ingredients and it must come out. He that abideth in Him will bring forth much fruit; and bringing forth much fruit is happiness. The infallible recipe for happiness, then, is to do good; and the infallible recipe for doing good is to abide in Christ.

The surest proof that all this is a plain matter of cause and effect is that men may try every other conceivable way of finding happiness, and they will fail. Only the right cause in each case can produce the right effect.

Then the Christian experiences are our own making? In the same sense in which grapes are our own making, and no more. All fruits *grow*—whether they grow in the soil or in the soul; whether they are the fruits of the wild grape or of the True Vine. No man can *make* things grow. He can *get them to grow by* arranging all the circumstances and fulfilling all the conditions. But the growing is done by God. Causes and effects are eternal arrangements, set in the constitution of the world; fixed beyond man's ordering. What man can do is to place himself in the midst of a chain of sequences. Thus he can get things to grow: thus he himself can grow. But the grower is the Spirit of God.

What more need I add but this—test the method by experiment. Do not imagine that you have got these things because you know how to get them. As well try to feed upon a cookery book. But I think I can promise that if you try in this simple and natural way, you will not fail. Spend the time you have spent in sighing for fruits in fulfilling the conditions of their growth. The fruits will come, must come. We have hitherto paid immense attention to *effects,* to the mere experiences themselves; we have described them, extolled them, advised them, prayed for them—done everything but find out what *caused* them. Henceforth let us deal with causes. "To be," says Lotze, "is to be in relations." About every other method of living the Christian life there is an uncertainty. About every other method of acquiring the Christian experiences there is a "perhaps." But in so far as this method is the way of nature, it cannot fail. Its guarantee is the laws of the universe, and these are "the hands of the Living God."

THE
IDEAL LIFE

THE IDEAL LIFE

December, 1897

INTRODUCTORY NOTE

The addresses which make up this volume were written by Professor Drummond between the years 1876 and 1881 and are now published to meet the wishes of those who heard some of them delivered, in the hope that they may continue his work.

They were never prepared for publication, and have been printed from his manuscripts with a few obvious verbal corrections. A few paragraphs used in later publications have been retained.

CHAPTER ONE
ILL-TEMPER
"THE ELDER BROTHER"

"He was angry, and would not go in."—Luke xv. 28.

Those who have studied the paintings of Sir Noel Paton must have observed that part of their peculiar beauty lies, by a trick of art, in their partial ugliness. There are flowers and birds, knights and ladies, gossamer-winged fairies and children of seraphic beauty; but in the corner of the canvas, or just at their feet, some uncouth and loathsome form—a toad, a lizard, a slimy snail—to lend, by contrast with its repulsiveness, a lovelier beauty to the rest. So in ancient sculpture the griffin and the dragon grin among the angel faces on the cathedral front, heightening the surrounding beauty by their deformity.

Many of the literary situations of the New Testament powerfully exhibit this species of contrast. The twelve disciples—one of them is a devil. Jesus upon the cross, pure and regal—on either side a thief. And here, as conspicuously, in this fifteenth chapter of Luke, the most exquisite painting in the Bible touched off at the foot with the black thundercloud of the elder brother—perfect, as a mere dramatic situation.

But this conjunction, of course, is more than artistic. Apart from its reference to the Pharisees, the association of these two characters—the prodigal and his brother—side by side has a deep moral significance.

When we look into sin, not in its theological aspects, but in its everyday clothes, we find that it divides itself into two kinds. We find that there are sins of the body and sins of the disposition. Or more narrowly, sins of the passions, including all forms of lust and selfishness, and sins of the temper. The prodigal is *the* instance in the New Testament of sins of passion; the elder brother, of sins of temper.

One would say, at a first glance, that it was the younger brother in this picture who was the thundercloud. It was he who had dimmed all the virtues, and covered himself and his home with shame. And men have always pointed to the runaway son in contrast with his domestic brother, as the type of all that is worst in human character. Possibly the estimate is wrong. Possibly the elder brother is the worse. We judge of sins, as we judge of most things, by their outward form. We arrange the vices of our neighbors according to a scale which society has tacitly adopted, placing the more gross and public at the foot, the slightly less gross higher up, and then by some strange process the scale becomes obliterated. Finally it vanishes into space, leaving lengths of itself unexplored, its sins unnamed, unheeded, and unshunned. But we have no balance to weigh sins. Coarser and finer are but words of our own. The chances are, if anything, that the finer are the lower. The very fact that the world sees the coarser sins so well is against the belief that they are the worst. The subtle and unseen sin, that sin in the part of the nature most near to the spiritual, ought to be more degrading than any other. Yet for many of the finer forms of sin society has yet no brand. This sin of the elder brother is a mere trifle, only a little bit of temper, and scarcely worthy the recording.

Now what was this little bit of temper? For Christ saw fit to record it. The elder brother, hard-working, patient, dutiful—let him get full credit for his virtues—comes in from his long day's work in the fields. Every night for years he has plodded home like this, heavy-limbed but light-hearted, for he has done his duty and honest sweat is on his brow. But a man's sense of responsibility for his character ends too often with the day's work. And we always meet the temptation which is to expose us when we least expect it. Tonight, as he nears the old homestead, he hears the noise of mirth and music. He makes out the strain of a dancing measure—a novel sound, surely, for the dull farm. "Thy brother is come," the servant says, "and they have killed the fatted calf." His brother! Happy hour! how long they mourned for him! How glad the old man would be! How the family prayer has found him out at last and brought the erring boy to his parents' roof! But no—there is no joy on that face. It is the thundercloud. "Brother, indeed," he mutters; "the scapegrace! Killed the fatted calf, have they? More than they ever did for me. I can teach them what I think of their merry-making. And talk of the reward of virtue! Here have I been all these years unhonored and ignored, and this young *roue* from the swine-troughs assembles the whole country-side to do him homage." "And he was angry, and would not go in."

"Oh, the baby!" one inclines to say at first; but it is more than this. It is the thundercloud, a thundercloud which has been brewing under all his virtues all his life. It is the thundercloud. The subtle fluids from a dozen sins have come together for once, and now they are scorching his soul. Jealousy, anger, pride, uncharity, cruelty, self-righteousness, sulkiness, touchiness, doggedness, all mixed up together into one—ill-temper. This is a fair analysis. Jealousy, anger, pride, uncharity, cruelty, self-righteousness, sulkiness, touchiness, doggedness,—these are the staple ingredients of ill-temper. And yet, men laugh over it. "Only temper," they call it: a little hot-headedness, a momentary ruffling of the surface, a mere passing cloud. But the passing cloud is composed of drops, and the drops here betoken an ocean, foul and rancorous, seething some-where within the life—an ocean made up of jealousy, anger, pride, un-charity, cruelty, self-righteousness, sulkiness, touchiness, doggedness, lashed into a raging storm.

This is why temper is significant. It is not in what it is that its significance lies, but in what it reveals. But for this it were not worth notice. It is the intermittent fever which tells of unintermittent disease; the occasional bubble escaping to the surface, betraying the rottenness underneath; a hastily prepared specimen of the hidden products of the soul, dropped involuntarily when you are off your guard. In one word, it is the lightning-form of a dozen hideous and unchristian sins.

One of the first things to startle us—leaving now mere definition—about sins of temper, is their strange *compatibility with high moral character.* The elder brother, without doubt, was a man of high principle. Years ago, when his father divided unto them his living, he had the chance to sow his wild oats if he liked. As the elder brother, there fell to him the larger portion. Now was his time to see the world, to enjoy life, and break with the monotony of home. Like a dutiful son he chose his career. The old home should be his world, the old people his society. He would be his father's right hand, and cheer and comfort his declining years. So to the servants he became a pattern of industry; to the neighbors an example of thrift and faithfulness; a model young man to all the country, and the more so by contrast with his vagabond brother. For association with lofty character is a painful circumstance of this deformity. And it suggests strange doubts as to the real virtue of much that is reckoned virtue and gets credit for the name. In reality we have no criterion for estimating at their true worth men who figure as models of all the virtues.

Everything depends on motive. The virtues may be real or only apparent, even as the vices may be real though not apparent. Some men, for instance, are kept from going astray by mere cowardice. They have not character enough to lose their character. For it often requires a strong character to go wrong. It demands a certain originality and courage, a pocketing of pride of which all are not capable, before a man can make up his mind to fall out of step with society and scatter his reputation to the winds. So it comes to pass that many very mean men retain their outward virtue. Conversely among the prodigal sons of the world are often found characters of singular beauty. The prodigal, no doubt, was a better man to meet and spend an hour with than his immaculate brother. A wealth of tenderness and generosity, truly sweet and noble dispositions, constantly surprise us in characters hopelessly under the ban of men. But it is an instance of misconception as to the nature of sin that with most men this counts for nothing; although in those whose defalcation is in the lower region it counts, and counts almost for every-thing. Many of those who sow to the flesh regard their form of sin as trifling compared with the inconsistent and unchristian graces of those who profess to sow to the spirit. Many a man, for example, who thinks nothing of getting drunk would scorn to do an ungenerous deed or speak a withering word. And, as already said, it is really a question whether he is not right. One man sins high up in his nature, the other low down; and the vinous spendthrift, on the whole may be a better man than the acid Christian. "Verily, I say unto you," said Jesus to the priests, "the publicans and the harlots go into the kingdom of God before you."

The fact, then, that there are these two distinct sets of sins, and that few of us indulge both, but most of us indulge the one or the other, explains the compatibility of virtuous conduct with much unloveliness of disposition. Now it is this very association which makes sins of temper appear so harmless. There cannot be much wrong, we fancy, where there is so much general good. How often it is urged as an apology for garrulous people, that they are the soul of kindness if we only knew them better. And how often it is maintained, as a set-off against crossness and pitiable explosions of small distempers, that those who exhibit them are, in their normal mood, above the average in demonstrative tenderness. And it is this which makes the cure so hard. We excuse the partial failure of our characters on the ground of their general success. We can afford to be a little bad who are so good. A true logic would say we can *only* afford to be a little better. If the fly in the ointment is a very small fly, why have a very small fly? Temper is the vice of the virtuous. Christ's sermon on the "elder brother" is evidently a sermon pointedly to the virtuous—not to make bad people good but to make good people perfect.

Passing now from the nature and relations of sins of this peculiar class, we come briefly to look at their effects. And these are of two kinds—the influence of temper on the intellect, and on the moral and religious nature.

With reference to the first, it has sometimes been taken for granted that a bad temper is a positive acquisition to the intellect. Its fieriness is supposed to communicate combustion to surrounding faculties, and to kindle the system into intense and vigorous life. "A man, when excessively jaded," says Darwin, "will sometimes invent imaginary offenses, and put himself into a passion unconsciously, for the sake of re-invigorating himself." Now, of course, passion has its legitimate place in human nature, and when really controlled instead of controlling, becomes the most powerful stimulus to the intellectual faculties. Thus it is this to which Luther refers when he says, "I never work better than when I am inspired by anger. When I am angry, I can write, pray, and preach well; for then my whole temperament is quickened, my understanding sharpened, and all mundane vexations and temptations depart."

The point, however, at which temper interferes with the intellect is in all matters of judgment. A quick temper really incapacitates for sound judgment. Decisions are struck off at a white heat, without time to collect grounds or hear explanations. Then it takes a humbler spirit than most of us possess to reverse them when once they are made. We ourselves are prejudiced in their favor simply because we have made them, and subsequent courses must generally do homage to our first precipitancy. No doubt the elder brother secretly confessed himself a fool the moment after his back was turned on the door. But he had taken his stand; he had said "I will not go in," and neither his father's entreaties nor his own sense of the growing absurdity of the situation—think of the man standing outside his own door—were able to shake him. Temptation betraying a man into an immature judgment, that quickly followed by an irrelevant action, and the whole having to be defended by subsequent conduct, after making such a fuss about it—such is the natural history on the side of intellect of a sin of temper.

Amongst the scum left behind by such an action, apart from the consequences to the individual, are results always disastrous to others. For this is another peculiarity of sins of temper, that their worst influence is upon others. It is generally, too, the weak who are the sufferers; for temper is the prerogative of superiors and inferiors, down to the bottom of the scale, have not only to bear the brunt of the storm, but to sink their own judgment and spend their lives in ministering to what they know to be caprice. So their whole training is systematically false, and their own mental habits become disorganized and ruined. When the young, again, are disciplined by the iron instead of by the golden rule, the consequences are still more fatal. They feel that they do not get a fair hearing. Their case is summarily dismissed untried; and that sort of nursery lynch law to which they are constantly subjected carries with it no explanation of moral principles, muzzles legitimate feelings, and really inflicts a punishment infinitely more serious than is intended, in crushing out all sense of justice.

But it is in their moral and social effects that the chief evil lies. It is astonishing how large a part of Christ's precepts is devoted solely to the inculcation of happiness. How much of His life, too, was spent simply in making people happy! There was no word more often on His lips than "blessed," and it is recognized by Him as a distinct end in life, the end for this life, to secure the happiness of others. This simple grace, too, needs little equipment. Christ had little. One need scarcely even be happy oneself. Holiness, of course, is a greater word, but we cannot produce that in others. That is reserved for God Himself, but what is put in our power is happiness, and for that each man is his brother's keeper. Now society is an arrangement for producing and sustaining human happiness, and temper is an agent for thwarting and destroying it. Look at the parable for a moment, and see how the elder brother's wretched pettishness, explosion of temper, churlishness, spoiled the happiness of a whole circle. First, it certainly spoiled his own. How ashamed of himself he must have been when the fit was over, one can well guess. Yet these things are never so quickly over as they seem. Self-disgust and humiliation may come at once, but a good deal else within has to wait till the spirit is tuned again. For instance, prayer must wait. A man cannot pray till the sourness is out of his soul. He must first forgive his brother who trespassed against him before he can go to God to have his own trespasses forgiven.

Then look at the effect on the father, or on the guests, or even on the servants. That scene outside had cast its miserable gloom on the entire company. But there was one other who felt it with a tenfold keenness—the prodigal son. We can imagine the effect on him. This was home, was it? Then, it was a pity he ever came. If this was to be the sort of thing, he had better go. Happier a thousand times among the swine than to endure the boorishness of his self-contained, self-righteous brother. Yes, we drive men from Christ's door many a time by our sorry entertainment. The Church is not spiritualized enough yet to entertain the world. We have no spiritual courtesies. We cultivate our faith and proclaim our hope, but forget that a greater than these is charity. Till men can say of us, "They suffer long and are kind; they are not easily provoked, do not behave themselves unseemly, bear all things, think no evil," we have no chance against the world. One repulsive Christian will drive away a score of prodigals. God's love for poor sinners is very wonderful, but God's patience with ill-natured saints is a deeper mystery.

The worst of the misery caused by ill-temper is that it does no good. Some misery is beneficial, but this is gratuitous woe. Nothing in the world causes such rankling, abiding, unnecessary and unblessed pain. And Christ's words, therefore, when He refers to the breach of the law of love, are most severe; "If any man offend one of these little ones," He says, "it were better for him that a millstone were hanged about his neck, and that he were cast into the depths of the sea." That is to say, it is Christ's deliberate verdict that it is better not to live than not to love.

In its ultimate nature distemper is a sin against love. And however impossible it may be to realize that now, however we may condone it as a pardonable weakness or small infirmity, there *is* no greater sin. A sin against love is a sin against God, for God is love. He that sinneth against love, sinneth against God.

This tracing of the sin to its root now suggests this further topic—its *cure*. Christianity professes to cure anything. The process may be slow, the discipline may be severe, but it can be done. But is not temper a constitutional thing? Is it not hereditary, a family failing, a matter of temperament, and can *that* be cured? Yes, if there is anything in Christianity. If there is no provision for that, then Christianity stands convicted of being unequal to human need. What course then did the father take, in the case before us, to pacify the angry passions of his ill-natured son? Mark that he made no attempt in the first instance to reason with him. To do so is a common mistake, and utterly useless both with ourselves and others. We are perfectly convinced of the puerility of it all, but that does not help us in the least to mend it. The malady has its seat in the affections, and therefore the father went there at once. Reason came in its place, and the son was supplied with valid arguments—stated in the last verse of the chapter—against his conduct, but he was first plied with love.

"Son," said the father, "thou art ever with me, and all that I have is thine." Analyze these words, and underneath them you will find the rallying cries of all great communities. There lie liberty, equality, and fraternity—the happy symbols with which men have sought to maintain governments and establish kingdoms. "Son"—there is liberty. "Thou art ever with me"—there is unity, fraternity. "All that I have is thine"—there is equality. If any appeal could rouse a man to give up himself, to abandon selfish ends, under the strong throb of a common sympathy, it is this formula of the Christian republic. Take the last, equality, alone—"All that I have is thine." It is absurd to talk of your rights here and your rights there. You have all rights. "All that I have is thine." There is no room for selfishness if there is nothing more that one can possess. And God has made the equality. God has given us all, and if the memory of His great kindness, His particular kindness to us, be once moved within, the heart must melt to Him, and flow out to all mankind as brothers.

It is quite idle, by force of will, to seek to empty the angry passions out of our life. Who has not made a thousand resolutions in this direction, only and with unutterable mortification to behold them dashed to pieces with the first temptation? The soul is to be made sweet not by taking the acidulous fluids out, but by putting something in—a great love, God's great love. This is to work a chemical change upon them, to renovate and regenerate them, to dissolve them in its own rich fragrant substance. If a man let this into his life, his cure is complete; if not, it is hopeless.

The character most hard to comprehend in the New Testament is the unmerciful servant. For his base extravagance his wife and children were to be sold, and himself imprisoned. He cries for mercy on his knees, and the 10,000 talents, a hopeless and enormous debt, is freely cancelled. He goes straight from the kind presence of his lord, and, meeting some poor wretch who owes him a hundred pence, seizes him by the throat and hales him to the prison cell, from which he himself had just escaped. How a man can rise from his knees, where, forgiven much already, he has just been forgiven more, and go straight from the audience chamber of his God to speak hard words and do hard things, is all but incredible. This servant truly in wasting his master's money must have wasted away his own soul. But grant a man any soul at all; love must follow forgiveness.

Being forgiven much, he *must* love much, not as a duty, but as a necessary consequence; he *must* become a humbler, tenderer man, generous and brotherly. Rooted and grounded in love, his love will grow till it embraces the earth. Then only he dimly begins to understand his father's gift—"All that I have is thine." The world is his: he cannot injure his own. The ground of benevolence is proprietorship. And all who love God are the proprietors of the world. The meek inherit the earth—all that He has is theirs. All that God has—what is that? Mountain and field, tree and sky, castle and cottage, white man, black man, genius and dullard, prisoner and pauper, sick and aged—all these are mine. If noble and happy, I must enjoy them; if great and beautiful, I must delight in them; if poor and hungry, I must clothe them; if sick and in prison, I must visit them. For they are all mine, all these, and all that God has beside, and I must love all and give myself for all.

Here the theme widens. From Plato to Herbert Spencer, reformers have toiled to frame new schemes of Sociology. There is none so grand as the sociology of Jesus. But we have not found out the New Testament sociology yet; we have spent the centuries over its theology. Surely man's relation to God may be held as settled now. It is time to take up the other problem, man's relation to man. With a former theology, man as man, as a human being, was of no account. He was a mere theological unit, the x of doctrine, an unknown quantity. He was taught to believe, therefore, not to love. Now we are learning slowly that to believe is to love; that the first commandment is to love God, and the second *like unto it*—another version of it—is to love man. Not only the happiness but the efficiency of the passive virtues, love as a power, as a practical success in the world, is coming to be recognized. The fact that Christ led no army, wrote no book, built no church, spent no money, but that He loved, and so conquered, this is beginning to strike men. And Paul's argument is gaining adherents that when all prophecies are fulfilled, and all our knowledge becomes obsolete, and all tongues grow unintelligible, this thing, Love, will abide and see them all out one by one into the oblivious past. This is the hope for the world, that we shall learn to love, and in learning that, unlearn all anger and wrath and evil-speaking and malice and bitterness.

And this will indeed be the world's future. This is heaven. The curtain drops on the story of the prodigal, leaving him *in,* but the elder brother out. And why is obvious. It is impossible for such a man to be in heaven. He would spoil heaven for all who were there. Except such a man be born again he cannot enter the kingdom of God. To get to heaven we must take it in with us.

There are many heavens in the world even now from which we all shut ourselves out by our own exclusiveness—heavens of friendship, of family life, of Christian work, of benevolent ministrations to the poor and ignorant and distressed. Because of some personal pique, some disapproval of methods, because the lines of work or some of the workers are not exactly to our taste, we play the elder brother, we are angry and will not go in. This is the naked truth of it, we are simply angry and will not go in. And this bears, if we could see it, its own worst penalty; for there is no severer punishment than just to be left outside, perhaps, to grow old alone, unripe, loveless and unloved. We are angry and will not go in. All sins mar God's image, but sins of temper mar God's image and God's work and man's happiness.

CHAPTER TWO
WHY CHRIST MUST DEPART
"A SERMON BEFORE COMMUNION"
"It is expedient for you that I go away."—John xvi. 7.

It was on a communion night like this that the words were spoken. They fell upon the disciples like a thunderbolt startling a summer sky.

Three and thirty years He had lived among them. They had lately learned to love Him. Day after day they had shared together the sunshine and the storm, and their hearts clung to Him with a strange tenderness. And just when everything was at its height, when their friendship was now pledged indissolubly in the first most solemn sacrament, the unexpected words come, "I must say goodbye; it is expedient for you that I go away." It was a crushing blow to the little band. They had staked their all upon that love. They had given up home, business, friends, and promised to follow Him. And now He says, "I must go!"

Let us see what He means by it. The words may help us to understand more fully our own relations with Him now that He is gone.

I. The first thing to strike one is the way Jesus took to break the news. It was characteristic. His sayings and doings always came about in the most natural way. Even His profoundest statements of doctrine were invariably *apropos* of some often trivial circumstance happening in the day's round. So now He did not suddenly deliver Himself of the doctrine of the Ascension. It leaked out as it were in the ordinary course of things.

The supper was over, but the friends had much to say to one another that night, and they lingered long around the table. They did not know it was the last supper, never dreamed of it, but there had been an unusual sweetness in their intercourse and they talked on and on. The hour grew late, but John still leaned on his Master's breast, and the others, grouped round in the twilight, drank in the solemn gladness of the communion evening. Suddenly a shadow falls over this scene. A sinister figure rises stealthily, takes the bag, and makes for the door unobserved. Jesus calls him and hands him the sop. The spell is broken. A terrible revulsion of feeling comes over Him—as if a stab in the dark had struck into His heart. He cannot go on now. It is useless to try. He cannot keep up the perhaps forced spirits.

"Little children," He says very solemnly, His voice choking, "yet a little while I am with you." And "Whither I go ye cannot come."

The hour is late. They think He is getting tired, He means to retire to rest. But Peter asks straight out, "Lord, whither goest Thou?" Into the garden? Back to Galilee? It never occurred to one of them that He meant the Unknown Land.

"Whither I go," He replies a second time, "Ye cannot follow Me now, but ye shall follow Me *afterward." Afterward!* The blow slowly falls. In a dim, bewildering way it begins to dawn upon them. It is separation.

We can judge of the effect from the next sentence. "Let not your heart be troubled," He says. He sees their panic and consternation, and doctrine has to stand aside till experimental religion has ministered. And then, it is only at intervals that He gets back to it; every sentence almost is interrupted. Questionings and misgivings are started, explanations are insisted on, but the terrible truth will not hide. He always comes back to that—He will not temper its meaning. He still insists that it is absolute, literal, and finally He states it in its most bare and naked form, "It is expedient for you that I go away."

II. Notice His reasons for going away. Why did Jesus go away? We all remember a time when we could not answer that question. We wished He had stayed, and had been here now. The children's hymn expresses a real human feeling, and our hearts burn still as we read it:—

> "I think, when I read that sweet story of old,
> How Jesus was here among men,
> How He called little children as lambs to His fold,
> I should like to have been with them then.
> I wish that His hands had been placed on my head,
> That His arms had been thrown around me,
> And that I might have seen His kind look as He said,
> 'Let the little ones come unto Me.' "

Jesus must have had reasons for disappointing a human feeling so deep, so universal, and so sacred. We may be sure, too, that these reasons intimately concern us. He did not go away because He was tired. It was quite true that He was despised and rejected of men; it was quite true that the pitiless world hated and spurned and trod on Him. But that did not drive Him away. It was quite true that He longed for His Father's house and pined and yearned for His love. But that did not draw Him away. No. He never thought of Himself. It is expedient for you, He says, not for Me, that I go.

1. The first reason is one of His own stating. "I go away *to prepare a place for you.*" And the very naming of this is a proof of Christ's considerateness. The burning question with every man who thought about his life in those days was, "Whither is this life leading?" The present, alas, was dim and inscrutable enough, but the future was a

fearful and unsolved mystery. So Christ put that right before He went away. He gave this unknown future form and color. He told us—and it is only because we are so accustomed to it that we do not wonder more at the magnificence of the conception—that when our place in this world should know us no more there would be another place ready for us. We do not know much about that place, but the best thing we do know, that *He* prepares it. Eye hath not seen, nor ear heard, nor hath it entered into the heart of man what the Lord went away to prepare for them that love Him. It is better to think of this, to let our thoughts rest on this, that He prepares it, than to fancy details of our own.

But that does not exhaust the matter. Consider the alternative. If Christ had not gone away, what then? We should not either. The circumstances of our future life depended upon Christ's going away to prepare them; but the fact of our going away at all depended on His going away. We could not follow Him hereafter, as He said we should, unless He led first. He had to be the Resurrection and the Life.

And this was part of the preparing a place for us—the preparing a way for us. He prepared a place for us by the way He took to prepare a place. It was a very wonderful way.

In a lonely valley in Switzerland a small band of patriots once marched against an invading force ten times their strength. They found themselves one day at the head of a narrow pass, confronted by a solid wall of spears. They made assault after assault, but that bristling line remained unbroken. Time after time they were driven back decimated with hopeless slaughter. The forlorn hope rallied for the last time. As they charged, their leader suddenly advanced before them with outstretched arms, and every spear for three or four yards of the line was buried in his body. He fell dead. But he prepared a place for his followers. Through the open breach, over his dead body, they rushed to victory and won the freedom of their country.

So the Lord Jesus went before His people, the Captain of our salvation, sheathing the weapons of death and judgment in Himself, and preparing a place for us with His dead body. Well for us not only that He went away, but that He went by way of the cross.

2. Another reason why He went away was to be very near. It seems a paradox, but He went away really in order to be near. Suppose, again, He had not gone away; suppose He were here now. Suppose He were still in the Holy Land, at Jerusalem. Every ship that started for the East would be crowded with Christian pilgrims. Every train flying through

Europe would be thronged with people going to see Jesus. Every mail-bag would be full of letters from those in difficulty and trial, and gifts of homage to manifest men's gratitude and love. You yourself, let us say, are in one of those ships. The port, when you arrive after the long voyage, is blocked with vessels of every flag. With much difficulty you land, and join one of the long trains starting for Jerusalem. Far as the eye can reach, the caravans move over the desert in an endless stream. You do not mind the scorching sun, the choking dust, the elbowing crowds, the burning sands. You are in the Holy Land, and you will see Jesus! Yonder, at last, in the far distance, are the glittering spires of the Holy Hill, above all the burnished temple dome beneath which He sits. But what is that dark seething mass stretching for leagues and leagues between you and the Holy City? They have come from the north and from the south, and from the east and from the west, as you have, to look upon their Lord. They wish "that His hands might be placed on their head; That His arms might be thrown around them." But it cannot be. You have come to see Jesus, but you will not see Him. They have been there weeks, months, years, and have not seen Him. They are a yard or two nearer, and that is all. The thing is impossible. It is an anti-climax, an absurdity. It would be a social outrage; it would be a physical impossibility.

Now Christ foresaw all this when He said it was expedient that He should go away. Observe, He did not say it was necessary—it was *expedient*. The objection to the opposite plan was simply that it would not have worked. So He says to you, "It is very kind and earnest of you to come so far, but you mistake. Go away back from the walls of the Holy City, over the sea, and you will find Me in your own home. You will find Me where the shepherds found Me, doing their ordinary work; where the woman of Samaria found Me, drawing the water for the forenoon meal; where the disciples found Me mending nets in their working clothes; where Mary found Me, among the commonplace household duties of a country village." What would religion be, indeed, if the soul-sick had to take their turn like the out-patients waiting at the poor-hour outside the infirmary? How would it be with the old who were too frail to travel to Him, or the poor who could not afford it? How would it be with the blind, who could not see Him, or the deaf, who could not hear Him? It would be physically impossible for millions to obey the Lord's command, "Come unto Me, and I will give you rest."

For their sakes it was expedient that He should go away. It was a great blessing for the world that He went. Access to Him is universally complete from every corner of every home in every part of the world. For the poor can have Him always with them. The soul-sick cannot be out of reach of the Physician. The blind can see His beauty now that He has gone away. The deaf hear His voice when all others are silent, and the dumb can pray when they cannot speak.

Yes the visible Incarnation must of necessity be brief. Only a small circle could enjoy His actual presence, but a kingdom like Christianity needed a risen Lord. It was expedient for the whole body of its subjects that He went away. He would be nearer man by being apparently further. The limitations of sense subjected Him while He stayed. He was subject to geography, locality, space, and time. But by going away He was in a spaceless land, in a timeless eternity, able to be with all men always even unto the end of the world.

3. Another reason why He went away—although this is also a para-dox—*was that we might see Him better.* When a friend is with us we do not really see him so well as when he is away. We only see points, details. It is like looking at a great mountain: you see it best a little way off. Clamber up the flanks of Mont Blanc, you see very little—a few rocks, a pine or two, a blinding waste of snow; but come down into the Valley of Chamounix and there the monarch dawns upon you in all his majesty.

Christ is the most gigantic figure of history. To take in His full pro-portions one must be both near and away. The same is true of all great-ness. Of all great poets, philosophers, politicians, men of science, it is said that their generation never knew them. They dawn upon us as time rolls past. Then their life comes out in its true perspective, and the symmetry of their work is revealed. We never know our friends, likewise, till we lose them. We often never know the beauty of a life which is lived very near our own till the hand of death has taken it away. It was expedient for us, therefore, that He should go—that we might see the colossal great-ness of His stature, appreciate the loftiness and massiveness of His whole character, and feel the perfect beauty and oneness of His life and work.

4. Still another reason. He went away that we might walk *by faith.* After all, if He had stayed, with all its inconveniences, we should have been walking by sight. And this is the very thing religion is continually trying to undo. The strongest temptation to every man is to guide himself by what he can see, and feel, and handle. This is the core of ritualism, the foundation of Roman Catholicism, the essence of idolatry. Men want to see God, therefore they make images of Him. We do not laugh at ritualism; it is intensely human. It is not so much a sin of presumption;

it is a sin of mistake. It is a trying to undo the going away of Christ. It is a trying to make believe that He is still here. And the fatal fallacy of it is that it defeats its own end. He who seeks God in tangible form misses the very thing he is seeking, for God is a Spirit. The desire burns within him to see God; the desire is given him to make him spiritual, by giving him a spiritual exercise to do; and he cheats himself by exercising the flesh instead of the spirit. Hunger and thirst after God are an endowment to raise us out of the seen and temporal. But instead of letting the spiritual appetite elevate us into the spirit, we are apt to degrade the very instrument of our spiritualization and make it minister to the flesh.

It was expedient in order that the disciples should be spiritualized that Jesus should become a Spirit. Life in the body to all men is short. The mortal dies and puts on immortality. So Christ's great aim is to strengthen the afterlife. Therefore He gave exercises in faith to be the education for immortality. Therefore Jesus went away to strengthen the spirit for eternity.

It is not because there is any deep mysterious value in faith itself that it plays so great a part in religion. It is not because God arbitrarily chooses that we should walk by faith rather than by sight. It is because it is essential to our future; it is because this is the faculty which of all others is absolutely necessary to life in the spirit.

For our true life will be lived in the spirit. In the hereafter there will be nothing carnal. Christ is therefore solicitous to educate our faith, for sight will be useless. There will be no eye, no pupil, no retina, no optic nerve in the hereafter, so faith is the spiritual substitute for them which Christ would develop in us by going away.

5. But the great reason has yet to be mentioned. He went away *that the Comforter might come.*

We have seen how His going away was a provision for the future life. The absent Lord prepares a place there; the absent Object of faith educates the souls of the faithful to possess and enjoy it. But He provides for the life that now is. And His going away has to do with the present as much as with the life to come. One day when Jesus was in Peroea, a message came to Him that a very dear friend was sick. He lived in a distant village with his two sisters. They were greatly concerned about their brother's illness, and had sent in haste for Jesus. Now Jesus loved Mary and Martha and Lazarus their brother, but He was so situated at the time that He could not go. Perhaps He was too busy, perhaps He had other similar cases on hand; at all events He could not go. When He went ultimately, it was too late. Hour after hour the sisters waited for Him. They could not believe He would not come; the slow hours dragged themselves along by the dying man's couch, and he was dead and laid in the grave before Jesus arrived. You can imagine one of His thoughts, at least, as He stands and weeps by that grave with the inconsolable sisters,—"It is expedient that I go away. I should have been present at his death-bed scene if I had been away. I will depart and send the Comforter. There will be no summons of sorrow which He will not be able to answer. He will abide with men forever. Everywhere He will come and go. He will be like the noiseless invisible wind, blowing all over the world wheresoever He listeth."

The doctrine of the Holy Ghost is very simple. Men stumble over it because they imagine it to be something very mysterious and unintelligible. But the whole matter lies here. Our text is the key to it. The Holy Spirit is just what Christ would have been had He been here. He ministers comfort just as Christ would have done—only without the inconveniences of circumstance, without the restriction of space, without the limitations of time. More: we need a personal Christ, but we cannot get Him, at least we cannot each get Him. So the only alternative is a spiritual Christ,—a Holy Spirit, and then we can all get Him. He reproves the world of sin, of righteousness, and of judgment. Christ had to go away to make room for a Person of the Trinity who could deal with the world. He Himself could only reprove the individual of sin, of righteousness, and of judgment. But work on a larger scale is done now that He is gone. This is what He refers to when He said, "Greater works than these shall ye do."

And yet Christ did not go away that the Spirit might take His place. Christ is with us Himself. He is with us and yet He is not with us, that is, He is with us by His Spirit. The Spirit does not reveal the Spirit. He speaks not of Himself, He reveals Christ. He is the nexus, the connection between the absent Christ and the world—a spiritual presence which can penetrate where the present Christ could not go. It was expedient for the present Christ to go away that the universal Christ might come to all.

Finally, if all this was expedient for us, this strange relation of Jesus to His people ought to have a startling influence upon our life. Expediency is a practical thing. It was a terrible risk going away. Has the expedient which Christ adopted been worthwhile to you and me? These three great practical effects at least are obvious.

(1) Christ ought to be as near to us as if He were still here. Nothing so simplifies the whole religious life as this thought. A present, personal Christ solves every difficulty, and meets every requirement of Christian

experience. There is a historical Christ, a national Christ, a theological Christ—we each want Christ. So we have Him. For purposes of expediency, for a little while, He has become invisible. It is our part to have Him.

"More present to Faith's vision keen;
Than any other vision seen;
More near, more intimately nigh
Than any other earthly tie."

(2) Then consider what an incentive to honest faithfulness this is. The kingdom of Heaven is like a man travelling into a far country. And before he went he called his servants and gave to every man his work.

Are we doing it faithfully? Are we doing it at all? The visible eye of the Master is off us. No-one inspects our work. Wood, hay, stubble, no man knows. It is the test of the absent Christ. He is training us to a kind of faithfulness whose high quality is unattained by any other earthly means. It was after the Lord was gone that the disciples worked. They grew fast after this—in vigor, in usefulness, in reliance, in strength of character. Hitherto they had rested in His love. Did you ever think what a risk it was for Him to go away? It was a terrible risk—to leave us here all by ourselves. And yet this was one of His ways of elevating us. Nothing exalts a man like confidence put in him. So He went away and let us try ourselves.

We cannot always sit at the communion table. We partake of the feast not so much as a luxury, though it is that, but to give us strength to work. We think our Sabbath services, our prayers, our Bible reading are our religion. It is not so. We do these things to help us to be religious in other things. These are the mere meals, and a workman gets no wages for his meals. It is for the work he does. The value of this communion is not estimated yet. It will take the coming week to put the value upon it. In itself it counts little; we shall see what it is, by what we shall be.

Every communicant is left by Christ with a solemn responsibility. Christ's confidence in us is unspeakably touching. Christ was sure of us: He felt the world was safe in our hands. He was away, but we would be Christs to it; the Light of the World was gone, but He would light a thousand lights, and leave each of us as one to illuminate one corner of its gloom.

(3) Lastly, He has only gone for a little while. "Behold, I come quickly." The probation will soon be past. "Be good children till I come

back," He has said, like a mother leaving her little ones, "and I will come again, and receive you unto Myself, that where I am, ye may be also." So we wait till He come again—we wait till it is expedient for Him to come back.

"So I am watching quietly
Every day.
Whenever the sun shines brightly,
I rise and say;
'Surely it is the shining of His face!'
And when a shadow falls across the window
Of my room
Where I am working my appointed task,
I lift my head to watch the door, and ask
If He is come."

CHAPTER THREE
GOING TO THE FATHER
"WRITTEN AFTER THE DEATH OF A FRIEND"
"I go to my Father."—John xiv. 12.

You can unlock a man's whole life if you watch what *words* he uses most. We have each a small set of words, which, though we are scarce aware of it, we always work with, and which really express all that we mean by life, or have found out of it. For such words embalm the past for us. They have become ours by a natural selection throughout our career of all that is richest and deepest in our experience. So our vocabulary is our history, and our favorite words are ourselves.

Did you ever notice Christ's favorite words? If you have you must have been struck by two things—their simplicity and their fewness. Some half-dozen words embalm all His theology and these are, without exception, humble, elementary, simple monosyllables. They are such words as these—world, life, trust, love.

But none of these was the greatest word of Christ. His great word was new to religion. There was no word there, when He came, rich enough to carry the new truth He was bringing to men. So He imported into religion one of the grandest words of human language, and transfigured it, and gave it back to the world illuminated and transformed, as the watchword of the new religion. That word was Father.

107

The world's obligation to the Lord Jesus is that He gave us that word. We should never have thought of it—if we had, we should never have dared to say it. It is a pure revelation. Surely it is the most touching sight of the world's past to see God's only begotten Son coming down from heaven to try to teach the stammering dumb inhabitants of this poor planet to say, "Our Father."

It is that word which has gathered the great family of God together. When we come face to face with the real, the solid, and the moving in our religion, it is to find all its complexity resolvable into this simplicity, that God, whom others call King Eternal, Infinite Jehovah, is, after all, our Father, and we are His children.

This, after all, is religion. And to live daily in this simplicity, is to live like Christ.

It takes a great deal to succeed as a Christian—such a great deal, that not many do succeed. And the great reason for want of success is the want of a central word. Men will copy anything rather than a principle. A relationship is always harder to follow than a fact. We study the details of Christ's actions, the point of this miracle and of that, the circumferential truth of this parable and of that, but to copy details is not to copy Christ. To live greatly like Christ is not to agonize daily over details, to make anxious comparisons with what *we* do and what *He* did, but a much more simple thing. It is to re-echo Christ's word. It is to have that calm, patient, assured spirit, which reduces life simply to this—a going to the Father.

Not one man in a hundred, probably, has a central word in his Christian life; and the consequence is this, that there is probably nothing in the world so disorderly and slipshod as personal spiritual experience. With most of us it is a thing without stability or permanence; it is changed by every trifle we meet, by each new mood or thought. It is a series of disconnected approaches to God, a disorderly succession of religious impulses, an irregulation of conduct, now on this principle, now on that, one day because we read something in a book, the next because it was contradicted in another. And when circumstances lead us really to examine ourselves, everything is indefinite, hazy, unsatisfactory, and all that we have for the Christian life are the shreds perhaps of the last few Sabbaths' sermons and a few borrowed patches from other people's experience. So we live in perpetual spiritual oscillation and confusion, and we are almost glad to let any friend or any book upset the most cherished thought we have.

Now the thing which steadied Christ's life was the thought that He was going to His Father. This one thing gave it unity, and harmony, and success. During His whole life He never forgot His Word for a moment. There is no sermon of His where it does not occur; there is no prayer, however brief, where it is missed. In that first memorable sentence of His, which breaks the solemn spell of history and makes one word resound through thirty silent years, the one word is this; and all through the after-years of toil and travail "the Great Name" was always hovering on His lips, or bursting out of His heart. In its beginning and in its end, from the early time when He spoke of His Father's business till He finished the work that was given Him to do, His life, disrobed of all circumstance, was simply this, "I go to My Father."

If we take this principle into our own lives, we shall find its influence tell upon us in three ways:

I. It explains life.
II. It sustains life.
III. It completes life.

I. It explains life. Few men, I suppose, do not feel that life needs explaining. We think we see through some things in it—partially; but most of it, even to the wisest mind, is enigmatic. Those who know it best are the most bewildered by it, and they who stand upon the mere rim of the vortex confess that even for them it is overspread with cloud and shadow. What is my life? Whither do I go? Whence do I come? These are the questions which are not worn down yet, although the whole world has handled them.

To these questions there are but three answers—one by the poet, the other by the atheist, the third by the Christian.

(*a*) The poet tells us, and philosophy says the same, only less intelligibly, that life is a sleep, a dream, a shadow. It is a vapor that appeareth for a little and vanisheth away; a meteor hovering for a moment between two unknown eternities; bubbles, which form and burst upon the river of time. This philosophy explains nothing. It is a taking refuge in mystery. Whither am I going? Virtually the poet answers, "I am going to the Unknown."

(*b*) The atheist's answer is just the opposite. He knows no unknown. He understands all, for there is nothing more than we can see or feel. Life is what matter is. The soul is phosphorus. Whither am I going? "I go to dust," he says; "death ends all." And this explains nothing. It is worse than mystery. It is contradiction. It is utter darkness.

(c) But the Christian's answer explains something. Where is he going? "I go to my Father." This is not a definition of His death—there is no death in Christianity; it is a definition of the Christian life. All the time it is a going to the Father. Some travel swiftly, some are long upon the road, some meet many pleasant adventures by the way, others pass through fire and peril; but though the path be short or winding, and though the pace be quick or slow, it is a going to the Father.

Now this explains life. It explains the two things in life which are most inexplicable. For one thing, it explains why there is more pain in the world than pleasure. God knows, although we scarce do, there is something better than pleasure—progress. Pleasure, mere pleasure, is animal. He gives that to the butterfly. But progress is the law of life to the immortal. So God has arranged our life as progress, and its working principle is evolution. Not that there is no pleasure in it. The Father is too good to His children for that. But the shadows are all shot through it, for He fears lest we should forget there is anything more. Yes, God is too good to leave His children without indulgences, without far more than we deserve; but He is too good to let them spoil us. Our pleasures therefore are mere *entertainments.* We are entertained like passing guests at the inns on the roadside. Yet after even the choicest meals we dare not linger. We must take the pilgrim's staff again and go on our way to the Father.

Sooner or later we find out that life is not a holiday, but a discipline. Earlier or later we all discover that the world is not a playground. It is quite clear God means it for a school. The moment we forget that, the puzzle of life begins. We try to play in school; the Master does not mind that so much for its own sake, for He likes to see His children happy, but in our playing we neglect our lessons. We do not see how much there is to learn, and we do not care. But our Master cares. He has a perfectly overpowering and inexplicable solicitude for our education, and because He loves us, He comes into the school sometimes and speaks to us. He may speak very softly and gently, or very loudly. Sometimes a look is enough, and we understand it, like Peter, and go out at once and weep bitterly. Sometimes the voice is like a thunderclap startling a summer night. But one thing we may be sure of: the task He sets us to is never measured by our delinquency. The discipline may seem far less than our desert, or even to our eye ten times more. But it is not measured by these—it is measured by God's solicitude for our progress; measured solely by God's love; measured solely that the scholar may be better educated when he arrives at his Father. The discipline of life is a preparation for meeting the Father. When we arrive there to behold His beauty, we must have the educated eye; and that must be trained here. We must become so pure in heart—and it needs much practice—that we shall see God. That explains life—why God puts man in the crucible and makes him pure by fire.

When we see Him, we must speak to Him. We have that language to learn. And that is perhaps why God makes us pray so much. Then we are to walk with Him in white. Our sanctification is a putting on this white. But there has to be much disrobing first; much putting off of filthy rags. This is why God makes man's beauty to consume away like the moth. He takes away the moth's wings, and gives the angel's, and man goes the quicker and the lovelier to the Father.

It is quite true, indeed, besides all this, that sometimes shadow falls more directly from definite sin. But even then its explanation is the same. We lose our way, perhaps, on the way to the Father. The road is rough, and we choose the way with the flowers beside it, instead of the path of thorns. Often and often thus, purposely or carelessly, we lose the way. So the Lord Jesus has to come and look for us. And He may have to lead us through desert and danger, before we regain the road—before we *are as we were*—and the voice says to us sadly once more, "This is the way to the Father."

The other thing which this truth explains is, why there is so much that is unexplained. After we have explained all, there is much left. All our knowledge, it is said, is but different degrees of darkness. But we know *why we do not know why*. It is because we are going to our Father. We are only going; we are not there yet. Therefore patience. "What I do thou knowest not now, but thou shalt know. Hereafter, thou shalt know." Hereafter, because the chief joy of life is to have something to look forward to. But, hereafter, for a deeper reason. Knowledge is only given for action. Knowing only exists for doing: and already nearly all men know to do more than they do do. So, till we do all that we know, God retains the balance till we can use it. In the larger life of the hereafter, more shall be given, proportionate to the vaster sphere and the more ardent energies.

Necessarily, therefore, much of life is still twilight. But our perfect refuge is to anticipate a little and go in thought to our Father, and, like children tired out with efforts to put together the disturbed pieces of a puzzle, wait to take the fragments to our Father.

And yet, even that fails sometimes. He seems to hide from us and the way is lost indeed. The footsteps which went before us up till then cease, and we are left in the chill, dark night alone. If we could only see the road, we should know it went to the Father. But we cannot say we are going to the Father; we can only say *we would like to go.* "Lord," we cry, "we know not whither Thou goest, and how can we know the way?" "Whither I go," is the inexplicable answer, "ye know not now." Well is it for those who at such times are near enough to catch the rest: "But ye shall know hereafter."

II. Secondly, and in a few words, this sustains life.

A year or two ago some of the greatest and choicest minds of this country labored, in the pages of one of our magazines, to answer the question, "Is life worth living?" It was a triumph for religion, some thought, that the keenest intellects of the nineteenth century should be stirred with themes like this. It was not so; it was the surest proof of the utter heathenism of our age. Is Life worth living? As well ask, is air worth breathing? The real question is this—taking the definition of life here suggested—Is it worthwhile going to the Father?

Yet we can understand the question. On any other definition we can understand it. On any other definition life is very far from being worth living. Without that, life is worse than an enigma; it is an inquisition. Life is either a discipline, or a most horrid cruelty. Man's best aims here are persistently thwarted, his purest aspirations degraded, his intellect systematically insulted, his spirit of inquiry is crushed, his love mocked, and his hope stultified. There is no solution whatever to life without this; there is nothing to sustain either mind or soul amid its terrible mystery but this; there is nothing even to account for mind and soul. And it will always be a standing miracle that men of powerful intellect who survey life, who feel its pathos and bitterness, and are shut up all the time by their beliefs to impenetrable darkness—I say it will always be a standing miracle how such men, with the terrible unsolved problems all around them, can keep reason from reeling and tottering from its throne. If life is not a going to the Father, it is not only not worth living, it is an insult to the living; and it is one of the strangest mysteries how men who are large enough in one direction to ask that question, and too limited in another to answer it, should voluntarily continue to live at all.

There is nothing to sustain life but this thought. And it does sustain life. Take even an extreme case, and you will see how. Take the darkest, saddest, most pathetic life of the world's history. That was Jesus Christ's. See what this truth *practically* was to Him. It gave Him a life of absolute composure in a career of most tragic trials.

You have noticed often, and it is inexpressibly touching, how as His life narrows, and troubles thicken around Him, He leans more and more upon this. And when the last days draw near—as the memorable chapters in John reveal them to us—with what clinging tenderness He alludes in almost every second sentence to "My Father." There is a wistful eagerness in these closing words which is strangely melting—like one ending a letter at sea when land is coming into sight.

This is the Christian's only stay in life. It provides rest for his soul, work for his character, an object, an inconceivably sublime object, for his ambition. It does not stagger him to be a stranger here, to feel the world passing away. The Christian is like the pearl-diver, who is out of the sunshine for a little, spending his short day amid rocks and weeds and dangers at the bottom of the ocean. Does he desire to spend his life there? No, but his Master does. Is his life there? No, his life is up above. A communication is open to the surface, and the fresh pure life comes down to him from God. Is he not wasting time there? He is gathering pearls for his Master's crown. Will he always stay there? When the last pearl is gathered, the "Come up higher" will beckon him away, and the weights which kept him down will become an exceeding weight of glory, and he will go, he and those he brings with him, to his Father.

He feels, to change the metaphor, like a man in training for a race. It is months off still, but it is nearer him than tomorrow, nearer than anything else. Great things are always near things. So he lives in his future. Ask him why this deliberate abstinence from luxury in eating and drinking. "He is keeping his life," he says. Why this self-denial, this separation from worldliness, this change to a quiet life from revelries far into the night? "He is keeping his life." He cannot have both the future and the present; he knows that every regulated hour, and every temptation scorned and set aside, is adding a nobler tissue to his frame and keeping his life for the prize that is to come.

Trial to the Christian is training for eternity, and he is perfectly contented; for he knows that "he who loveth his life in this world shall lose it—but he that hateth his life in this world shall keep it unto life eternal." He is keeping his life till he gets to the Father.

III. Lastly, in a word, this completes life.

Life has been defined as a going to the Father. It is quite clear that there must come a time in the history of all those who live this life when they reach the Father. This is the most glorious moment of life. Angels attend at it. Those on the other side must hail the completing of another soul with ineffable rapture. When they are yet a great way off, the Father runs and falls on their neck and kisses them.

On this side we call that death. It means reaching the Father. It is not departure, it is arrival; not sleep, but waking. For life to those who live like Christ is not a funeral procession. It is a triumphal march to the Father. And the entry at the last in God's own chariot is the best hour of all. No, as we watch a life which is going to the Father, we cannot think of night, of gloom, of dusk and sunset. It is life which is the night, and death is sunrise.

"Pray moderately," says an old saint, "for the lives of Christ's people." *Pray moderately.* We may want them on our side, he means. but Christ may need them on His. He has seen them a great way off, and set His heart upon them, and asked the Father to make them come quickly. "I will," He says, "that such a one should be with Me where I am." So it is better that they should go to the Father.

These words have a different emphasis to different persons. There are three classes to whom they come home with a peculiar emphasis:—

1. They speak to those who are staying away from God. "I do not wonder at what men suffer," says Ruskin, "I wonder often at what they lose." My fellow pilgrim, you do not know what you are losing by not going to the Father. You live in an appalling mystery. You have nothing to explain your life, nor to sustain it; no boundary line on the dim horizon to complete it. When life is done you are going to leap into the dark. You will cross the dark river and land on the further shore alone. No one will greet you. You and the Inhabitant of eternity will be strangers. Will you not today arise and go to your Father?

2. They speak, next, to all God's people. Let us remember that we are going to the Father. Even now are we the sons of God. Oh, let us live like it—more simple, uncomplaining, useful, separate—joyful as those who march with music, yet sober as those who are to company with Christ. The road is heavy, high road and low road, but we shall soon be home. God grant us a sure arrival in our Father's house.

3. And this voice whispers yet one more message to the mourning. Did death end all? Is it well with the child? It is well. The last inn by

the roadside has been passed—that is all, and a voice called to us. "Good-bye! I go to my Father."

CHAPTER FOUR

THE ECCENTRICITY OF RELIGION

"They said, He is beside Himself,"—Mark iii. 21.

The most pathetic life in the history of the world is the life of the Lord Jesus. Those who study it find out, every day, a fresh sorrow. Before He came it was already foretold that He would be acquainted with grief, but no imagination has ever conceived the darkness of the reality.

It began with one of the bitterest kinds of sorrow—the sorrow of an enforced silence. For thirty years He saw, but dared not act. The wrongs He came to redress were there. The hollowest religion ever known—a mere piece of acting—was being palmed off around Him on every side as the religion of the living God. He saw the poor trodden upon, the sick untended, the widow unavenged, His Father's people scattered, His truth misrepresented, and the whole earth filled with hypocrisy and violence. He saw this, grew up amongst it, knew how to cure it. Yet He was dumb, He opened not His mouth. How He held in His breaking spirit, till the slow years dragged themselves done, it is impossible to comprehend.

Then came the public life, the necessity to breathe its atmosphere: the temptation, the contradiction of sinners, the insults of the Pharisees, the attempts on his life, the dullness of His disciples, the Jews' rejection of Him, the apparent failure of His cause, Gethsemane, Calvary. Yet these were but the more marked shades in the darkness which blackened the whole path of the Man of Sorrows.

But we are confronted here with an episode in His life which is not included in any of these—an episode which had a bitterness all its own, and such as has fallen to the lot of few to know. It was not the way the world treated Him; it was not the Pharisees; it was not something which came from His enemies; it was something His friends did. When He left the carpenter's shop and went out into the wider life, His friends were watching Him. For some time back they had remarked a certain strangeness in His manner. He had always been strange among His brothers, but now this was growing upon Him. He had said much stranger things of late, made many strange plans, gone away on curious

115

errands to strange places. What did it mean? Where was it to end? Were the family to be responsible for all this eccentricity? One sad day it culminated. It was quite clear to them now. He was not responsible for what He was doing. It was His mind, alas, that had become affected. He was beside Himself. In plain English, *He was mad!*

An awful thing to say when it is true, a more awful thing when it is not; a more awful thing still when the accusation comes from those we love, from those who know us best. It was the voice of no enemy; it came from His own home. It was His own mother, perhaps, and His brethren, who pointed this terrible finger at Him; apologizing for Him, entreating the people never to mind Him, He was beside Himself—He was mad.

There should have been one spot surely upon God's earth for the Son of Man to lay His head—one roof, at least, in Nazareth, with mother's ministering hand and sister's love for the weary Worker. But His very home is closed to Him. He has to endure the furtive glances of eyes which once loved Him, the household watching Him and whispering one to another, the cruel suspicion, the laying hands upon Him, hands which were once kind to Him, and finally, the overwhelming announcement of the verdict of His family, "He is beside Himself." Truly He came to His own, and His own received Him not.

What makes it seemly to dig up this harrowing memory today, and emphasize a thought which we cannot but feel lies on the borderland of blasphemy? Because the significance of that scene is still intense. It has a peculiar lesson for us who are to profess ourselves followers of Christ—a lesson in the counting of the cost. Christ's life, from first to last, was a dramatized parable—too short and too significant to allow even a scene which well might rest in solemn shadow to pass by unimproved.

I. Observe, from the world's standpoint, *the charge is true.* It is useless to denounce this as a libel, a bitter, blasphemous calumny. It is not so—it is true. There was no alternative. Either He was the Christ, the Son of the living God, or He was beside Himself. A holy life is always a phenomenon. The world knoweth it not. It is either supernatural or morbid.

For what is being beside oneself? What is madness? It is eccentricity—ec-centr-icity—having a different center from other people. Here is a man, for instance, who devotes his life to collecting objects of antiquarian interest, old coins perhaps, or old editions of books. His center is odd; his life revolves in an orbit of his own. Therefore, his friends say he is eccentric. Or here is an engine with many moving wheels, large and small, cogged and plain, but each revolving upon a central axis, and describing a perfect circle. But at one side there is one small wheel which does not turn in a circle. Its motion is different from all the rest, and the changing curve it describes is unlike any ordinary line of the mathematician. The engineer tells you that this is *the eccentric,* because it has a peculiar center.

Now when Jesus Christ came among men He found them nearly all revolving in one circle. There was but one center to human life—self. Man's chief end was to glorify himself and enjoy himself forever. Then, as now, by the all but unanimous concensus of the people, this present world was sanctioned as the legitimate object of all human interest and enterprise. By the whole gravitation of society, Jesus—as a man—must have been drawn to the very verge of this vast vortex of self-indulgence, personal ease and pleasure, which had sucked in the populations of the world since time began. But He stepped back. He refused absolutely to be attracted. He put everything out of His life that had even a temptation in it to the world's center. He humbled Himself—there is no place in the world's vortex for humbleness; He became of no reputation—nor for namelessness. He emptied Himself—gravitation cannot act on emptiness. So the prince of this world came, but found nothing in Him. He found nothing, because the true center of that life was not to be seen. It was with God. The unseen and the eternal moved Him. He did not seek His own happiness, but that of others. He went about doing good. His object in going about was not gain, but to do good.

Now all this was very eccentric. It was living on new lines altogether. He did God's will. He pleased not Himself. His center was to one side of self. He was beside Himself. From the world's viewpoint it was simply madness.

Think of this idea of His, for instance, of starting out into life with so quixotic an idea as that of doing good; the simplicity of the expectation that the world ever would become good; this irrational talk about meat to eat that they knew not of, about living water; these extraordinary beatitudes predicating sources of happiness which had never been heard of; these paradoxical utterances of which He was so fond, such as that the way to find life was to lose it, and to lose life in this world was to keep it to life eternal. What could these be but mere hallucination and dreaming! It was inevitable that men should laugh and sneer at Him. He was unusual. He would not go with the multitude. And men were expected to go with the multitude. What the multitude thought, said, and did, were the right things to have thought, said, and done. And if anyone thought, said, or did differently, his folly be on his own head—he was beside himself, he was mad.

II. *Every man who lives like Christ produces the same reaction upon the world.* This is an inevitable consequence. What men said of Him, if we are true to Him, they will say of you and me. The servant is not above his master. If they have persecuted Me, they will also persecute you. A Christian must be different from other people. Time has not changed the essential difference between the spirit of the world and the spirit of Christ. They are radically and eternally different. And from the world's standpoint still Christianity is eccentricity. For what, again, is Christianity? It is the projection into the world of these lines along which Christ lived. It is a duplicating in modern life of the spirit, the method, and the aims of Jesus, a following through the world the very footprints He left behind. And if these footprints were at right angles to the broad beaten track the world went along in His day, they will be so still. It is useless to say the distinction has broken down. These two roads are still at right angles. The day may be, when the path of righteousness shall be the glorious highway for all the earth. But it is not now. Christ did not expect it would be so. He made provision for the very opposite. He prepared His Church beforehand for the reception it would get in the world. He gave no hope that it would be an agreeable one. Light must conflict with darkness, truth with error. There is no sanctioned place in the world as yet for a life with God as its goal, and self-denial as its principle. Meekness must be victimized; spirituality must be misunderstood; true religion must be burlesqued. Holiness must make a strong ferment and reaction in family or community, office or workshop, wherever it is introduced. "Think not that I am come to send peace on earth, I came not to send peace, but a sword. For I am come to set a man at variance against his father, and the daughter against her mother, and the daughter-in-law against her mother-in-law, and a man's foes (He might well say it) shall be they of his own household."

True religion is no milk-and-water experience. It is a fire. It is a sword. It is a burning, consuming heat, which must radiate upon everything around. The change to the Christlike Life is so remarkable that when one really undergoes it, he cannot find words in common use by which he can describe its revolutionary character. He has to recall the very striking phrases of the New Testament, which once seemed such exaggerations:—"A new *man,* a new *creature;* a new *heart;* a new *birth."* His very life has been taken down and re-crystallized round the new center. He has been born again.

The impression his friends receive from him now is the impression of eccentricity. The change is bound to strike them, for it is radical, central. They will call in unworthy motives to account for the difference. They will say it is a mere temporary fit, and will pass away. They will say he has shown a weakness which they did not expect from him, and try to banter him out of his novel views and stricter life. This, in its mildest form, is the modern equivalent of "He is beside himself." And it cannot be helped. It is the legitimate reproach of the cross. The words are hard, but not new. Has it not come down that long line of whom the world was not worthy? Its history, alas, is well known. It fell on the first Christians in a painful and even vulgar form.

The little Church had just begun to live. The disciples stood after the great day of Pentecost contemplating that first triumph of Christ's cause with unbounded joy. At last an impression had been made upon the world. The enterprise was going to succeed, and the whole earth would fill with God's glory. They little calculated that the impression they made on the world was the impression of their own ridiculousness. "What meaneth this?" the people asked. "It means," the disciples would have said, "that the Holy Ghost, who was to come in His name, is here, that God's grace is stirring the hearts of men and moving them to repent." The people had a different answer. "These men," was the coarse reply, "are full of new wine." Not mad this time—they are intoxicated!

Time passed, and Paul tells us the charge was laid at his door. He had made that great speech in the hall of the Caesarean palace before Agrippa and Festus. He told them of the grace of God in his conversion, and closed with an eloquent confession of his Lord. What impression had he made upon his audience? The impression of a madman. "As he thus spake for himself, Festus said with a loud voice, 'Paul, thou art beside thyself, much learning hath made thee mad.'" Poor Paul! How you feel for him when the cruel blow was struck. But there was no answer to it. From their viewpoint it was perfectly true. And so it has been with all saints to the present hour. It matters not if they speak like Paul the words of soberness. It matters not if they are men of burning zeal like Xavier and Whitfield, men of calm spirit like Tersteegen and à Kempis, men of learning like Augustine, or of ordinary gifts like

Wesley—the effect of all saintly lives upon the world is the same. They are to the Jews a stumbling-block and to the Greeks foolishness.

It is not simply working Christianity that is an offense. The whole spiritual life, to the natural man, is an eccentric thing. Take such a manifestation, for instance, as prayer. The scientific men of the day have examined it and pronounced it hallucination. Or take public prayer. A congregation of people with bowed heads, shut eyes, hushed voices, invoking, confessing, pleading, entreating One who, though not seen, is said to see, who, speaking not, is said to answer. There is no other name for this incantation from the world's standpoint than eccentricity, delusion, madness. We are not ashamed of the terms. They are the guarantee of quality. And all high quality in the world is subject to the same reproach. For we are discussing a universal principle. It applies to inventors, to discoverers, to philosophers, to poets, to all men who have been better or higher than their time. These men are never understood by their contemporaries. And if there are martyrs of science, the centers of science being in this world, seen, demonstrated, known, how much more must there be martyrs for religion whose center is beyond the reach of earthly eye?

III. It follows from this, that *the more active religion is, the more unpopular it must be.*

Christ's religion did not trouble His friends at first. For thirty years, at all events, they were content to put up with it. But as it grew in intensity they lost patience. When He called the twelve disciples, they gave Him up. His work went on, the world said nothing for some time. But as His career became aberrant more and more, the family feeling spread, gained universal ground. Even the most beautiful and tender words He uttered were quoted in evidence of His state. For John tells us that after that exquisite discourse in the tenth chapter about the Good Shepherd, there was a division among the Jews for these sayings: "And many of them said, He hath a devil and is mad. Why hear ye Him?" It seemed utter raving.

Have you ever noticed—and there is nothing more touching in history—how Christ's path narrowed?

The first great active period is called in books the year of public favor. On the whole it was a year of triumph. The world received Him for a time. Vast crowds followed Him. The Baptist's audience left him and gathered round the new voice. Palestine rang with the name of Jesus.

Noblemen, rulers, rabbis, vied with one another in entertaining Him. But the excitement died down suddenly and soon.

The next year is called the year of opposition. The applause was over. The crowds thinned. On every hand He was obstructed. The Sadducees left Him. The Pharisees left Him. The political party was roused into opposition. The Jews, the great mass of the people, gave Him up. His path was narrowing.

With the third period came the end. The path was very narrow now. There were but twelve left to Him when the last act of the drama opens. They are gathered on the stage together for the last time. But it must narrow still. One of the disciples, after receiving the sop, goes out. Eleven are left Him. Peter soon follows. There are but ten. One by one they leave the stage, till all forsook Him and fled, and He is left to die alone. Well might He cry, as He hung there in this awful solitude—as if even God had forgotten Him, "My God, my God, why hast Thou forsaken Me?"

But this is not peculiar to Jesus. It is typical of the life of every Christian. His path too, must narrow. As he grows in grace, he grows in isolation. He feels that God is detaching his life from all around it and drawing him to Himself for a more intimate fellowship. But as the communion is nearer, the chasm which separates him from his fellow man must widen. The degree of a man's religion, indeed, is to be gauged by the degree of his rejection by the world. With the early Christians was not this the commonest axiom, "We told you before," did not Paul warn them, "that we should suffer?" "Unto some it was given in the behalf of Christ not only to believe on Him, but also to suffer for His sake." It was the position of honor, as it were, in the family of God to be counted worthy of being persecuted for the sake of Christ.

It is a sad reflection that, as in the case of Christ, the keenest suffering may come sometimes still from one's own family circle. Among our friends there may be one on whom we all look askance—one who is growing up in the beauty of holiness, and we not knowing what it is that makes him strange. It often needs death to teach us the beauty of a life which has been lived beside our own; and we only know the worth of it when God proves it by taking it to Himself.

Finally, it may be objected to all this that if eccentricity is a virtue, it is easily purchased. Anyone can set up for an eccentric character. And if that is the desideratum of religion we shall have candidates enough for the office. But it remains to define the terms on which a Christian should be eccentric—Christ's own terms. And let them be guides to us in our eccentricity, for without them we shall be not Christians, but fanatics.

The qualities which distinguish the eccentricity of godliness from all other eccentricities are three, and we gather them all from the life of Christ.

(1) Notice, His eccentricity *was not destructive.* Christ took the world as He found it, He left it as it was. He had no quarrel with existing institutions. He did not overthrow the church—He went to church. He said nothing against politics—He supported the government of the country. He did not denounce society—His first public action was to go to a marriage. His great aim, in fact, outwardly, and all along, was to be as normal, as little eccentric as possible. The true fanatic always tries the opposite. The spirit alone was singular in Jesus; a fanatic always spoils his cause by extending it to the letter. Christ came not to destroy, but to fulfill. A fanatic comes not to fulfill, but to destroy. If we would follow the eccentricity of our Master, let it not be in asceticism, in denunciation, in punctiliousness, and scruples about trifles, but in largeness of heart, singleness of eye, true breadth of character, true love to men, and heroism for Christ.

(2) *It was perfectly composed.* We think of eccentricity as associated with frenzy, nervousness, excitableness, ungovernable enthusiasm. But the life of Jesus was a calm. It was a life of marvelous composure. The storms were all about it, tumult and tempest, tempest and tumult, waves breaking over Him all the time till the worn body was laid in the grave. But the inner life was as a sea of glass. It was a life of perfect composure. To come near it even now is to be calmed and soothed. Go to it at any moment and the great calm is there. The request to "come" at any moment was a standing invitation all through His life. Come unto Me at My darkest hour, in My heaviest trial, on My busiest day, and I will give you rest. And when the very bloodhounds were gathering in the streets of Jerusalem to hunt Him down, did He not turn to the quaking group around Him and bequeath to them—a last legacy—"My peace"?

There was no frenzy about His life, no excitement. In quietness and confidence the most terrible days sped past. In patience and composure the most thrilling miracles were wrought. Men came unto Him, and they found not restlessness, but rest. Composure is to be had for faith. We shall be worse than fanatics if we attempt to go along the lonely path with Christ without this spirit. We shall do harm, not good. We shall leave half-done work. We shall wear out before our time. Do not say, "Life is short." Christ's life was short; yet He finished the work that was given Him to do. He was never in a hurry. And if God has given us anything to do for Him, He will give time enough to finish it with a repose like Christ's.

(3) *This life was consistent.*

From the Christian standpoint a consistent life is the only sane life. It is not worthwhile being religious without being thorough. An inconsistent Christian is the true eccentric. He is the true phenomenon in the religious world; to his brother Christian the only madman. For madness, in a sense, is inconsistency; madness is incoherency, irrelevancy, disconnectedness; and surely there is nothing more disconnected than a belief in God and eternity and no corresponding life. And that man is surely beside himself who assumes the name of Christ, pledges perhaps in sacramental wine to be faithful to His name and cause, and who from one year to another never lifts a finger to help it. The man who is really under a delusion, is he who bears Christ's name, who has no uneasiness about the quality of his life, nor any fear for the future, and whose true creed is that

> He lives for himself, he thinks for himself,
> For himself, and none beside;
> Just as if Jesus had never lived,
> As if He had never died.

Yes, a consistent eccentricity is the only sane life. "An enthusiastic religion is the perfection of common sense." And to be beside oneself for Christ's sake is to be beside Christ, which is man's chief end for time and eternity.

CHAPTER FIVE
"TO ME TO LIVE IS CHRIST"
Philippians i. 21. In connection with Acts ix. 1—18.

There is no more significant sign of the days in which we live than the interest society seems to be taking in the biographies of great men. Almost all the more popular recent books, for instance—the books which everyone is reading and has to read—come under the category of biography; and, to meet the demand, two or three times in each season the market has to be supplied with the lives, in minute detail, of men who but for this would perhaps have lain in unnoticed graves.

This thirst for memoirs and lives and letters is not all to be put down to the hero worship which is natural to every heart. It means, perhaps, a higher thing than that. It means, in the first place, that great living is being appreciated for its own sake; in the second, that great living is being imitated. If it is true that any of us are beginning to appreciate greatness for its own sake—greatness, that is to say, in the sense of great and true living—it is one of the most hopeful symptoms of our history. And, further, if we are going on from the mere admiration of great men to try and live like them, we are obeying one of the happiest impulses of our being. There is indeed no finer influence abroad than the influence of great men in great books, and all that literature can do in supplying the deformed world with worthy and shapely models is entitled to gratitude and respect.

But a shadow sometimes comes over this thought of the magnetic attraction which greatness is having upon our age—the further thought how hard it is to get our greatness *pure*. The well is deep, maybe, and the fountain sparkles to the eye; but we ask perhaps in vain for a guarantee of quality. Each new ideal we adjust our life to copy turns out to have its adulteration of selfishness or pride, like the one we studied last, till the pattern we sought to follow surprises us by becoming a beacon for us to shun.

There are a few biographies, however, where men may find their greatness pure; amongst them is one familiar writing which, though seldom looked at as biographical in this sense, really contains the life and letters of the greatest man probably of human history. That man was Paul. The life of Paul the man, apart from the theology of Paul the apostle, is a legitimate and fruitful study from the mere standpoint of the biography of a great and successful life. Judged by his influence on human history, no single life is entitled to more admiration for what it has done, or is indeed more worthy of imitation for what it was. And in our quest after a true life, a worthy and satisfying life, there may be some light for us in this old biography which we have missed perhaps in the lives of later men.

If we were to begin by seeking an appropriate motto for Paul's life, we should not need to go further than the quotation which forms our text. This fragment from one of his own letters lets us in at once to his whole secret. The true discovery of a character is the discovery of its ideals. Paul spares us any speculation in his case. "To me to live," he says, "is Christ." This is the motto of his life, the ruling passion of it, which at once explains the nature of his success and accounts for it. He lives for Christ. "To me to live is Christ."

Now here at the outset is a valuable practical point settled in this biography. When we turn to the biographies of most great men, we find either no key or a very complex one; and we rise from the perusal with nothing more than a vague desire to do better, but with no discovery *how*. We gain stimulus, indeed, but no knowledge and this is simply injurious. We are braced up enthusiastically for a little, and then do nothing. At the end of it all we are not better, we are only exhausted. This is the reason why biography-hunters often, after long dogging the footsteps of greatness, find that they are perhaps no further on the road to it themselves, but rather more inclined than before to lie down where they were.

But Paul explicitly announces to us the working principle of his life. If the lines are great lines, there is nothing mysterious about them. If we want to live like Paul, we have simply to live for Christ; Christ our life on one side, our life for Christ on the other, and both summed up together in Paul's epitome: "To me to live is Christ."

This being the clue to Paul's life, the instructive question next arises, What exactly did Paul mean by this principle, and how did he come to find it out? But the question, "What is this object of life?" is so closely bound up with how Paul came to have this object of life, that the answer to the last question will form at once an explanation and an illustration of the first.

Therefore let us go at once for the answer to the life itself. Great principles are always best and freshest when studied from the life, and it so happens that a circumstance in Paul's life makes it peculiarly easy to act on this rule here.

That circumstance was that Paul had two lives. Many men besides Paul have had two lives, but the line is cleaner cut in Paul's case than in almost any other biography. Both lives were somewhere about the same length, so far as we know, but so distinct in their general features and details that Paul had not only two lives, but, as if to mark the distinction more strikingly, two names. Let us look for a moment at the first of these lives—the reason will appear presently.

Paul's first life, as we all know, was spent under the most auspicious circumstances, and it will be worthwhile running over it. Born of a family which belonged to the most select theological school of that day, the son was early looked upon as at once the promise of his parents and the hope of their religion. They sent him when a mere lad to Jerusalem, and enrolled him as a student in the most distinguished college of the time. After running a brilliant college career, and sitting for many years at the feet of the greatest learning the Jewish capital could boast, we find him bursting upon the world with his splendid talents, and taking a place at once in the troubled political movements of the day. It was impossible for such a character with his youth's enthusiasm and his Pharisee's pride to submit to the tame life of a temple Rabbi, and he sees his opportunity in the rise of the Christian sect. Here, at last, he would match his abilities in a contest which would gain him at once a field of exercise and a name. So far, doubtless, he thought his first life great.

Into his work of persecution he seems now to have entered with all an inquisitor's zest. His conspicuous place among the murderers of the first martyr stamped him forthwith as a leader, and gave him the foretaste of a popularity which, but for the interruption of the hand of God, might have ended disastrously to the struggling Christian church. His success as an inquisitor is recognized in the highest quarters of the land; and the young man's fortune is made. Perhaps no Rabbi of that time had such prospects now as Saul. "He is a man raised up for the emergency," said all Jerusalem, and henceforth the Jewish world was at his feet. Courted as the rising man of his day and flushed with success, he left no stone unturned to find fresh opportunities of adding to his influence and power. And as he climbed each rung of the ladder of fame, we can imagine, as a great student of Paul has said, how his heart swelled within him when he read these words at night from the Book of Wisdom: "I shall have estimation among the multitude, and honor with the elders, though I be young. I shall be found of a quick conceit in judgment, and shall be admired in the sight of great men. When I hold my tongue, they shall abide my leisure, and when I speak, they shall give good ear unto me." Such was the man who afterwards said, "To me to live is Christ."

Upon the little church at Jerusalem, he has already wreaked his vengeance to the full. The town and neighborhood at last are well nigh ridded of the pest; and—unlooked-for calamity—in the height of his triumph Saul finds his occupation gone. Dispersed in all directions, members of the little band have made their way in secret through Judaea and Samaria, through Syria and Phoenicia, even into strange cities. And Saul finds round-about Jerusalem no fuel to feed the martyrs' fire, and thus to add more lustre to his own name.

But there is no pause in the pursuit of human fame. The young lawyer's reputation can never end in an anti-climax like this. And with the ambition which knows not how to rest, and in the pride of his Pharisee's heart, he strikes out the idea to reverse the maxim of the crucified Leader of the hated sect and to go into all the world and suppress the gospel in every creature. He applies to the high priest for commission and authority, and, breathing out threatenings and slaughter, the man who is going to live for Christ starts out on his Christless mission to make havoc of the church.

This is the last act of Paul's first life. Let us note it carefully. We are on the bridge which separates Paul's two lives. What marks the transition is this: hitherto his life has been spent in public. It has been one prolonged whirl of excitement and applause. But no sooner have the gates of Jerusalem closed upon him than Saul begins to think. The echoes of the people's praises have died away one by one. He has gone out into the great desert. It is strangely silent and soothing, and the lull has come at last upon his soul. It is a long while, perhaps, since he has had time to think, but Saul was far too great a man to live long an unthinking life. His time for reflection has come. And as he wanders with his small escort along the banks of the Jordan or across the solitary hills of Samaria, his thoughts are busy with the past. And if Saul was far too great a man to live an unthinking life, he was also too great a man to think well of his life when he did think. Each new day as he journeyed away from the scene of his triumph, and looked back upon it all from that distance— which always gives the true perspective to man's life—his mind must have filled with many a sad reproach. And as he lay down at night in the quiet wilderness his thoughts must often have turned on the true quality of the life to which he was sacrificing his talents and his youth. With his quick perception, with his keen trained intellect, with his penetration, he must have seen that after all this life was a mistake. Minds of lesser caliber in the applauding world which he had left had told him he was great. Now, in his calmer moments, he knew he was not great. The eternal heavens stretching above him pointed to an infinity which lay behind them all; the stars and the silence spoke to him of God. He felt that his life was miserably small. Saul's thoughts were greater than Saul's life. How he had been living beneath himself—how he had wasted the precious years of his youth—how he had sold his life for honor and reputation, and bartered the talents God had given him for a name, he must have seen. He had been dazzled, and that was all. He had nothing really to show for his life, nothing that would stand the test of solid thought. It was all done for himself. He, Saul of Tarsus, the rising man of his time, was the sole center of it. "After all," perhaps he cried in agony, "To me to live is Saul. To me to live is Saul."

Paul's first great discovery, as we have seen—and it is the discovery which precedes every true reformation of life—was the discovery of himself. When Paul said, "To me to live is *myself*," his conversion was begun. There was no retreat then for a man like him. He was too great to have such a little center to his life; or rather, he felt life too great to be absorbed with even such a personality as his.

But the next element in the case was not so easily discovered, and it is of much more importance than the first. His first achievement was only to discover himself. His second was to discover someone better than himself. He wanted a new center to his life—where was he to find it? The unseen hand which painted his own portrait in its true colors on the dark background of his mind had painted every other life the same. The high priests at Jerusalem, the members of the Sanhedrim, his own father at Tarsus—all the men he knew were living lives like himself: They were no better—most of them worse. Must the old center of Paul's life remain there still? Is there nothing better in all the world than himself?

It may be conjecture, or it may be nearer truth, that while such questionings passed through the mind of Paul, there came into his thoughts as he journeyed some influences from another life—a life like that for which his thoughts had longed. Paul's best known journeys are his missionary tours, and we generally associate him in our thoughts with the countries of Asia and Italy and Greece. But this time his way leads through the Holy Land. He has entered the country of Christ. He is crossing the very footsteps of Jesus. The villages along his route are fragrant still with what Jesus said and did—not the bitter things that Saul had heard before. Kind words are repeated to him, and tender acts which Jesus did are told. The peasants by the way-side and the shepherds on the hills are full of stories of a self-denying life which used to pass that way a year or two ago, but now will come no more. And the mothers at the cottage doors remember the Stranger who suffered their little children to come unto Him, and get them to repeat to Saul, perhaps, the children's blessing which He left behind. Perhaps, in passing through Samaria, the traveller meets a woman at a well, who tells her strange tale for the thousandth time, of a weary Man who had sat there once and said He was the Christ. And Galilee and Capernaum, and Bethsaida, and the lake shore at Gennesaret, are full of memories of the one true life which surely even then had begun to cast a sacred influence over Saul. At all events, there seems a strange preparedness in his mind for the meeting on the Damascus road, as if the interview with Jesus then were not so much the first of his friendship as the natural outcome of something that had gone before. And no doubt the Spirit's silent working had been telling on his mind during all these quiet days, leading up his thoughts to the revelation that was to come and preparing a pathos for the memorable question, with its otherwise unaccountable emphasis, "Why persecutest thou *Me?*"

What went on between Paul's heart and God we do not know. We do not know how deep repentance ran, nor where nor how the justifying grace came down from heaven to his soul. Whether just then he went through our formula of conversion—the process which we like to watch and describe in technical words—we do not know. But we know this— there came a difference into his life. His life was changed. It was changed at its most radical part. He had changed centers. During the process, whatever it was, this great transfer was effected. Paul deliberately removed the old center from his life, and put a new one in its place. Instead of "to me to live is Saul." It was now, "to me to live is Christ."

Of course, when the center of Paul's life was changed, he had to take his whole life to pieces and build it up again on a totally different plan. This change, therefore, is not a mere incident in a man's life. It is a revolution, a revolution of the most sweeping sort. There never was a life so filled up with anti-Christian thoughts and impulses, brought so completely to a halt. There never was such a total eclipse of the most brilliant worldly prospects, nor such an abrupt transition from a career of dazzling greatness to humble and obscure ignominy.

Let those who define conversion as a certain colorless experience supposed to go on in the feelings, blind themselves to the real transition in this life if they will. Let them ask themselves if there ever was a more sweeping revolution in any life, for any cause, than in Paul's, when he abandoned himself, literally abandoned himself, and subordinated everything, evermore, to this one supreme passion—"to live for Christ."

The stages by which this transcendent standpoint is to be reached are now plainly before us. They are the discovery of self and the discovery of Christ. These two discoveries between them exhaust the whole of life. No man truly lives till both these discoveries are made—for many discover themselves who have not yet discovered Christ. But he that hath not the Son hath not life. Whatever he has—existence, continuity—he has not life. The condition of living at all is to live for Christ. "He that hath the Son," and he alone, and no one else, "hath life."

1. Paul takes special care indeed that we should fully understand the altogether different quality of the two lives which a man may live. In his view, the first life, the ordinary life of men, was altogether a mistake. "What things were gain to me" he tells us, "I counted loss for Christ." That brilliant career of his was loss; that mission, noble and absorbing once, was mere waste energy and misspent time. And he goes further still. His life was death. It was selfishness pure and simple; it was the carnal mind pure and simple; and to be carnally minded is death. We shall understand the theology of these letters better if we think of the writer as a man escaping death. And with this horrible background to his life we can see the fuller significance of his words, that for him to live was Christ.

Another thing is also made plain to us.

The ceaseless demand of the New Testament for regeneration is plain to us when we study the doctrine in such a life as this. It was not Saul who wrote the letters; it was a different man altogether—Paul. It was one who was in a totally different world from the other. If it were Saul, he must have been born again before he could have done it. Nothing less could account for it. His interests were new, his standpoint, his resources, his friendships. All old things, in fact, had passed away. All things had become new. In a word, he was a new creature. The pool, polluted and stagnant, had found its way at last into the wide, pure sea; the spirit, tired of its narrow prison, disgusted with ambition which ended with itself, reaches out to the eternal freedom, and found a worthy field of exercise in the great enterprise of Christ.

There is one class to whom this biography of Paul has a special message. The people who need Paul's change most are not those, always, who are most thought to need it. The really difficult cases—to others, but especially to themselves—are the people who fail to see really that their life could be much better. There are thousands who do not see exactly what conversion could do to them. And their great difficulty in changing their life has just been this: "What, after all, should we really have to change? Our lives at present can scarcely be distinguished from the real Christians around us. Had we been irreligious, or profane, or undutiful, or immoral, conversion might do something for us; but we belong to the class who feel how well we have been brought up, how much our interests are gathered round religion, and, generally, how circumspect and proper our entire outward life has been. We do not really see, indeed, what change conversion could make." Now this is a class who seldom get any sympathy, and none deserve it more. Religious people and religious books are always saying hard things of the "religiously brought up"— bitterly hard and undeserved things—until they almost come to feel as if their goodness were a crime. But there are secret rendings of the heart within these ranks—longings after God perhaps purer than anywhere else outside God's true family. And there are those who feel the difficulty of changing amid surroundings so Christian-like as theirs; who feel it so keenly that despair sometimes leads them to the dark thought of almost envying the prodigal and the open sinner, who seem to have more chance of finding the kingdom than they.

Now the change in Paul's life is exactly the case in point for them. Paul himself was one of these characters who wondered what use conversion could ever be to him. He was one of the "religiously brought up." Touching the law he was blameless. There was no man stricter with his religion in all Jerusalem than Saul. No man took his place more regularly in the temple, or kept the Sabbath with more scrupulous care. Touching the law he was blameless—just the man you would have said who never would be changed, who was far too good to be susceptible of a change. But this is the man—not far from the kingdom of God, as everyone thought him to be—who found room in his most religious heart for the most sweeping reform that ever occurred in a life.

Let those who really do not know very well what religion could do for them take a little quiet thought like Paul. Let them look once more, not at the circumference, but at the center of their life. Let them ask one question about it: "Is it Christ?" There is no middle way in religion— self or Christ. The quality of the selfishness—intellectual, literary, artistic—the fact that our self's center may be of a superior order of self, does nothing to destroy this grave distinction. It lies between all self and Christ. For the matter of that no center could have been more disciplined or cultured than Paul's. In its place it was truly great and worthy, but its place was anywhere else than where Paul had it for the full half of his life. This question, then, of centers is the vital question. "To me to live is"—what?-"To me to live is myself!" Suppose that it is so. What kind of an aim for a life is this? How much nobler a center our life is worthy of—our one life, which is to live forevermore; which is to live with a great center or a mean one—meanly or greatly forevermore!

Think of living with oneself forever and forever. Think of having lived, living now, and evermore living only for this. Consider Him who endured such contradiction of sinners for our sake, who made Himself of no reputation, who gave up form and comeliness; who humbled Himself and emptied Himself for us. Then look, if we can, with complacency on such a life—

> "I lived for myself, I thought for myself,
> For myself, and none beside,
> Just as if Jesus had never lived,
> As if He had never died.

2. This leads naturally to the other point—the discovery of Christ. And here once more we draw abundant encouragement from our biography of Paul. And it brings us not only to a hopeful thought, but to a very solemn thought. We have all in some way made the discovery of Christ; we know more about Christ than Paul did when he became a Christian. When he made Him the center of his life, he knew less of Him perhaps than most of us. It is a startling truth, at all events, that we are as near the center of life—the center of the universe—as Paul. We have heard of Him from our infancy; the features of His life are as familiar as our own; we have no hatred to Him as Paul had once. And if the few days' quietness in the Holy Land, which Paul had on the threshold of his change, were in any way a preparation for the crisis of his life, how much more has our past life been a preparation for a change in ours! We call Paul's change a sudden conversion—we do not know how sudden it was. But if our life were changed today, it would be no sudden conversion. Our whole past has been leading up to these two discoveries of life. Our preparation, so far as knowledge of the new center goes, is complete. The change, so far as that is concerned, might happen *now*. We have the responsibility of being so near eternal life as that.

The question comes to be then, finally, a simple question of transfer. To me to live is myself, or to me to live is Christ. To live for Christ is not simply the sublime doctrine which it includes of *Christ our life*. It is not so much Christ our life, but rather *our life for Christ*.

Shall it be, then, our life for Christ? "To me to live is Christ." Contrast it with all the other objects of life; take all the centers out of all the great lives, and compare them one by one. Can you match the life-creed of Paul—"to me to live is Christ"?

"To me to live is—business"; "to me to live is—pleasure," "to me to live is—myself." We can all tell in a moment what our religion is really worth. "To me to live is"—what? What are we living for? What rises naturally in our heart when we press it with a test like this: "to me to live is"—what? First thoughts, it is said, are best in matters of conscience. What was the first thought that came into our heart just then? What word trembled first on our lips just now—"to me to live is"—was it business, was it money, was it myself, was it Christ?

The time will come when we shall ask ourselves why we ever crushed this infinite substance of our life within these narrow bounds, and centred that which lasts forever on what must pass away. In the perspective of eternity all lives will seem poor, and small, and lost, and self-condemned beside a life for Christ. There will be plenty then to gather round the cross. But who will do it now? Who will do it now? There are plenty of men to die for Him, there are plenty to spend eternity with Christ; but where is the man who will *live* for Christ? Death and eternity come in their place. Christ wants lives. There is no fear about death being gain if we have lived for Christ. So, let it be: "To me to live is Christ."

There is but one alternative—Paul's alternative, the discovery of Christ. We have all in some sense, indeed, already made that discovery. We may be as near it now as Paul when he left Jerusalem. There was no notice given that he was to change masters. The new Master simply crossed his path one day, and the great change was come. How often has He crossed our path? We know what to do the next time: we know how our life can be made worthy and great—how only; we know how death can become gain—how only. Many, indeed, tell us death must be gain. Many long for life to be done that they may rest, as they say, in the quiet grave. Let no cheap sentimentalism deceive us. Death can only be gain when to have lived was Christ.

CHAPTER SIX
CLAIRVOYANCE

"We look not at the things which are seen, but at the things which are not seen: for the things which are seen are temporal; but the things which are not seen are eternal."—2 Cor. iv. 18.

"Everything that is, is double."—Hermes Trismegistus.

"Look not at the things which are seen." How can we look not at the things which are seen? If they are seen, how can we help looking at them? "Look at the things which are not seen." How can we look at things which are not seen? Has religion some magic wishing-cap, making the solid world invisible, or does it supply some strange clairvoyance power to see that which is unseen?

This is one of those alluring paradoxes which all great books delight in, which baffle thought while courting it, but which disclose to whoever picks the lock the rarest and profoundest truth. The surface meaning of a paradox is either nonsense, or it is false. In this case it is false. One would gather, at first sight, that we had here another of those attacks upon the world, of which the Bible is supposed to be so fond. It reads as a withering contrast between the things of time and the things of eternity—as an unqualified disparagement of this present world. The things which are seen are temporal—not worth a moment's thought, not even to be looked at.

In reality, this is neither the judgment of the Bible nor of reason.

There are four reasons why we should look at the things which are seen—

1. First, *because God made them.* Anything that God makes is worth looking at. We live in no chance world. It has been all thought out. Everywhere work has been spent on it lavishly—thought and work—loving thought and exquisite work. All its parts together, and every part separately, are stamped with skill, beauty, and purpose. As the mere work of a great master, we are driven to look—deliberately and long—at the things which are seen.

2. But, second, *God made us to look at them.* He who made light made the eye. It is a gift of the Creator on purpose that we may look at the things which are seen. The whole mechanism of man is made with reference to the temporal world—the eye for seeing it, the ear for hearing it, the nerve for feeling it, the muscle for moving about on it and getting more of it. He acts contrary to his own nature who harbors even a suspicion of the things that are seen.

3. But again, thirdly, God has not merely made the world, but *He has made it conspicuous.* So far from lying in the shade, so far from being constituted to escape observation, the whole temporal world clamors for it. Nature is never and nowhere silent. If you are apathetic, if you will not look at the things which are seen, they will summon you. The bird will call to you from the tree-top, the sea will change her mood for you, the flower looks up appealingly from the wayside, and the sun, before he sets with irresistible coloring, will startle you into attention. The

Creator has determined that, whether He be seen or no, no living soul shall tread His earth without being spoken to by these works of His hands. God has secured that. And even those things which have no speech nor language, whose voice is not heard, have their appeal going out to all the world, and their word to the end of the earth. Had God feared that the visible world had been a mere temptation to us, He would have made it less conspicuous. Certainly He has warned us not to love it, but nowhere not to look at it.

4. The last reason, fourthly, is the greatest of all. Hitherto we have been simply dealing with facts. Now we come to a principle. Look at the things that are seen, because *it is only by looking at the things that are seen that we can have any idea of the things that are unseen.* Our whole conception of the eternal is derived from the temporal.

Take any unseen truth, or fact, or law. The proposition is that it can be apprehended by us only by means of the seen and temporal. Take the word *eternal* itself. What do we know of eternity? Nothing that we have not learned from the temporal. When we try to realize that word there rises up before us the spaceless sea. We glide swiftly over it day after day, but the illimitable waste recedes before us, knowing no end. On and on, week and month, and there stretches the same horizon vague and infinite, the far-off circle we can never reach. We stop. We are far enough. This is eternity!

In reality, this is not eternity; it is mere water, the temporal, liquid and tangible. But by looking at this thing which is seen we have beheld the unseen. Here is a river. It is also water. But its different shape mirrors a different truth. As we look, the opposite of eternity rises up before us. There is time, swift and silent; or life, fleeting and irrevocable. So one might run over all the material of his thoughts, all the groundwork of his ideas, and trace them back to things that are temporal. They are really material, made up of matter, and in order to think at all, one must first of all see.

Nothing could illustrate this better, perhaps, than the literary form of our English Bible. Leaving out for the present the language of symbol and illustration which Christ spoke, there is no great eternal truth that is not borne to us upon some material image. Look, for instance, at its teaching about human life. To describe that, it does not even use the words derived from the temporal world. It brings us face to face with the temporal world, and lets us abstract them for ourselves. It never uses the word "fleeting" or "transitory." It says life is a vapor that appeareth for a little and vanisheth away. It likens it to a swift post, a swift ship, a tale that is told.

It never uses the word "irrevocable." It speaks of water spilt on the ground that cannot be gathered up again—a thread cut by the weaver. Nor does it tell us that life is "evanescent." It suggests evanescent things—a dream, a sleep, a shadow, a shepherd's tent removed. And even to convey the simpler truth that life is short, we find only references to short things that are seen—a handbreadth, a pilgrimage, a flower, a weaver's shuttle. The Bible in these instances is not trying to be poetical; it is simply trying to be true. And it distinctly, unconsciously, recognizes the fact that truth can be borne into the soul only through the medium of things. We must refuse to believe, therefore, that we are not to look at the things which are seen. It is a necessity, for the temporal is the husk and framework of the eternal. And the things which are not seen are made of the things which do appear. "All visible things," said Carlyle, "are emblems. What thou seest is not there on its own account; strictly speaking, it is not there at all. Matter exists only spiritually, and to represent some idea and body it forth." And so John Ruskin:—"The more I think of it, I find this conclusion more impressed upon me—that the greatest thing a human soul ever does in this world is to *see* something and tell what it *saw* in a plain way. Hundreds of people can talk for one who can think; thousands can think for one who can see. To see clearly is poetry, prophecy, and religion—all in one."

From this point we can now go on from the negative of the paradox to the second and positive term—"Look at the things which are not seen." We now understand how to do this. Where is the eternal? Where are the unseen things, that we may look at them? And the answer is— *in the temporal.* Look then at the temporal, but do not pause there. You must penetrate it. Go through it and see its shadow, its spiritual shadow, on the further side. Look upon this shadow long and earnestly, till that which you look through becomes the shadow, and the shadow merges into the reality. Look through till the thing you look through becomes dim, then transparent, and then invisible, and the unseen beyond grows into form and strength. For, truly, the first thing seen is the shadow, the thing on the other side the reality. The thing you see is only a solid, and men mistake solidity for reality. But that alone is the reality—the eternal which lies behind. Look, then, not at the things which are seen, but look through them to the things that are unseen.

The great lesson which emerges from all this is as to the religious use of the temporal world. Heaven lies behind earth. This earth is not merely a place to live in, but to see in. We are to pass through it as clairvoyants, holding the whole temporal world as a vast transparency, through which the eternal shines.

Let us now apply this principle briefly to daily life. To most of us, the most practical division of life is threefold: the working life, the home life, and the religious life. What do these yield us of the eternal, and how?

1. *The Working Life.* To most men, work is just work—manual work, professional work, office work, household work, public work, intellectual work. A yellow primrose is just a yellow primrose; a spade is a spade; a ledger is a ledger; a lexicon is a lexicon. To a worker with this mind, so far as spiritual uses are concerned therefore, work is vanity—an unaccountable squandering of precious time. He must earn his success by the sweat of his brow; that is all he knows about it. It is a curse, lying from the beginning upon man as man. So, six days each week, he bends his neck to it doggedly; the seventh God allows him to think about the unseen and eternal.

Now God would never unspiritualize three-fourths of man's active life by work, if work were work, and nothing more.

A second workman sees a little further. His work is not a curse exactly; it is his appointed life, his destiny. It is God's will for him, and he must go through with it. No doubt its trials are good for him; at all events, God has appointed him this sphere, and he must accept it with Christian resignation.

It is a poor compliment to the divine arrangements if they are simply to be acquiesced in. The all-wise God surely intends some higher outcome from three-fourths of life than bread and butter and resignation.

To the spiritual man, next, there lies behind this temporal a something which explains all. He sees more to come out of it than the year's income, or the employment of his allotted time, or the benefiting of his species. If violins were to be the only product, there is no reason why Stradivarius should spend his life in making them. But work is an incarnation of the unseen. In this loom man's soul is made. There is a subtle machinery behind it all, working while he is working, making or unmaking the unseen in him. Integrity, thoroughness, honesty, accuracy, conscientiousness, faithfulness, patience—these unseen things which complete a soul are woven into it in work. Apart from work, these things are not. As the conductor leads into our nerves the invisible electric force, so work conducts into our spirit all high forces of character, all essential qualities of life, truth in the inward parts. Ledgers and lexicons, business letters, domestic duties, striking of bargains, writing of examinations, handling of tools—these are the conductors of the eternal. So much the conductors of the eternal, that without them there is no eternal. No man *dreams* integrity, accuracy, and so on. He cannot learn them by reading about them. These things require their wire as much as electricity. The spiritual fluids and the electric fluids are under the same law; messages of grace come along the lines of honest work to the soul like the invisible message along the telegraph wires. Patience, spiritually, will travel along a conductor as really as electricity.

A workshop, therefore, or an office, or a school of learning, is a gigantic conductor. An office is not a place for making money—it is a place for making character. A workshop is not a place for making machinery—it is a place for making men: not for turning wood, for fitting engines, for founding cylinders—to God's eye, it is a place for founding character; it is a place for fitting in the virtues to one's life, for turning out honest, modest-tempered God-fearing men. A school of learning is not so much a place for making scholars, as a place for making souls. And he who would ripen and perfect the eternal element in his being will do this by attending to the religious uses of his daily task, recognizing the unseen in its seen, and so turning three-fourths of each day's life into an ever-acting means of grace.

We say some kinds of work are immoral. A man who is turning out careless, imperfect work, is turning out a careless imperfect character for himself. He is touching deceit every moment, and this unseen thing rises up from his work like a subtle essence, and enters and poisons his soul. We say piece-work is immoral—it makes a man only a piece of a man, shuts him out from variety, and originality, and adaptation, narrowing and belittling his soul. But we forget the counter-truth, that honest and good work makes honesty and goodness, integrity and thoroughness— nay that it alone makes them. And the man who would ripen and perfect his soul must attend to the religious uses of his daily work—seeing the unseen in its seen—heeding it, not with a dry punctiliousness, but lovingly, recognizing its dignity, not as a mere making of money, but as an elaborate means of grace, occupying three-fourths of life.

2. *The Family Life.* Next, life is so ordered that another large part of it is spent in the family. This also, therefore, has its part to play in the completing of the soul. The working life could never teach a man all the lessons of the unseen. A whole set of additional messages from the

eternal have to be conducted into his soul at home. This is why it is not good for a man to be alone. A lonely man is insulated from the eternal—inaccessible to the subtle currents which ought to be flowing hourly into his soul.

Here, too, is a higher source of spirituality than work. It is here that life dawns, and the first mold is given to the plastic substance. Home is the cradle of eternity. It has been secured, therefore, that the first laws stamped here, the first lines laid down, the permanent way for the future soul, should be at once the lines of the eternal. Why do all men say that the family is a divine institution? Because God instituted it? But what guided Him in constituting it as it is? Eternity. Home is a preliminary heaven. Its arrangements are purely the arrangements of heaven. Heaven is a Father with His children. The parts we shall play in that great home are just the parts we have learned in the family here. We shall go through the same life there—only without the matter. This matter is a mere temporary quality to practice the eternal on—as wooden balls are hung up in a schoolroom to teach the children numbers till they can think them for themselves.

When a parent wishes to teach his child form and harmony, the properties of matter, beauty, and symmetry—all these unseen things—what does he do but give his child things that are seen, through which he can see them? He gives him a box of matter, bricks of wood, as playthings, and the child, in forming and transforming these, in building with them lines and squares, arches and pillars, has borne into his soul regularity and stability, form and symmetry. So God deals with us. The material universe is a mere box of bricks. We exercise our growing minds upon it for a space, till in the hereafter we become men, and childish things are put away. The temporal is but the scaffolding of the eternal; when the last immaterial souls have climbed through this material to God, the scaffolding shall be taken down, and the earth dissolved with fervent heat—not because it is evil, but because its work is done.

The mind of Christ is to be learned in the family. Strength of character may be acquired at work, but beauty of character is learned at home. There the affections are trained—that love especially which is to abide when tongues have ceased and knowledge fails. There the gentle life reaches us, the true heaven-life. In one word, the family circle is the supreme conductor of Christianity. Tenderness, humbleness, courtesy, self-forgetfulness, faith, sympathy; these ornaments of a meek and quiet spirit are learned at the fireside, round the table, in commonplace houses, in city streets. We are each of us daily embodying these principles in our soul, or trampling them out of it, in the ordinary intercourse of life. As actors in a charade, each member of the house each day, consciously or unconsciously, acts a word. The character is the seen, the word the unseen, and whether he thinks of the word at night or not, the souls of all around have guessed it silently. When the material mask and costume are put away, and their circumstances long years forgotten, that word of eternity lives on to make or mar the player, and all the players with him, in that day's game of life.

To waken a man to all that is involved in each day's life, in even its insignificant circumstance and casual word and look, surely you have but to tell him all this—that in these temporals lie eternals; that in life, not in church, lies religion; that all that is done or undone, said or unsaid, of right or wrong, has its part, by an unalterable law, in the eternal life of all.

3. We now come to *religion*. And we shall see further how God has put even that for us into the temporal. Reflect for a moment upon the teaching of Christ. All that He had to say of the eternal He put up in images of the temporal world. What are all His parables, His allusions to nature, His illustrations from real life, His metaphors and similes, but disclosures to our blind eyes of the unseen in the seen? In reality, the eternal is never nearer us than in a material image. Reason cannot bring religion near us—only things can. So Christ never demonstrated any- thing. He did not appeal to the reasoning power in man, but to the seeing power—that power of imagination which deals with images of things.

That is the key to all Christ's teaching—that He spoke not to the reason but to the imagination. Incessantly he held up *things* before our eyes—things which in a few days or years would smoulder into dust— and told us to look there at the eternal. He held up bread. "I am the bread," He said. And if you think over that for a lifetime, you will never get nearer to the truth than through that thing, bread. That temporal is so perfect an image of the eternal, that no reading, or thinking, or argu- ing, or sermonizing, can get us closer to Christ.

Hence the triumphant way in which He ransacked the temporal world, and—what we, with our false views of spirituality, had never dared—marked off for us all its common and familiar things as mirrors of the eternal. So light, life, vine, bread, water, physician, shepherd, and a hundred others, have all become transformed with a light from the other world. Observe, Christ does not say He is *like* these things, He *is* these things. Look through these things, right through, and you will see

Him. We disappoint our souls continually in trying, by some other way than through these homely temporals, to learn the spiritual life.

It is the danger of those who pursue the intellectual life as a specialty to miss this tender and gracious influence. The student of the family, by a generous though perilous homage paid to learning is allowed to be an exception to family life. He dwells apart, goes his own way, lives his own life; unconsciously, and to his pain, he finds himself, perhaps, gradually looking down on its homelier tasks and less transcendent interests. In society, it is for the scholar we make allowances, but the eccentricities which we condone on account of their high compensations often mark an arrested development of what is really higher. And there is nothing so much to fear in oneself, and to check with more resolute will, than the unconscious tendency in all who pursue culture to get out of step with humanity, and be not at home at home.

A very remarkable instance of Christ's use of this principle is the sacraments. His design there was to perpetuate in the most luminous and arresting way, the two grandest facts of the spiritual world. How did He proceed? He made them visible. He associated these facts with the two commonest things in the world, *water* and *bread and wine*—the everyday diet at every peasant's board. By these sacraments, the souls of men are tied down at the most sacred moments of life to the homeliest temporal things; so that the highest spirituality, by Christ's own showing, comes to God's children through lowly forms of the material world. Transcendentalism in religion is a real mistake. True spirituality is to see the divinity in common things.

But, yet again, there is a more wonderful exhibition of this law than the sacraments. God furnished the world with a temporal thing for every eternal thing save one. Every eternal truth had its material image in the world, every eternal law had its working-model among the laws of nature. But there was one thing wanting. There was no temporal for the eternal God Himself. And man missed it. He wished to see even this unseen in something seen. In the sea, he saw eternity; in space, infinity; in the hills, sublimity; in the family, love; in the state, law. But there was no image of God. One speaks of what follows with bated breath. *God gave it!* God actually gave it! God made a seen image of Himself—not a vision, not a metaphor—an express image of His person. He laid aside His invisibility; He clothed Himself with the temporal; He took flesh and dwelt among us. The Incarnation was the eternal become temporal for a little time, that we might look at it.

141

It was our only way of beholding it, for we can only see the unseen in the seen. The word "God" conveyed no meaning; there was no seen thing to correspond to that word, and no word is intelligible till there is an image for it. So God gave religion its new word in the intelligible form—a Word in flesh—that, henceforth, all men might behold God's glory, not in itself, for that is impossible, but in the face of Jesus. This is the crowning proof of the religious use of the temporal world.

Three classes of men, finally, have taken up their position in recent years with reference to this principle of the eternal uses of the temporal world.

One will not look at the unseen at all—the materialist. He is utterly blind to the eternal. The second is utterly blind to the temporal—the mystic. He does not look for the unseen in the seen, but apart from the seen. He works, or tries to work, by direct vision. The third is neither blind to the unseen nor to the seen, but shortsighted to both. The ritualist selects some half-dozen things from the temporal world, and tries to see the unseen in them. As if there were only some half-dozen things—crosses and vestments, music and stained glass—through which the eternal shone! The whole world is a ritual—that is the answer. If a man means to evade God, let him look for Him in some half-dozen forms; he *will* evade Him, he will not see Him anywhere else. But let him who wishes to get near God, and be with God always, move in a religious atmosphere always; let him take up his position beside this truth. Worldliness has been defined as a looking at the things that are seen, but *only closely enough to see their market value.* Spirituality is that further look which sees their eternal value, which realizes that:

"Earth's crammed with Heaven,
And every common bush afire with God."

CHAPTER SEVEN
THE THREE FACTS OF SIN
"Who forgiveth all thine iniquities;
Who healeth all thy diseases;
Who redeemeth thy life from destruction."—Ps. ciii. 3, 4.

There is one theological word which has found its way lately into nearly all the newer and finer literature of our country. It is not only one of the words of the literary world at present, it is perhaps *the* word. Its reality, its certain influence, its universality, have at last been recognized, and in spite of its theological name have forced it into a place which nothing but its felt relation to the wider theology of human life could ever have earned for a religious word. That word, it need scarcely be said, is *sin*.

Even in the lighter literature of our country, and this is altogether remarkable, the ruling word just now is *sin*. Years ago it was the gay term *chivalry* which held the foreground in poem and ballad and song. Later still, the word which held court, in novel and romance, was *love*. But now a deeper word heads the chapters and begins the cantos. A more exciting thing than chivalry is descried in the arena, and love itself fades in interest before this small word, which has wandered out of theology, and changed the face of literature, and made many a new book preach.

It is not for religion to complain that her vocabulary is being borrowed by the world. There may be pulpits where there are not churches, and it is a valuable discovery for religion that the world has not only a mind to be amused but a conscience to be satisfied. But religion has one duty in the matter—when her words are borrowed, to see that they are borrowed whole. Truth which is to pass into such common circulation must not be mutilated truth; it must be strong, ringing, decided, whole; it must be standard truth; in a word, it must be Bible truth.

Now the Bible truth about this word is in itself interesting and very striking. In David especially, where the delineations are most perfect and masterly, the reiteration and classification of the great facts and varieties of sin form one of the most instructive and impressive features of the sacred writings. The Psalms will ever be the standard work on sin—the most ample analysis of its nature, its effects, its shades of difference, and its cure.

And yet, though it is such a common thing, I daresay many of us, perhaps, do not know anything about it. Somehow, it is just the common things we are apt not to think about. Take the commonest of all things—air. What do we know about it? What do we know about water?—that great mysterious sea, on which some of you spend your lives, which moans all the long winter at your very doors. Sin is a more common thing than them all; deeper than the sea, more subtle than the air; mysterious indeed, moaning in all our lives, through all the winter and summer of our past—that shall last, in the undying soul of man, when there shall

143

be no more sea. To say the least of it, it is unreasonable that a man should live in sin all his life without knowing in some measure what he is about.

And as regards the higher bearings of the case, it is clear that without the fullest information about sin no man can ever have the fullest information about himself, which he ought to have; and what is of more importance, without understanding sin no man can ever understand God. Even the Christian who has only the ordinary notions of sin in the general, can neither be making very much of himself nor of his theology; for as a rule, a man's experience of religion and of grace is in pretty exact proportion to his experience of sin.

No doubt, the intimate knowledge of themselves which the Old Testament writers possessed, had everything to do with their intimate knowledge of God. David, for instance, who had the deepest knowledge of God, had also the deepest knowledge of his own heart. If there is one thing more conspicuous than another in the writings he has left us, it is the ceaseless reiteration of the outstanding facts of sin—the cause, the effects, the shades of difference, and the cure of sin.

In the clause which forms our text today, David has given us in a nutshell the whole of the main facts of sin. And for any one who wishes to become acquainted with the great pivots on which human life turns, and on which his own life turns; for anyone who wishes to understand the working of God's grace; for anyone who wishes to examine himself on the great facts of human Sin, there is no more admirable summary than these words:

> "Who forgiveth all thine iniquities;
> Who healeth all thy diseases;
> Who redeemeth thy life from destruction."

These facts of sin, when we pass it through the prism of the text, may be said to be *three* in number: the guilt of sin, the stain of sin, the power of sin.

And these three correspond roughly with the natural divisions of the text:

> Who forgiveth all thine iniquities = the guilt of sin.
> Who healeth all thy diseases = the stain of sin.
> Who redeemeth thy life from destruction = the power of sin.

The best fact to start with will perhaps be the last of these, and for this reason the word *life* is in it. "Who redeemeth thy *life* from destruction." We have all a personal interest in anything that concerns life. We can understand things—even things in theology—if they will only bear upon our life. And to anything which in anyway comes home to life, in influencing it, or bettering it, or telling upon it in anyway whatever, we are always ready, for our life's sake, to give a patient hearing. We feel prepared to take kindly to almost any doctrine if it will only bear upon our life. And surely in the whole range of truth none has more points of contact with the heart of man than the doctrine of the power of sin.

(1) In the first place, then, let us notice that sin is a *power,* and a power which concerns *life.*

There is an old poem which bears the curious title of "Strife in Heaven," the idea of which is something like this. The poet supposes himself to be walking in the streets of the New Jerusalem, when he comes to a crowd of saints engaged in a very earnest discussion. He draws near, and listens. The question they are discussing is which of them is the greatest monument of God's saving grace. After a long debate, in which each states his case separately, and each claims to have been by far the most wonderful trophy of God's love in all the multitude of the redeemed, it is finally agreed to settle the matter by a vote. Vote after vote is taken, and the list of competition is gradually reduced until only two remain. These are allowed to state their case again, and the company stand ready to join in the final vote. The first to speak is a very old man. He begins by saying that it is a mere waste of time to go any further; it is absolutely impossible that God's grace could have done more for any man in heaven than for him. He tells again how he had led a most wicked and vicious life—a life filled up with every conceivable indulgence, and marred with every crime. He had been a thief, a liar, a blasphemer, a drunkard, and a murderer. On his deathbed, at the eleventh hour, Christ came to him and he was forgiven. The other is also an old man who says, in a few words, that he was brought to Christ when he was a boy. He had led a quiet and uneventful life, and had looked forward to heaven as long as he could remember.

The vote is taken; and, of course, you would say it results in favor of the first. But no, the votes are all given to the *last.* We might have thought, perhaps, that the one who led the reckless, godless life—he who had lied, thieved, blasphemed, murdered; he who was saved by the skin of his teeth, just a moment before it might have been too late—had the most to thank God for. But the old poet knew the deeper truth. It required great grace verily to pluck that withered brand from the burning. It required depths, absolutely fathomless depths, of mercy to forgive that veteran in sin at the close of all those guilty years. But it required more grace to keep that other life from guilt through all those tempted years. It required more grace to save him from the sins of his youth, and keep his Christian boyhood pure, to steer him scathless through the tempted years of riper manhood, to crown his days with usefulness and his old age with patience and hope. Both started in life together; to one grace came at the end, to the other at the beginning. The first was saved from the guilt of sin, the second from the power of sin as well. The first was saved from dying in sin. But he who became a Christian in his boyhood was saved from living in sin. The one required just one great act of love at the close of life; the other had a life full of love. It was a greater salvation by far. His soul was forgiven like the other, but his life was redeemed from destruction.

The lesson to be gathered from the old poet's parable is that sin is a question of power as much as a question of guilt,—that salvation is a question of life perhaps far more than a question of death. There is something in every man's life which he needs saving from, something which would spoil his life and run off with it into destruction if let alone. This principle of destruction is the first great fact of sin—its *power*.

Now any man who watches his life from day to day, and especially if he is trying to steer it towards a certain moral mark which he has made in his mind, has abundant and humiliating evidence that this power is busily working in his life. He finds that this power is working against him in his life, defeating him at every turn, and persistently opposing all the good he tries to do. He finds that his natural bias is to break away from God and good. Then he is clearly conscious that there is an acting ingredient in his soul which not only neutralizes the inclination to follow the path which he knows to be straightest and best, but works continually and consistently against his better self, and urges his life onwards towards a broader path which leads to destruction.

Now it was this road which David had in his mind when he thanked God that his life had been redeemed, or kept back from destruction. It was a beaten track we may be sure in those times, as it is today, and David knew perfectly well when he penned these words that God's hand had veritably saved him from ending his life along that road. It was not enough in summing up his life in his old age, and calling upon his soul to bless the Lord for all His benefits, to thank Him simply for the forgiveness of his sins. God has done far more for him than forgive him his sins. He has redeemed his life from destruction. He has saved him from the all but omnipotent power of sin. What that power was, what that power might have become, how it might have broken loose and wrecked his life a thousand times, let those who remember the times when it did break loose in David's life, recall. How little might we have guessed that there was anything in the psalmist's life to make him thank God at its close for keeping it back from destruction. Brought up in the secluded plains of Bethlehem, and reared in the pure atmosphere of country innocence, where could the shepherd lad get any taint of sin which could develop in after years to a great destroying power? And yet he got it—somehow, he got it. And even in his innocent boyhood, the fatal power lurked there, able enough, willing enough, vicious enough, to burst through the boundaries of his life and wreck it before it reached its prime. All the time he was walking with God; all the time he was planning God's temple; all the time he was writing his holy psalms—which make all men wonder at the psalmist's grace; while he was playing their grave sweet melody upon his harp in the ear of God, the power of sin was seething and raging in his breast, ready to quench the very inspiration God was giving him, and ruin his religion and his soul forevermore. God kept His hand, we may be sure, through David's life, on the springs of David's sin; and there was nothing so much to thank God for, in taking the retrospect of his eventful course, than that his life had been redeemed from this first great fact of sin.

David's salvation, to round off the point with an analogy from the old poet, was a much more wonderful thing than, say, the dying thief's salvation. David cost grace far more than the dying thief. The dying thief only needed dying grace. David needed living grace. The thief only needed forgiving grace; David needed forgiving grace and restraining grace. He needed grace to keep in his life, to keep it from running away. But the thief needed no restraining grace. The time for that was past. His life had run away. His wild oats were sown, and the harvest was heavy and bitter. Destruction had come upon him already in a hundred forms. He had had no antidote to the power of sin, which runs so fiercely in every vein of every man, and he had destroyed himself. His character was ruined, his soul was honey-combed through and through with sin. He could not have joined in David's psalm that his life was saved from destruction. His death was, and the wreck of his soul was, but his life was lost to God, to the world, and to himself. His life had never been redeemed as David's was, so David was the greater debtor to God's grace, and few men have had greater reason than he to praise God in old age for redeeming their life from destruction.

Yes, there is more in salvation than forgiveness. And why? Because there is more in sin than guilt. "If I were to be forgiven today," men who do not know this say, "I should be as bad as ever tomorrow." No, that is based on the fallacy, on the heresy, that there is no more for a man in religion than forgiveness of sins. If there were not, I say it with all solemnity, it would be very little use to me. It would have been little use to a man like David. And David's life would have been incomplete, and David's psalm would have been impossible, had he not been able to add to the record of God's pardon the record of God's power in redeeming his life from destruction. We have all thanked God for the dying thief—have we ever thanked God for redeeming our life from destruction? Destruction is the natural destination of every human soul. It is as natural for our soul to go downward as for a stone to fall to the ground. Do we ever thank God for redeeming our soul from that? And when we thank God we are saved, do we mean we are saved from hell, or do we think sometimes how He has rescued our life from the destroying power of sin?

(2) *The Stain of Sin.*

The power of sin could never run through a man's life without leaving its mark behind. Nothing in the world ever works without friction. A mountain torrent digs a glen in the mountain side; the sea cuts a beach along the shore; the hurricane leaves a thousand fallen witnesses behind to mark its track. And the great river of sin, as it rolls through a human life, leaves a pile of ruins here and there as melancholy monuments to show where it has been. Nature, with all its strength, is a wonderfully delicate machine, and everything has its reaction somewhere and some time. Nothing is allowed to pass, and nothing has so appalling a reaction upon everyone and everything as sin.

History is an undying monument of human sin. The most prominent thing on its pages are the stains—the stains of sin which time has not rubbed out. The history of the world, for the most part, has been written in the world's blood; all the reigns of all its emperors and kings will one day be lost in one absorbing record of one great reign—the one long reign of sin. As it has been with history so it is in the world today. The surface of society is white with leprosy. Take away the power of sin tomorrow, the stain of sin remains. Whatever the world may suffer from want of conviction of the guilt of sin, it will never be without conviction of its stain. We see it in one another's lives. We see it in one another's faces. It is the stain of the world's sin that troubles the world's conscience. It is the stain of the world's sin that troubles philanthropy; that troubles the parliament of the country; that troubles the press of the country. It is the stain of the world's sin especially that is making a place in literature for this word sin. It is this side of sin that is absorbing the finest writing of the day; that is filling our modern poetry; that is making a thousand modern books preach the doctrine of retribution, which simply means the doctrine of the stain of sin. Society is not wise enough to see the power of sin, or religious enough to see the guilt of sin, but it cannot fail to see the stain of sin. It does not care for the power or the guilt of sin; it cares for the stain of sin, because it must. That troubles society. That lies down at its doors, and is an eyesore to it. It is a loathsome thing to be lying there, and society must do something.

So this is what it does with it: on one corner it builds a prison—this will rid the world of its annoyance. In another corner it plants a madhouse—the sore may fester there unseen. In another it raises a hospital; in a fourth it lays out a graveyard. Prisons, mad-houses, hospitals—these are just so much roofing which society has put on to hide the stain of sin. It is a good thing in some ways that sin has always its stain. Just as pain is a good thing to tell that something is wrong, so the stain of sin may be a good thing to tell that the power has broken loose. Society might never trouble itself if it were not for the stain. And in dealing with the stain of sin it sometimes may do a very little to maim its power. But it is a poor, poor remedy. If it could only see the power and try to deal with that—try to get God's grace to act on that, the world might be redeemed from destruction after all. But it only sees the stain when it is too late—the stain which has dropped from the wound after the throat of virtue has been cut. Surely, when the deed is done, it is the least it can do to remove the traces of the crime.

But one need not go to society or history to see the stains of sin. We see it in one another's lives and in our own lives. Our conscience, for instance, is not so quick as it might have been—the stains of sin are there, between us and the light. We have ignored conscience many a time when it spoke, and its voice has grown husky and indistinct. Our intellectual life is not so true as it might have been—our intellectual sins have stained it and spoilt our memory, and taken the edge off our sympathy, and filled us with suspicion and one-sided truths, and destroyed the delicate power of faith.

There are few more touching sights than to see a man in mature life trying to recover himself from the stains of a neglected past. The past itself is gone, but it remains in dark accumulated stains upon his life, and he tries to take them off in vain. There was a time once, when his robe was white and clean. "Keep your garment unspotted from the world," they said to him, the kind home-voices, as he went out into life. He remembers well the first spot on that robe. Even the laden years that lie between have no day so dark—no spot now lies so lurid red upon his soul as that first sin. Then the companion stain came, for sins are mostly twins. Then another, and another, and many more, till count was lost, and the whole robe was patterned over with sin-stains. The power of God has come to make a new man of him, but the stains are sunk so deeply in his soul that they are living parts of him still. It is hard for him to give up the world. It is hard for him to be pure. It is hard for him to forget the pictures which have been hanging in the galleries of his imagination all his life—to forget them when he comes to think of God; to forget them when he kneels down to pray; to forget them even when he comes to sit in church. The past of his life has been all against him; even if his future is religious, it can never be altogether unaffected by the stain of what has been. It is the stain of sin which makes repentance so hard in adult life, which yields the most impressive argument to the young to remember their Creator in their youth. For even "the angels," says Ruskin, "who rejoice over repentance, cannot but feel an uncomprehended pain as they try and try again in vain whether they may not warm hard hearts with the brooding of their kind wings."

But if the stain of sin is invisible in moral and intellectual life, no one can possibly be blind to it in bodily life. We see it in one another's lives, but more than that, we see it in one another's faces. Vice writes in plain characters, and all the world is its copybook. We can read it everywhere and on everything around, from pole to pole. The drunkard, to take the conspicuous example, so stains his bodily life with his sin that the seeds of disease are sown which, long after he has reformed, will germinate in his death. If all the drunkards in the world were to be changed tomorrow, the stains of sin in their bodies even would doubtless bring a large majority—in a few years, less or more—to what was after all really a drunkard's grave.

There is a physical demonstration of sin as well as a religious; and no sin can come in among the delicate faculties of the mind, or among the coarser fibres of the body, without leaving a stain, either as a positive injury to the life, or, what is equally fatal, as a predisposition to commit the same sin again. This predisposition is always one of the most real and appalling accompaniments of the stain of sin. There is scarcely such a thing as an isolated sin in a man's life. Most sins can be accounted for by what has gone before. Every sin, so to speak, has its own pedigree, and is the result of the accumulated force, which means the accumulated stain of many a preparatory sin.

Thus when Peter began to swear in the High Priest's palace, it was probably not the first time Peter swore. A man does not suddenly acquire the habit of uttering oaths; and when it is said of Peter, "Then began he to curse and to swear," it does not at all mean by "then" and "began" that he had not begun it long ago. The legitimate inference is, that in the rough days of his fisherman's life, when the nets got entangled perhaps, or the right wind would not blow, Peter had come out many a time with an oath to keep his passion cool. And now, after years of devoted fellowship with Christ, the stain is still so black upon his soul that he curses in the very presence of his Lord. An outbreak which meets the public eye is generally the climax of a series of sins, which discretion has been able, till then, to keep out of sight. The doctrine of the stain of sin, has no exceptions; few men, we may be sure, can do a suddenly notorious wrong without knowing something in private of the series to which it belongs.

But the most solemn fact about this stain of sin is that so little can be done for it. It is almost indelible. There is a very solemn fact about this stain of sin—it can never be altogether blotted out. The guilt of sin may be forgiven, the power of sin may be broken, but the stains of sin abide. When it is said, "He healeth our diseases," it means indeed that we may be healed; but the ravages which sin has left must still remain. Small-pox may be healed, but it leaves its mark behind. A cut limb may be cured, but the scar remains forever. An earthquake is over in three minutes, but centuries after the ground is still rent into gulfs and chasms which ages will never close. So the scars of sin on body and mind and soul live with us in silent retribution upon our past, and go with us to our graves.

And the stain does not stop with *our* lives. Every action of every man has an ancestry and a posterity in other lives. The stains of life have power to spread. The stains of other lives have crossed over into our lives, stains from our lives into theirs. "I am a part," says Tennyson, "of all that I have met." A hundred years hence we all must live again—in thoughts, in tendencies, in influences, perhaps in sins and stains in other lives. The sins of the father shall be visited on the children. The blight on the vicious parent shall be visited on the insane offspring. The stain on the intemperate mother shall reappear in the blasted lives of her drunken family. Finer forms of sin reappear in the same way—of companion on companion, of brother on sister, of teacher on pupil. For God Himself has made the law, that the curse must follow the breach; and even He who healeth our diseases may never interfere with the necessary stain of a sinful life.

"Take my influence," cried a sinful man, who was dying; "take my influence, and bury it with me." He was going to be with Christ; his influence had been against Him; he was leaving it behind. As a conspirator called by some act of grace to his sovereign's table remembers with unspeakable remorse the assassin whom he left in ambuscade at his king's palace gate, so he recalls the traitorous years and the influences which will plot against his Lord when he is in eternity. Oh, it were worth being washed from sin, were it only to escape the possibility of a treachery like that. It were worth living a holy and self-denying life, were it only to "join the choir invisible of those immortal dead who live again in lives made better by their presence."

(3) But now, lastly, we come to the third great fact of sin, *its guilt.* And we find ourselves face to face with the greatest question of all, "What has God to say to all this mass of sin?"

Probably everyone will acknowledge that his life bears witness to the two first facts of Sin. Starting with this admission, a moment's thought lands us in a greater admission. We all acknowledge sin. Therefore we must all acknowledge ourselves to be guilty. Whether we feel it or no, Guilt is inseparable from sin. Physical evil may make a man sorry, but moral evil makes him guilty. It may not make him *feel* guilty—we are speaking of facts—he *is* guilty. So we are guilty for our past lives. We may be sorry for the past. But it is not enough that we are sorry, we are guilty for the past. We are more than sinners, we are criminals. This is where the literary conception of sin is altogether defective and must be supplemented. It knows nothing, and can teach nothing, of the guilt of a sinner's soul. It is when we come to God that we learn this. God is our Father, but God is our Judge. And when we know that, our sin takes on a darker coloring. It grows larger than our life, and suddenly seems to be infinite. The whole world, the whole universe, is concerned in it. Sin only made us recoil from ourselves before; now it makes God recoil from us. We are out of harmony with God. Our iniquities have separated us from God, and in some mysterious way we have come to be answerable to Him. We feel that the Lord has turned and looked upon us as He looked at Peter, and we can only go out and weep bitterly.

If these experiences are foreign to our souls, we must feel our sense of guilt when we come to look at Christ. Christ could not move through the world without the mere spectacle of His life stirring to their very depths the hearts of everyone whose path He crossed. And Christ cannot move through the chambers of our thoughts without the dazzling contrast to ourselves startling into motion the sense of burning shame and sin. But, above all, Christ could not die upon the cross without witnessing to all eternity of the appalling greatness of human guilt. And it is the true climax of conviction which the prophet speaks of: "They shall look on Me whom they have pierced, and they shall *mourn*."

This conviction of sin, in this the deepest sense, is not a thing to talk about, but to feel. And when it is felt, it cannot be talked about. It is too deep for words. It comes as an unutterable woe upon the life, and rests there, in dark sorrow and heaviness, till Christ speaks peace.

Such, in outline, are the three facts of sin. They are useful in two ways: they teach us ourselves, and they teach us God. It is along these three lines that you will find salvation. Run your eye along the first—the power of sin—and you will understand Jesus. "Thou shalt call His name Jesus, for He shall save His people from their sins." Look at the second—the stain of sin—and you will understand the righteousness of Christ. You will see the need of the one pure life. You will be glad that there has been One who has kept His garment unspotted from the world.

Look at the third, and you will see the Lamb of God taking away the sin of the world. You will understand the atonement. You will pray:—

> Let the water and the blood,
> From Thy riven side which flowed,
> Be of sin the double cure,
> Cleanse me from its guilt and power.

CHAPTER EIGHT

THE THREE FACTS OF SALVATION
SUPPLEMENT TO "THE THREE FACTS OF SIN"

"Who forgiveth all thine iniquities;
Who healeth all thy diseases;
Who redeemeth thy life from destruction."—Ps. ciii. 3, 4.

Last Sabbath we were engaged with the three facts of sin. Today we come to the three facts of salvation.

The three facts of sin were:—

1. The guilt of sin—"Who forgiveth all thine iniquities."
2. The stain of sin—"Who healeth all thy diseases."
3. The power of sin—"Who redeemeth thy life from destruction ."

And now we come to the three facts of Salvation—the emphasis on the first words of each clause instead of the last.

1. He forgiveth.
2. He healeth.
3. He redeemeth.

Every one who comes into the world experiences less or more of the three facts of sin; and everyone is allowed to live on in the world mainly that he may also experience the three great facts of salvation. God keeps the most of us alive from day to day with this one object. Sin has got hold of us, and He is giving us time—time for grace to get the upper hand of it, time to work out the three facts of salvation in our lives with fear and trembling against the three facts of sin. Our being, therefore, lies between these two great sets of facts, the dark set and the bright: and life is just the battlefield on which they fight it out. If the bright side wins, it is a bright life—saved. If the dark side, it is a dark life—lost.

We have seen how the three dark facts have already begun to work upon our life and that they are not only working at our life, but sapping it, and preying upon it every hour of the day. And now we stand face to face with the question which is wrung out from our life by the very sin which is destroying it, "What must I do to be saved?"

The first fact about which we ask this question—to begin once more with the fact which most conspicuously concerns life—is the fact of the power of sin. What must I do to be saved from the power of sin? What most of us feel we really want religion to do for us, though it is not the deepest experience, is to save us from something which we feel in our life—a very terrible something which is slowly dragging our life downward to destruction. This something has gained an unaccountable hold upon us; it seems to make us go wrong whether we will or no, and instead of exhausting itself with all the attempts it has made upon our life in the past, it seems to get stronger and stronger every day. Even the Christian knows that this strange wild force is just at his very door, and if he does not pray tomorrow morning, for instance, before the day is out it will have wrought some mischief in his life. If he does not pray, in the most natural way in the world, without any effort of his own, without even thinking about it, this will necessarily come to the front and make his life go wrong. Now, wherever this comes from, or whatever it is, it is a great *fact*, and the first practical question in religion that rises to many a mind is this, "What must I do to be saved from this inevitable, and universal, and terrible fact of sin?"

We have probably all made certain experiments upon this fact already, and we could all give some explanation, at least, of what we are doing to be saved.

If some of us were asked, for instance, what was our favorite fact of salvation for resisting the power of sin, we might say the fact that we were doing our best. Well, it is a great thing for any man to be doing his best. But two questions will test the value of this method of resisting the power of sin. In the first place: How is your best doing? In the second place, Do you think you could not do better? As to how your best is doing, you would probably admit that, in fact, if you were to be candid, has not been much to boast of after all. And as regards to not doing better, you might also admit that in some ways, perhaps, you could. The fact of salvation then is evidently a poor one, as far as results are concerned, and may be judiciously laid aside.

Then another experiment people try to break the power of sin is to get thoroughly absorbed in something else—business, or literature, or some favorite pursuit. It is in our spare hours sin comes to us, and we try to have no sin by having no spare hours. But our very preoccupation may then be one continuous sin. And besides, if a man have no spare hours, he will have spare minutes, and sin comes generally in a minute. Most sins, indeed, are done in minutes. They take hours to execute, it may be; but in a moment the plot is hatched, the will consents, and the deed is done. Preoccupation then is clearly no savior.

Then there are others who withdraw from the world altogether, to break with sin, and live the solitary life of the recluse. But they forget that sin is not in the sinful world without, but in the sinful heart within, and that it enters the hermit's solitary cell as persistently as the wicked world around. So solitude comes to be no savior.

And there are still others who take refuge in religiousness—in going to church, for instance, and in religious society and books. But there is not necessarily any more power to resist sin within the four walls of a church or the pages of a religious book, than between the walls of a theater or the covers of a novel. There may be less temptation there, not necessarily more power. For there is no strength in mere religious ceremonies to cancel the power of sin, and many a man proves this, after years and years of church, by wakening to find the power of sin in his breast unchanged, and breaking out, perhaps, in every form of vice. Neither is religiousness, therefore, any escape from the dominion of sin.

And lastly, some of us have resorted to doctrines. We have got the leading points of certain doctrines worn into our minds, and because these have a religious name we are apt to think they have also a religious power. In reality, while dealing with the theory of sin, we may leave the power to resist it untouched. And many a pen has been busy with a book on the doctrine of sin while the life which employed it was going to destruction for want of salvation from its power.

There is one doctrine especially with which the word salvation is most often connected and to which many look for their deliverance from the power of indwelling sin. And it may seem a startling statement to make, but it will emphasize a distinction which cannot be too clearly drawn, that even the atonement itself is not the answer to the question, "What must I do to be saved from the power of sin?" The answer entirely depends on the atonement, but it is not the atonement. The atonement is *not* the fact of salvation which saves the sinner from the power of sin. If you believed in the atonement today, if you were absolutely assured that your past sins were all forgiven, that would be no criterion that you would not be as bad as ever again tomorrow. The atonement, therefore, is not the fact which deals with the power of sin. The atonement deals with a point. We are coming to that. Just now we are talking of a life. We are looking out for something which will deal with something in our life—something which will redeem our life from destruction. And a man may believe the atonement whose life is *not* redeemed from destruction.

You have gone out into the country on a summer morning, and as you passed some little rustic mill, you saw the miller come out to set his simple machinery agoing for the day. He turned on the sluice, but the water-wheel would not move. Then, with his strong arm, he turned it once or twice, then left it to itself to turn busily all the day. It is a sorry illustration in detail, but its principle means this, that the atonement is the first great turn as it were which God gives in the morning of conversion to the wheel of the Christian's life. Without it nothing more would be possible: alone it would not be enough. The water of life must flow in a living stream all through the working day and keep pouring its power into it ceaselessly till the life and the work are done.

Now, practically everything in salvation depends upon the clearness with which this great truth is recognized. Sin is a power in our life: let us fairly understand that it can only be met by another power. The fact of sin works all through our life: the fact of salvation which is to counteract it, must act all through life. The death of Christ, which is the atonement, reconciles us to God, makes our religion possible, puts us in the way of the power which is to come against our sin and deliver our life from destruction. But the water of life, which flows from the life of Christ, is the power itself. He redeemeth my life, by His life, from destruction. This is the power, Paul says, which redeemed his life from destruction. Christ's life, not His death, living in his life, absorbing it, impregnating it, transforming it: "Christ," as he confessed, "in me." And this, therefore, is the meaning of a profound sentence in which Paul states the true answer to the question, What must I do to be saved? records this first great fact of salvation and pointedly distinguishes it from the other. "If when we were enemies we were reconciled to God by the *death* of His Son, much more, being reconciled, *we shall be saved by His life*" (Rom. v. 10).

"We shall be saved by His life," says Paul. Paul meant no disrespect to the atonement when he said, "We shall be saved by His life." He was bringing out in relief one of the great facts of salvation. If God gives atoning power with one hand, and power to save the life from destruction with the other, there is no jealousy between. Both are from God. If you call the one justification and the other sanctification, God is the author of them both. If Paul seems to take something from the one doctrine and add it to the other, he takes nothing from God. atonement is from God. Power to resist sin is from God. When we say we shall be saved by the death of Christ, it is true. When Paul says, "We shall be saved by His life," it is true. Christ is all and in all, the beginning and the end. Only when we are speaking of one fact of sin, let us speak of the corresponding fact of grace. When the thing we want is power to redeem our life from destruction, let us apply the gift which God has given us for our life, and for guilt the gift for guilt. When an Israelite was bitten in the wilderness, he never thought of applying manna to the wound. The manna was for his life. But he did think of applying the brazen serpent. The manna would never have cured his sin, nor would the brazen serpent have kept him from starving. Suppose he had said, "Now I am healed by this serpent, I feel cured, and I need not eat this manna anymore. The serpent has done it all, and I am well." The result would have been, of course, that he would have died. The man to be sure was cured, but he has to live, and if he eats no manna his life must languish, go to destruction, die. Without taking any trouble about it, simply by the inevitable processes of nature, he would have died. The manna was God's provision to redeem his life from destruction, after the serpent had redeemed it from death. And if he did nothing to stop the natural progress of destruction, in the natural course of things, he must die. Now there is no jealousy between these two things—the manna is from God and the serpent is from God. But they are different gifts for different things. The serpent gave life, but could not keep life; the manna kept life, but could not give life. Therefore, the Israelites were saved by the serpent, but they did not try to eat the serpent.

To apply this to the case in hand. The atonement of Christ is the brazen serpent. Christ's life is the manna—the bread of life. Our sins are not forgiven by bread, nor are our lives supported by death. Our life is not redeemed from destruction by the atonement, nor kept from day to day from the power of sin by the atonement. Our life is not redeemed from destruction by the death of Christ, nor kept from day to day by the death of Christ. But we are saved, as Paul says, by His life. We cannot live upon death. *Mors janua vitae*—death is the gate of life. And after we have entered the gateway by the death of Christ, we shall be saved by His life.

It is one thing, therefore, to be saved by the death of Christ, and another to be saved by His life; while both expressions are correct, to talk of being saved by the death of Christ is not so scriptural as to talk of being saved by the life of Christ; and Paul, with his invariable conciseness on important points, has brought out the facts of salvation with profound insight in the pregnant antithesis already quoted, "When we were enemies we were reconciled by the death of Christ, now we shall be saved by His life."

The first fact of salvation, therefore, which is to be brought to bear upon the first great fact of sin, is not our own efforts, our own religiousness, our own doctrine, the atonement, or the death of Christ, but the power of the life of Christ. He redeems my life from destruction. How? By His life. This is the fact of salvation. It takes life to redeem life—power to resist power. Sin is a ceaseless, undying power in our life. A ceaseless, undying power must come against it. And there is only one such power in the universe—only one, which has a chance against sin: the power of the living Christ. God knew the power of sin in a human soul when He made so great provision. He knew how great it was; He calculated it. Then He sent the living Christ against it. It is the careful and awful estimate of the power of sin. God saw that nothing else would do. It would not do to start our religion, and then leave us to ourselves. It would not do with hearts like ours, yearning to sin, to leave us with religiousness or moral philosophy or doctrine. Christ must come Himself, and live with us. He must come and make His abode with us. So that when we live, it shall be not we that live, but Christ living in us, and the life which we are now living in the flesh must be lived by the power of the Son of God.

What, then, must I do to be saved? Receive the Lord Jesus Christ, and thou shalt be saved. Slave of a thousand sins, receive the Lord Jesus Christ into thy life, and thy life, thy far-spent life, shall yet be redeemed from destruction. Receive the Lord Jesus Christ, and thou who hast lived in the far famine land shalt return and live once more by thy Father's side. Thou seekest not a welcome to thy Father's house—of thy welcome thou hast never been afraid. But thou seekest a livelihood; thou seekest *power.* Thou seekest power to be pure, to be true, to be free from the power of sin. "What must I do to be saved from that? What power will free me from that?" The power of the living Christ. "As many as received Him, to them gave He *power* to become the sons of God." "Power to become the sons of God"—the great fact of salvation. Receive the Lord Jesus Christ, and thou shalt be saved.

Christ, therefore, is the power of God unto salvation—the counterfact to the power of sin unto destruction. Christ is the Way—He is also the Truth and the *Life.* This power, this life, is within our reach each moment of our life; as near, as free, as abundant as the air we breathe. A breath of prayer in the morning, and the morning life is sure. A breath of prayer in the evening, and the evening blessing comes. So our life is redeemed from destruction. Breath by breath our life comes into us.

Inch by inch it is redeemed. So much prayer today—so many inches redeemed today. So much water of life today—so many turns of the great wheel of life today. Therefore, if we want to be saved—whosoever will, let him take of the water of life freely. If you want to be saved, breathe the breath of life. And if you cannot breathe, let the groans which cannot be uttered go up to God, and the power will come. To all of us alike, if we but ask we shall receive. For God makes surpassing allowances, and He will do unto the least of us exceeding abundantly above all that we ask or think.

Secondly, and more briefly, the second fact of sin is the stain of sin, the second fact of salvation, "He healeth all thy diseases." The stain of sin is a very much more complicated thing even than the power of sin; and for this reason—most of it lies outside our own life. If it only lay in dark blotches upon our own life, we might set to work to rub it out. But it has crossed over into other lives all through the years that have gone, and left its awful mark—*our* mark, on every soul we touched since the most distant past.

A young man once lay upon his deathbed. He was a Christian, but for many days a black cloud had gathered upon his brow. Just before his last breath, he beckoned to the friends around his bed. "Take my influence," he said, "and bury it with me." He stood on the very threshold of glory. But the stain of sin was burning hot upon his past. Bury his influence with him! No, his influence will remain. His life has gone to be with God, who gave it; but his influence—he has left no influence for Christ. His future will be forever with the Lord. The unburied past remains behind, perhaps, forever to be against him. The black cloud which hangs over many a dying brow means the stain of an influence lost for Christ—means with many a man who dies a Christian, that though his guilt has been removed and his life redeemed from destruction, the infection of his past lurks in the world still, and his diseases fester in open sore among all the companions of his life.

What must I do to be saved from the stain of sin? Gather up your influence, and see how much has been for Christ. Then undo all that has been against Him. It will never be healed till then. This is the darkest stain upon your life. The stain of sin concerns your own soul, but that is a smaller matter. That can be undone—in part. There are open sores enough in our past life to make even heaven terrible. But God is healing them. He is blotting them from His own memory and from ours. If the stains that were there had lingered, life would have been a long sigh of agony. But salvation has come to your soul. God is helping you to use the means for repairing a broken life. He restoreth thy soul, He healeth all thy diseases. But thy brother's soul, and thy brother's diseases? The worst of thy stains have spread far and wide without thyself; and God will only heal them, perhaps, by giving you grace to deal with them. You must retrace your steps over that unburied past, and undo what you have done. You must go to the other lives which are stained with your blood-red stains and rub them out. Perhaps you did not lead them into their sin, but you did not lead them out of it. You did not show them you were a Christian. You left a worse memory with them than your real one. You pretended you were just like them—that your sources of happiness were just the same. You did not tell them you had a power which kept your life from sin. You did not take them to the closet you had at home, and let them see you on your knees, nor tell them of your Bible which was open twice a day. And all these negatives were stains and sins. It is a great injustice to do to anyone we know—the worst turn we could do a friend, to keep the best secret back, and let him go as calmly to hell as we are going to heaven.

If we cannot bury our influence, thank God if here and there we can undo it still. The other servant in the kitchen, the clerk on the next stool, the lady who once lived in the next house, we must go to them, by the grace of God, and take the stain away. And let the thought that much that we have done can never be undone, that many whose lives have suffered from our sins have gone away into eternity with the stains still unremoved. When we all stand round the throne together, even from the right hand of the judgment seat of Christ, we may behold on the left among the lost the stains of our own sin, still livid on some soul—let this quicken our steps as we go to obliterate the influence of our past, and turn our fear into a safeguard as we try to keep our future life for Christ.

The second fact of salvation, therefore, is to be effected by God in part and by ourselves in part. By God as regards ourselves; by God and ourselves as regards others. He is to heal our diseases, and we are to spread the balm He gives us wherever we have spread our sin.

Lastly, the third great fact of Sin is Guilt—the third fact of salvation is forgiveness. "He forgiveth all thine iniquities." The first question we asked came out of our life; the second mostly from our memory; but the third rises up out of conscience.

Our first cry, as we looked at our future, was, "Where can I get power?" Now we are looking at our past, and the question is, "Where can I get pardon?" The questions which conscience sends up to us are always the deepest questions. And the man who has never sent up the question. "Where can I get pardon?" has never been into his conscience to find out the deepest want he has. It is not enough for him to look lifeward; he must also look Godward. And it is not enough to discover the stain of his past, and cry out, "I have sinned." But he must see the guilt of his life and cry, "I have sinned *against God.*" The fact of salvation which God has provided to meet the fact of guilt, although it is the most stupendous fact of all, only comes home to man when he feels a criminal and stands, like a guilty sinner, for pardon at God's bar.

It is enough for him then to invoke God's strength against the power of sin. Just as the fact which meets the guilt of sin, as we have seen, can never meet the power of sin, so the fact which meets the power of sin can never meet the fact of guilt: manna was what was required for a man's life, but it was no use against his guilt. It is nothing that he makes a good resolution not to do wrong anymore, that he asks Christ to come and live with him and break the power of sin, and redeem his life from destruction. God has something to say to him before that. Something must happen to him before that. He must come and give an account of himself before that. The good resolution is all very laudable for the days to come, but what about the past? God wants to know about the past. It may be convenient for us to forget the past, but God cannot forget it. We have done wrong, and wrongdoing must be punished. Wrongdoing must be punished—*must;* this is involved in one of the facts of sin. Therefore the punishment of wrongdoing must be involved in one of the facts of salvation. It is not in the first two. It must be somewhere in this.

Now the punishment of sin is death. "In the day that thou eatest thereof thou shalt surely die." Therefore death is the punishment which must be in one of the facts of salvation. It was not in the other two. It must be somewhere in this. It will not meet the case if the sinner professes his penitence and promises humbly never to do the like again. It will not meet the case if he comes on his knees to apologize to God, and ask Him simply to forget that he has sinned, or beg Him to have pity on the misfortunes of his past. God did not say, "In the day thou eatest thereof I will pity thy misfortunes. In the day thou eatest thereof thou shalt surely *apologize,* or thou shalt surely *repent.*" But "in the day thou eatest thereof thou shalt surely *die.*" So death, and nothing less than death, must be in the fact of salvation from the guilt of sin, if such salvation is to be.

This fact, this most solemn necessity understood and felt, the rest is plain. We all know who deserved to die. We all know who *did* die. We know *we* were not wounded for our transgressions, we were not bruised for our iniquities. But we know who was. The Lord hath not dealt with us according to our iniquities; but we know with whom He has. We know who bare our sins in His own body on the tree—One who had no sins of His own. We know who was lifted up like the serpent in the wilderness—He who died, the just for the unjust. If we know this, we know the great fact of salvation, for it is here.

It only remains to answer one question more: How is a poor sinner to make this great fact his? And the answer is, by trusting Christ. He has nothing else wherewith to make it his. The atonement is a fact. Forgiveness is a fact. Let him believe it. He does not understand it. He is not asked to understand it. The proper way to accept a fact is to believe it; and whosoever believeth in Him shall not perish, but have everlasting life. It is well to understand it, and you may try to understand it, if you can, but till then you must believe it. For it is a fact, and your understanding it will not make it less or more a fact. The death of Christ will always be a fact. Forgiveness of sins will always be a fact. You accept the facts of sin: accept the facts of grace. The atonement, you say, confuses you. You do not understand its bearings; the more you think and hear and read, the more mysterious it becomes. And well it may, well it may!

A student went to a professor of theology not long ago, and asked him how long it took him to understand the atonement. He answered, all his life. Thinking perhaps there might be some mistake, the young man went to another professor, who taught the very doctrine in his class. "How long did it take you, sir," he asked, "to understand the atonement?" The professor thought a moment, and looked him in the face. *"eternity,"* he said, *"Eternity;* and I shall not understand it then."

We have been dealing today with facts; we need not be distressed if we do not understand them. God's love—how could we? God's forgiveness—how could we? "He forgiveth all mine iniquities." It is a fact. What proof could commend itself if God's fact will not do? Verify the fact as you may, find out as much about it as you may; only accept it— accept it first. You are keeping your life waiting while you are finding out about it. You are keeping your salvation waiting. And it is better to spend a year in ignorance than live a day unpardoned. You are staining other lives while you are waiting; your influence is against Christ while you are waiting, and it is better to spend your life in ignorance than let your influence be against Christ. Most things in religion are matters of simple faith. But when we come to the atonement, somehow we all become rationalists. We want to see through it and understand it—as if it were finite like ourselves, as if it could ever be compassed by our narrow minds—as if God did not know that we never could fathom it when He said, "believe it," instead of "understand it." We are not rationalists when we come to the love of God, or to faith, or to prayer. We do not ask for a theory of love before we begin to love, or a theory of prayer before we begin to pray. We just begin. Well, just begin to believe in forgiveness. When they brought the sick man once to Jesus, He just said, "Man, thy sins are forgiven thee," and the man just believed it. He did not ask, "But why should you forgive me, and how do you mean forgive me? I don't see any connection between your forgiveness and my sin." No; he took the fact. "*Immediately* he rose up, and departed to his own house, glorifying God." The fact is, if we would come to Christ just now, we should never ask any questions. Our minds would be full of Him. We should be in the region of eternal facts, and we should just believe them. At least, we should believe *Him;* and He is the Savior, the sum of all the facts of salvation—the one Savior from all the facts of sin. If you will not receive salvation as a fact, receive the Lord Jesus Christ as a gift—we ask no questions about a gift. Receive the Lord Jesus Christ as a gift, and thou shalt be saved from the power and the stain and the guilt of sin, for His is the power and the glory. Amen.

<h3 style="text-align:center">CHAPTER NINE</h3>
<h3 style="text-align:center">MARVEL NOT</h3>

"Marvel not that I said unto thee, Ye must be born again."—John iii. 7.

Every man comes into the world wrapped in an atmosphere of wonder—an atmosphere from which his whole afterlife is a prolonged effort to escape. The moment he opens his eyes this sense of wonder is upon him, and it never leaves him till he closes them on the greatest wonder—death. Between these wonders, the first awaking and the last sleep, his life is spent—a long-drawn breath of mystery.

This sense of wonder is not an evil thing, although it is a thing to escape from. It is one of God's earliest gifts, and one of God's best gifts; but its usefulness to childhood or to manhood depends on the mind escaping from wonder into something else—on its passing out from wonder into knowledge. Hence God has made the desire to escape as natural to us as the desire to wonder.

Everyone has been struck with the wonderment of a little child; but its desire to escape out of wonderment is a more marvelous thing. Its wonder becomes to it a constant craving for an entrance into the rest of information and fact. Its eager questionings, its impatience of its own ignorance, its insatiable requests for knowledge, these are alike the symptoms of its wonder and the evidences of its efforts to escape. And although, in adult life, the developed man is too cautious or too proud to display his wonder like the child, it is there in its thin disguise as inquiry, or investigation, or doubt. And there is no more exuberant moment in a man's life than when this wonder works until it passes into truth, when reason flashes a sudden light into a groping mind, and knowledge whispers, *"Marvel not!"*

There are three possible ways in which different minds attempt to escape from this sense of wonder. They take refuge in knowledge, or in mystery, or in ignorance. The first of these, knowledge, satisfies the sense of wonder. The second, mystery, deepens it. The third, ignorance, crushes it. Marvel not at all, says ignorance, because you cannot know at all. Marvel more, says mystery, because you cannot know more. Marvel not, says knowledge, because you know enough. Christ in our text says, *"Marvel not."*

It is the custom with most people, on every subject except one, to let their wonder escape in the last and only reasonable way—knowledge. The exception is religion. Men will not trouble themselves with thorough knowledge about it. They protest it is too marvelous. When a man wonders at anything secular, he proceeds to inquire about it, and takes refuge in information. But when he wonders at anything sacred, he is wont to take refuge in mystery which is just his wonder deepened, or in ignorance, which is just his wonder neglected. Religion has been always treated by the world as if it contained no human, commonsense principles; and however right it may be to rank it on a platform by itself, it has probably suffered as much from having been regarded as too exclusively supernatural, as too exclusively natural. Men who would be very much ashamed to confess ignorance in secular things, have no scruples in saying, "I do not know" in religious things. Men who would consider it intellectual treason to permit their minds to be put off with inexactness or evasion in an intellectual question, feel it no disloyalty, on encountering a religious difficulty, to pass it by on the other side. The inscrutableness of God is made a veil for the neglect of God, the divine infinity becomes a plea for human ignorance, and the spirituality of the laws of heaven an excuse for failure and irresponsibility on earth. So there are times when Christ has to put His finger on this wonder, and tell us to wonder not.

Of all the subjects which men have found it convenient to banish into these regions of the unknowable, none suffer so frequently as this question of being born again. The elements of mystery which are supposed to cluster about it are reckoned an ample excuse for even the most intelligent minds not trying to understand it, and more than a justification of anyone who makes the attempt and fails.

The famous Rabbi, indeed, who was honored with all this immortal discourse on Regeneration is a case in point. He was just on the verge of losing himself in this most treasonable despair. Never was man more puzzled than Nicodemus at the initial statement of this truth. Never was man's sense of wonder more profoundly excited, more in danger of losing itself in the mazes of mystery, nearer taking the easy escape of drowning itself in ignorance, than when Jesus rallied the escaping faculties of the Jewish ruler by the message, *"Marvel not."* The background working of that mind during its strange night-interview with Christ is full of suggestion and meaning. Twice already during the conversation had the great Teacher said in substance, "Ye must be born again." And one of the strongest intellects of its time stood literally petrified before the words. Nicodemus first tries to summon courage and frame a wondering question in reply: "How can a man be born when he is old?"— less a question, perhaps, than a soliloquy of his own. He has heard the great Teacher's statement, and he thinks upon it aloud, turning it over in his calm Hebrew mind till his very question returns upon himself and plunges him in deeper wonderment than before: "How can a man be born again when he is old?"

Next time he will venture no remark, and the Teacher's words fall uninterrupted on the puzzled scholar's ear: "Except a man be born again, he cannot see the kingdom of God." He has given him the key to it. But Nicodemus sees it not. He seems to have plunged into a dream. His reverie has deepened till he stands absorbed in thought, with down-turned eyes, before his Master. Jesus stands by in silence, and reads the wonder and perplexity in the gathering blackness of his brow. Nicodemus is despairing, perhaps. He is going to give it up. He is utterly baffled with the strange turn the conversation has taken. There is no satisfaction to be got from this clandestine meeting after all, and puzzled, and beaten, and crestfallen, he prepares to take his leave. But Jesus will not let the divine sense of wonder be aroused to end like this. It must end in knowledge, not in ignominy. It must escape into spiritual truth, not into intellectual mystery. So He says, "Wonder not; Marvel not. Here is nothing so very mysterious that I cannot make you know. You will understand it all if you come and think of it. You need not *marvel* that I said, 'Ye must be born again.'"

Thus Jesus saved Nicodemus from relapsing into ignorance of the greatest truth the world had known till then, or lulling his wonder to sleep forever in mystery or despair.

Now for the sake of those of us who have been tempted to pause—where Nicodemus so nearly lost himself—on the threshold of this truth: for the sake of those of us who have almost felt drawn into the intellectual sin of drowning our wonder at this truth in despair of it, let us ask ourselves very shortly why Christ said, "Marvel not." And it may be convenient in following up the subject from this side in a few words, to divide the answer into three short heads.

    I. "Marvel not"—as if it were unintelligible.
    II. "Marvel not"—as if it were impossible.
    III. "Marvel not"—as if it were unnecessary.

To begin with the first of these:—

I. Marvel not—as if it were unintelligible. There is nothing more unintelligible in the world than *how* a soul is born again. There is nothing more intelligible than that it *is*. We can understand the fact, however, without necessarily understanding the act. The act of being born again is as mysterious as God. All the complaints which have been showered upon this doctrine have referred to the act—the act with which we have really nothing to do, which is a process of God, the agency of the unseen wind of the Spirit, and which Jesus Himself has expressly warned us not to expect to understand. "Thou canst not tell," He said, "whence it cometh or whither it goeth."

But there is nothing to frighten search in this. For precisely the same kind of mystery hangs over every process of nature and life. We do not understand the influence of sunshine on the leaves of a flower at this springtime, any more than we do the mysterious budding of spiritual life within the soul; but botany is a science for all that.

We do not give up the study of chemistry as hopeless because we fail to comprehend the unseen laws which guide the delicate actions and reactions of matter. Nor do we disbelieve in the influence of food on the vital frame because no man has found the point exactly at which it passes from dead nourishment into life. We do not avoid the subject of electricity because electricity is a mystery, or heat because we cannot see heat, or meteorology because we cannot see the wind. Marvel not then, from the analogy of physical nature, if, concerning this spirit of regeneration, we cannot tell whence it cometh and whither it goeth. It is not on that account unintelligible that a man should be born again.

If we care again to take the analogy from the moral and intellectual nature, the same may be said with even greater emphasis. The essence of regeneration is a change from one state to another—from an old life to a new one. Spiritually, its manifestation is in hating things once loved, or loving things once hated. God is no longer avoided, but worshipped; Christ no longer despised, but trusted.

Now, intellectually, changes at least in some way similar are happening every day. You rose up yesterday, bitterly opposed, let us say, to such and such a scheme. You were so strong in your opinion that nothing would ever shake you. You would never change, you said—you never could. But you met a friend, who began to talk about it. You listened, then wavered, then capitulated. You allowed yourself to be talked round, as you expressed it. You were *converted* to the other side. And in the evening your change of mind was so complete that you were literally born again—you were literally another man; you were in a new world of ideas, of interests, of hopes, with all the old dislikes in that special connection reversed, and the old loves turned into hates.

Something like this goes on, only with a higher agency, in the regeneration of the soul. Hence it is called by similar names—a change of heart, or a turning round or a conversion to the other side. And just as talking round will change a man's opinion or convert him intellectually, so turning round by the Spirit of God will change his heart or convert him spiritually. When you are told, therefore, that your heart may be changed by the Spirit, even as your mind was changed by your friend, *marvel not,* as if it were unintelligible. What a few hours' conversation could do in making you love the side you hated, and hate the side you loved, marvel not at what more the power of God could do in turning round your being from the old life to the new. And one might even press the analogy a little further, and add, if a few minutes' conversation with a fellowman overturned the stubborn mountain of your mind, how much more should a few minutes' conversation with Christ—such as Nicodemus had, and which overthrew his strongest Messianic views, and changed the current of his life forever from that hour—change your life the moment it touched you?

To Nicodemus, indeed, even the conception itself of being born again should have seemed no mystery. It was already a familiar thought in another sense to every Jewish heart—nothing more or less, indeed, than one of the common political phrases of the day. The custom in these times was to regard as unclean the foreigner who came to reside in a Jewish town. He was held at arm's length; he was a man of different caste, the Jew had no dealings with the Samaritan. But if he wished to leave his gods and share the religious hopes and civil privileges of the Jews, there was one way out of the old state into the new—just one way—he must be born again. He was baptized with water, and passed through certain other rites, till finally reckoned clean, when he became as truly one of the chosen people as if he had been the lineal son of Abraham. And the process of initiation from the Gentile world into the kingdom of the Jew was called a regeneration, or a being born again. There was nothing, therefore, in the thoughtful consideration of the new birth for the Jew to marvel at. "Art thou a Master in Israel," Jesus might well ask, "and understandest not these things?" A Master in Israel stumbling at an everyday illustration, marveling as if it were unintelligible! "Marvel not that I said unto thee, Ye must be born again."

What the Jews did to a stranger in admitting him to their kingdom corresponds exactly with what we do in our process of naturalization. Naturalization—spiritualization if we would be exactly accurate—is the idea, then, expressed in the "born again" of Christ. When we trace the expression back to its setting in Jewish politics, it yields the beautiful conception that God calls man—the foreigner, the stranger, the wanderer—to forsake the far country, and having been purified by initiatory rites from all uncleanness, to be translated into the kingdom of His dear Son. And though there may be, indeed, reasons why we should be so slow to understand it, and regions of rightful wonder in the deeper workings of the thought which we have not yet explored, there is at least this much clear, that we need *not* marvel as if it were unintelligible.

II. Marvel not—as if it were impossible. There is a name for God which men, in these days, have many temptations to forget—God the *Creator* of heaven and earth. It was the name, perhaps, by which we first knew God—God had made our earth, our house; God had made us. He was our Creator—God. We thought God could make anything then, or do anything, or do everything. But we lost our happy childhood's faith; now we wonder what things God can do, as if there were many things He could not.

But there is one thing we have little difficulty in always referring to the creating hand of God—*life*. No one has ever made life but God. We call Him the Author of life, and the Author of life is a wondrously fertile author. He makes much life—life in vast abundance. There is nothing so striking in nature as the prodigality—the almost reckless prodigality— of life. It seems as if God delighted Himself in life. So the world is filled with it. In the woods, in the air, in the ocean-bed, everywhere teeming life, superabundance of life, which God has made.

Well, if God can give life, He can surely add life. Regeneration is nothing in principle but the adding of more life. It is God adding life to life—more life to a man who has some life. The man has life which God gave him once; but part of him—the best part of him—is dead. His soul is dead in trespasses and sins. God touches this, and it lives. Even as the body was dead and God breathed upon it till it lived, so God will breathe upon the soul, and more life and better life will come.

So there is nothing impossible in being born again, anymore than there is the impossible in being born at all. What did Christ come into the world for? To give life, He said, even more abundant life. And Christ giving life—that is regeneration. It was not more knowledge Nicodemus wanted, though he thought so, but more life; and the best proof that life was possible was that life was granted. So the best proof of Christianity is a Christian; the best proof of regeneration is a man who has been regenerated. Can a man be born again when he is old? Certainly. For it has been done. Think of Bunyan the sinner and Bunyan the saint; think of Newton the miscreant and Newton the missionary; think of Paul the persecutor and Paul the apostle; and marvel not, as if it were impossible that a man should be born again.

III. Marvel not—as if it were unnecessary. Regeneration is more than intelligible and possible—it is necessary, to enter the kingdom of

God. "Except a man be born again, he *cannot* see the kingdom of God." Jesus says it *is* necessary. A man cannot *see* the kingdom of God except he be born again. He not only cannot enter it; Jesus says he cannot *see* it. It is actually invisible to him. This is why the world says of religion, "We do not understand it; we do not make it out; we do not *see it.*" No, of course they do not see it; they *cannot* see it; first, it is necessary to be born again.

When men come into the world, they are born outside of the kingdom of God, and they cannot see into it. They may go round and round it, and examine it from the outside, and pass an opinion on it. But they are no judges. They are not seeing what they are speaking about. For that which is born of spirit is spirit, that which is born of flesh is flesh; they can only give a criticism which is material on a thing which is spiritual. Therefore the critical value of a worldly man's opinion on religious matters is nothing. He is open to an objection which makes his opinion simply ludicrous—he is talking about a thing which he has never seen. So far as one's experience of religion goes, regeneration makes all the difference. It is as if someone had been standing outside some great cathedral. He has heard that its windows are of stained glass and exceeding beauty. He walks all around it and sees nothing but dull, unmeaning spaces—an iron grating over each, to intensify the gloom that seems to reign within. There is nothing worth seeing there, but everything to repel. But let him go in. Let him see things from the inside. And his eye is dazzled with the gorgeous play of colors; and the miracles and the parables are glowing upon the glass; and the figure of Jesus is there, and the story of His love is told on every pane—and there are choirs of angels, and cherubim and seraphim, and an altar where, in light which is inaccessible, is God.

So let a man enter into the kingdom of heaven—let a man be born again and enter—and he will *see* the kingdom of God. He will see the miracles and the parables which were meaningless, colorless once; he will see the story of the cross, which was a weariness and an offence; he will see the person of Christ and the King in His beauty, and beholding as in a glass the glory of the only begotten, he shall be changed into the same image from glory to glory. Marvel not if it is necessary, to see all this, that he must be born again.

Within this great world there are a number of little worlds, to which entrance is only attainable by birth. There is the intellectual world, for instance, which requires the birth of brains; the artistic world, which requires the birth of taste; and the dramatic world, which requires the birth of talent; the musical world, which requires the gift of harmony and ear. A man cannot enter the intellectual world except he have brains, or the artistic world except he have taste. And he cannot make or find brains or taste. They must be born in him. A man cannot make a poetical mind for himself. It must be created in him. Hence "the poet is born—not made," we say. So the Christian is born, not made.

There remains one other imperative protest against regeneration being unnecessary. Human nature demands regeneration as if it *were* necessary. No man who knows the human heart or human history will marvel as if it were unnecessary that the world must be born again. Every other conceivable measure has been tried to reform it. Government has tried it, philosophy has tried it, philanthropy has tried it, and failed. The heart—the national heart or the individual heart—remains deceitful above all things and desperately wicked. Reformation has been of little use to it; for every reformation is but a fresh and unguaranteed attempt to do what never has been done. Reconstruction has been of little use to it; for reconstruction is an ill-advised endeavor to rebuild a house, which has fallen a thousand times already with the same old bricks and beams. Man has had every chance from the creation to the present moment to prove that regeneration was not the one necessity of the world—and, again, has utterly failed.

We are still told, indeed, that all the world needs is just to get a start. Once set a man on his feet, or a universe, with a few good guiding principles. Give human nature fair play, and it must win in the end. But no. The experiment has been tried. God tried it Himself. It was fairly done, and it failed. The wickedness of man had waxed great throughout the land. So God said He would destroy all living flesh, and select a picked few of the best inhabitants to start the world afresh. A fair experiment. So all the world was drowned except a little nucleus in an ark—the picked few who were to found Utopia, who were to reconstruct the universe, who were to begin human life again, and make everything so much better than it was before. But the experiment failed. The picked few failed. Their children failed. Their children's children failed. Things got no better; only worse, perhaps, and worse; and no man ever really knew the cause till Jesus told the world that it *must*—absolutely and imperatively must—be born again.

If human nature makes it necessary, much more does the Divine nature. When Christ shall present His Church to God, it must be as a spotless Bride. In that eternal kingdom saints are more than subjects: they are the companions of the King. They must be a select number. They must be a highborn company. Marvel not if you and I are to be there—as if it were unnecessary that we must be born again. "Lord, who shall abide in Thy tabernacle—who shall dwell in Thy holy hill? He that hath clean hands and a pure heart." "There shall in no wise enter into it anything that defileth." Marvel not as if it were unnecessary that our robes should be washed white.

Marvel not, as if it were unintelligible.

Marvel not, as if it were impossible.

Marvel not, as if it were unnecessary that ye must be born again.

But marvel if you are. Marvel if you are not. Marvel that you may be today.

CHAPTER TEN

PENITENCE

"And the Lord turned, and looked upon Peter . . . and Peter went out, and wept bitterly."—Luke xxii. 61, 62.

Every man at some time in his life has fallen. Many have fallen many times; few, few times. And the more a man knows his life and watches its critical flow from day to day, larger seems to grow the number of these falls, and more often reaches out to God his penitential prayer, "Turn yet again, O Lord!"

We have all shuddered before this as we read the tale of Peter's guilt. Many a time we have watched the plot as it thickens round him, and felt the almost unconscious sympathy which betrayed of itself how like the story was to one that had sometimes happened with ourselves. And we knew, as we followed the dreary stages of his fall, that the same well-worn steps had been traced since then by every human foot. How Peter could have slept in the garden, when he should have watched and prayed, all men who have an inner history can understand. The faithlessness that made him follow Christ far off, instead of keeping at his Master's side, not the best of us will challenge. For we too know what it is sometimes to get out of step with Christ. We shall be the last to stop and ask his business in that worldly company who warmed themselves by the fire. And none who know that the heart is deceitful above all things, will wonder that this man who had lived so long in the inner circle of fellowship with Christ, whose eyes were familiar with miracles, who was one of that most select audience who witnessed the glory of the transfiguration—that this man, when his ears were yet full of the most solemn words the world had ever heard, when his heart was warm still with communion-table thoughts, should have turned his back upon his Lord, and, almost ere the sacramental wine was dry upon his lips, have cursed Him to His face. Such things, alas, are not strange to those who know the parts in the appalling tragedy of sin.

But there is a greater fact in Peter's life than Peter's sin—a much less known fact—Peter's penitence. All the world is at one with Peter in his sin; not all the world is with him in his penitence. Sinful Peter is one man, and repentant Peter is another; and many who kept his company along these worn steps to sin have left him to trace the tear-washed path of penitence alone. But the real lesson in Peter's life is the lesson in repentance. His fall is a lesson in sin which requires no teacher, but his repentance is a great lesson in salvation. And Peter's penitence is full of the deepest spiritual meaning to all who have ever made Peter's discovery—that they have sinned.

The few words which form the pathetic sequel to the tale of Peter's sin may be defined as the "ideal progress of Christian penitence." They contain materials for the analysis of the most rare and difficult grace in spiritual experience. And lying underneath these two simple sentences are the secrets of some of the most valuable spiritual laws. We find here four outstanding characteristics of the state of penitence:

(1) It is a *divine thing*. It began with God. Peter did not turn. But "the Lord turned and looked upon Peter."

(2) It is a *very sensitive thing*. A look did it. "The Lord looked upon Peter."

(3) It is a *very intense thing*. "Peter went out and wept bitterly."

(4) It is a *very lonely thing*. "Peter went out"—out into the quiet night, to be alone with his sin and God.

These are characteristic not only of the penitential state, but of all God's operations on the soul.

(1) To take the first of these, we find that the beginning of this strange experience came from God. It was not Peter who turned. The Lord turned and looked upon Peter. When the cock crowed, that might have recalled him to himself. But he was just in the very act of sin. And when a man is in the thick of his sin his last thought is to throw down his arms and repent. So Peter never thought of turning, but the Lord turned; and when Peter would rather have looked anywhere else than at

the Lord, the Lord looked at Peter. And this scarce-noticed fact is a great sermon to everyone who sins—that the Lord turns first.

Now the result of this distinction is that there are two kinds of sorrow for sin. And these are different in their origin, in their religious value, and in their influence on our life. The commoner kind is when a man does wrong, and, in the ordinary sense of the word, is sorry that he has done it. We are always easier in such a case when this sorrow comes. It seems to provide a sort of guarantee that we are not disposed to do the same again, and that our better self is still alive enough to enter its protest against the sin the lower self has done. And we count this feeling of reproach which treads so closely on the act as a sort of compensation or atonement for the wrong. This is a kind of sorrow which is well known to all who examine themselves, and in any way struggle with sin. It is a kind of sorrow which is coveted by all who examine themselves; which gives relief to what is called a penitential heart, and lends a fervor to many a penitential prayer. But it is a startling truth that there is no *religion* in such a state. There is no real penitence there. It may not contain even one ingredient of true repentance. It is all many know of repentance, and all many have for repentance. But it is no true sorrow for sin. It is wounded self-love. It is sorrow that we were weak enough to sin. We thought we had been stronger men and women, and when we were put to the test we found to our chagrin that we had failed. And this chagrin is what we are apt to mistake for penitence. But it is no divine gift of grace, this penitence—it is merely wounded pride—sorrow that we did not do better, that we were not so good as ourselves and our neighbors thought. It is just as if Peter turned and looked upon Peter. And when Peter turns and looks upon Peter, he sees what a poor, weak creature Peter is. And if God had not looked upon Peter he might have wept well-nigh as bitterly, not because he had sinned against his God, but because he, the great apostle, had done a weak thing—he was weak as other men.

The fit of low spirits which comes to us when we find ourselves overtaken in a fault, though we flatter ourselves to reckon it a certain sign of penitence, and a set-off to the sin itself which God will surely take into account, is often nothing more than vexation and annoyance with ourselves, that, after all our good resolutions and attempts at reformation, we have broken down again.

Contrast for a moment with such a penitence the publican's prayer of penitence in the temple. It was neither chagrin nor wounded pride with him. And we feel as we read the story that the Lord must have turned and looked upon the publican, when he cried "God"—as if God were looking right down into the man's eyes—"God be merciful to me, a sinner!" Stricken before his God, this publican had little thought of the self-respect he had lost, and felt it no indignity to take the culprit's place and be taught the true divinity of a culprit's penitence.

Now it will be seen at once that the difference between the publican's penitence and the first-named sorrow is just the difference between the divine and the human. The one is God turning and looking upon man, the other is man turning and looking upon himself. There is no wrong in a man turning and looking upon himself—only there is danger. There is the danger of misinterpreting what he sees and what he feels. What he feels is the mortification, the self-reproach of the sculptor who has made an unlucky stroke of the chisel; the chagrin of the artist who has spoilt the work of weeks by a clumsy touch. Apart altogether from religion we must feel mortified when we do wrong. Life, surely, is a work of art; character-building, soul-culture are the highest kind of art; and it would be strange indeed if failure passed unresented by the mind.

But what is complained of is not that it passes unresented by the mind, but that it passes unresented by the soul. Penitence of some sort there must be, but in the one case it is spiritual, in the other purely artistic. And the danger is the more subtle because the higher the character is the more there must necessarily be of the purely artistic penitence.

The effect is, that self gets in to what ought to be the most genuine experience of life, makes the most perfect imitation of it, and transforms the greatest opportunities for recovery into the basest ministry to pride. The true experience, on the other hand, is a touching lesson in human helplessness; teaching how God has to come to man's relief at every turn of his life, and how the same Hand which provides his pardon has actually to draw him to the place of penitence.

It is God looking into the sinner's face that has introduced a Christian element into human sorrow. And Paul, in making the Christian vocabulary, had to coin a word which was strange to all the philosophies of the world then, and is so still, when he joined the conceptions of God and sorrow into one, and told us of the Godly sorrow which has the marvelous virtue of working repentance not to be repented of. And it is this new and sacred sorrow which comes to sinful men as often as the Lord turns and looks upon their life; it is this which adds the penitential incense to the sacrifice of a broken and contrite heart. That was a great distinction which Luke brings out, in the prodigal's life, between coming to himself and coming to his father. "He came to himself," and then "he came to his father." So we are always coming to ourselves. We are always finding out, like the prodigal, the miserable bargains we have made. But it is only when we come to our Father that we can get them undone and the real debt discharged.

(2) But now, secondly, we come to the sensitiveness of penitence. Or rather, perhaps, we should talk of the sensitiveness of the penitent human soul. The Lord turned and looked upon Peter. There is nothing more sensitive in all the world than a human soul which has once been quickened into its delicate life by the touch of the divine. Men seldom estimate aright the exquisite beauty and tenderness of a sinner's heart. We apply coarse words to move it, and coarse, harsh stimulants to rouse it into life. And if no answer comes we make the bludgeon heavier and the language coarser still, as if the soul were not too fine to respond to weapons so blunt as these. There is coarseness in the fibres of the body, and these may be moved by blows; and there is coarseness in human nature, and that may be roused with threats; but the soul is fine as a breath, and will preserve, through misery and cruelty and sin, the marvellous delicacy which tells how near it lies to the spirit of God who gave it birth. Peter was naturally, perhaps, the coarsest of all the disciples. Our picture of him is of a strong-built, sun-tanned fisherman; robust, and fearless in disposition, quick-tempered and rash, a man who would bluster and swear—as we know he did—a wild man who had the making of a memorable sinner had not God made him a memorable saint. But inside this wild breast there lay a most lovely and delicate plant—the most tender plant, perhaps, but one which God had growing on the earth. With His own hand He had placed it there. With His own breath He nourished it from day to day; and already the storms in the wild breast were calmed and tempered for the holy flower which had begun to send a perfume through even coarse Peter's life. It always purifies a man to have a soul, and there is no such beauty of character as that which comes out in unconscious ways from a life made fine by Christ.

So God did not thunder and lighten to make Peter hear His voice. God knew that though Peter was blustering and swearing with his lips, there was dead silence in his soul. A whisper at that moment—that moment of high-strung feeling—a whisper even was not fine enough in its touch for this exquisitely sensitive spirit; so the Lord turned and *looked.* A look, and that was all. But it rent his heart as lightning could not, and melted into his soul.

There is a text in the Psalms which uses the strange expression, the *gentleness* of God. We wonder sometimes when God is so great, so terrible in majesty, that He uses so little violence with us, who are so small. But it is not His way. His way is to be gentle. He seldom drives; but draws. He seldom compels; but leads. He remembers we are dust. We think it might be quicker work if God threatened and compelled us to do right. But God does not want quick work, but good work. God does not want slave work, but free work. So God is gentle with us all—molding us and winning us many a time with no more than a silent look. Coarse treatment never wins souls. So God did not drive the chariot of His omnipotence up to Peter and command him to repent. God did not threaten him with thunderbolts of punishment. God did not even speak to him. That one look laid a spell upon his soul which was more than voice or language through all his afterlife.

Here, then, are two great lessons—the gentleness of God, and the gentleness of the soul—the one as divine a marvel as the other. God may be dealing with us in some quiet way just now and we do not know it. So mysteriously has all our life been shaped, and so unobtrusive the fingers which mold our will, that we scarce believe it has been the hand of God at all. But it is God's gentleness. And the reason why God made Peter's heart sensitive, and yours and mine, was to meet this gentleness of His.

Yes; we misunderstand God altogether, and religion, if we think God deals coarsely with our souls. If we ask ourselves what things have mainly influenced our life, we find the answer in a few silent voices which have preached to us, and winds which passed across our souls so gently that we scarce could tell when they were come or gone. The great physical forces of the world are all silent and unseen. The most ponderous of all—gravitation—came down the ages with a step so noiseless that centuries of wise men had passed away before an ear was quick enough to detect its footfall. And the great spiritual forces which startle men into thoughts of God and righteousness, which make men remember, in the rush of the world's life, that they have souls, which bring eternity near to us, when time is yet sweet and young, are not so much the warnings from the dead who drop at our side, nor the threats of judgment to come, nor the retributions of the life that is; but still small voices, which penetrate like Peter's look from Christ, and turn man's sensitive heart to God. The likeness of a long-dead mother's face; the echo of a children's hymn laden with pure memories coming over the guilty years which lie between; the fragments of an old, forgotten text— these are the messengers which heaven sends to call the world to God.

Let those who are waiting for Christ to thunder at their door before they will let Him in, remember that the quiet service of the Sabbath Day, and the soft whisper of text and Psalm, and the plaint of conscience, and the deep, deep heart-wish to be whole, are Christ's ways of looking for them. Let workers for Christ remember this. Let those who try to keep their influence for Christ, ponder Christ's methods of influence. Let those who live in the shade, whose lives are naturally bounded by timidity and reserve, be glad that, in the genius of Christianity, there is a place for even the gospel of the face. And let those who live in the battle, when coarser weapons fail, discern the lesson of Elijah: "A great and strong wind rent the mountains, and brake in pieces the rocks before the Lord; but the Lord was not in the wind: and after the wind, an earthquake; but the Lord was not in the earthquake: and after the earth-quake, a fire; but the Lord was not in the fire: and after the fire, a still, small voice" (I Kings xix. 11).

(3) Thirdly and briefly, for the truth is obvious, we learn from Peter's recovery that spiritual experience is intense. Peter wept bitterly. And this short sentence forever settles the question of emotion in religion. When the Lord turned and looked upon Peter, and memory crushed into one vivid moment the guilt of those never-to-be-forgotten hours, what else could Peter do than weep bitterly? Let memory so work on any of our lives today, and let the eye of the Eternal bring the naked truth from out our past, and let us ask if "bitterly" is a word too strong to express the agony of God's discovery of our sin. Much need, indeed, had Peter to weep bitterly; and if there are no bitter tears at times in our religious life, it is not because we have less of Peter's sin, but little of Peter's grace.

It is vain to console ourselves by measuring, as we try to do, the small size of the slips we make as compared with his. There is such a thing in the world as a great sin, but there is no such thing as a small sin. The smallest sin is a fall, and a fall is a fall from God, and to fall from God is to fall the greatest height in the universe. The publicity of a sin has nothing to do with its size. Our fall last week, or yesterday, or today, was just as great, perhaps, as Peter's fall, or David's, or Noah's, or Jacob's, or the many private sins of which history has made public examples, or the Bible placed as beacons to all the race.

Every sin that was ever done demands a bitter penitence. And if there is little emotion in a man's religion, it is because there is little introspection. *Religion without emotion is religion without reflection.* Let a man sit calmly down to think about his life. Let him think how God has dealt with him since ever he lisped God's name. Let him add to that how he has dealt with God since ever he could sin. And as he turns over the secrets of his past, and forgotten sins come crowding one by one into his thoughts, can he help a strong emotion rising in his heart, and shedding itself in tears? Yes; religion without emotion is religion without reflection. And, conversely, the man who gives himself to earnest thought upon his ways will always have enough emotion to generate religious fervor in his soul.

Only let religious emotion run in the right channel, let it work itself out in action and not in excited feeling, let it be something more than nervous agitation or a mere selfish fear, and there is no experience more purifying to the soul. No doubt it was a great thing for Peter that he wept bitterly, and no doubt from the bitterness of that night of penitence came much of the sweetness that hallowed his afterlife.

(4) Fourthly, and lastly, penitence is a lonely thing. Peter went out. When the Lord turned, He looked upon *Peter.* No one else noticed the quiet glance that was exchanged. But it did its work. It singled out one man in a moment, and cut him off from all the rest of the world. "*And Peter went out.*" And there was no man beneath the firmament of God that night so much alone as Peter with his sin.

Men know two kinds of loneliness, it has been said,—a loneliness of space and a loneliness of spirit. The fisherman in his boat on the wide sea knows loneliness of space. But it is no true loneliness. For his thoughts have peopled his boat with forms of those he loves. But Peter's was loneliness of spirit. A distance wider than the wide sea cut off the denier from all fellowship of man, and left him to mourn alone.

When God speaks He likes no other voice to break the stillness but His own. And hence the place that has always been given to solitude in all true religious life. It can be overdone, but it can be grossly underdone. And there is no lesson more worth insisting on in days like ours than this, that when God wants to speak with a man He wants that man to be alone. And God develops the germ of the recluse enough in all true Christian hearts to see that it is done. "Talent forms itself in solitude," says the German poet; "character amidst the storms of life." And if religious character is developed and strengthened in the battle of the world, it is no less true that religious talents are cultivated in quiet contemplation and communion alone with God. There are none more profoundly to be pitied than the worshippers who do all their religion in public; and he who knows not what it is to go out from the crowd sometimes and be alone with God is a stranger to the most divine experience that comes to sanctify a Christian's heart.

But what gave the beauty to Peter's loneliness was this—that he took God's time to be alone. Peter's penitence was not only an intense thing and a lonely thing, it was an immediate thing. Peter need not have gone out that time. He might have stood where he was, and braved it out. God has looked at us when we were sinning; and we did not do as Peter did. He lost no time between his penitence and his sin. But we spoil the grace of our penitence many a time by waiting till the sin grows old. We do it on purpose. Time seems to smooth the roughness off our sin and take its bitterness away. And we postpone our penitence till we think the edge is off the sharpness of the wrong. As if time, as if eternity could ever make a sinner's sin less black. Sin is always at its maximum. And no man ever gets off with penitence at its minimum. The time for penitence is just the time when we have sinned. And that perhaps is now. Peter's penitence came sharp upon his sin. It was not on his death-bed nor in his afterlife. But just when he had sinned. Many a man who postpones his penitence till he cannot help it, postpones his penitence till it cannot help him, and will not see the Lord turning till He turns and looks upon him in judgment. Then, indeed, he goes out to weep. But it is out into that night which knows no dawn.

Such are the lessons from Peter's penitence. Just one word more.

When God speaks He speaks so loud that all the voices of the world seem dumb. And yet when God speaks He speaks so softly that no one hears the whisper but yourself. Today, perhaps, as the service has gone on, the Lord has turned and looked on someone here. And the soul of some one has gone out to weep. No one noticed where the Lord's glance fell, and no one knows in the church that it was—*you.* You sit there in your wonted place. But your spirit is far away just now, dealing with some old sin, and God is giving you a lesson Himself—the bitterest, yet the sweetest lesson of your life, in heartfelt penitence. Come not back into the crowd till the Lord has turned and looked on you again, as He looked at the thief upon the cross, and you have beheld the "glory of the love of God in the face of Jesus."

CHAPTER ELEVEN

THE MAN AFTER GOD'S OWN HEART
A BIBLE STUDY ON THE IDEAL OF A CHRISTIAN LIFE

"A man after mine own heart, who shall fulfill all my will."—Acts xiii. 22.

No man can be making much of his life who has not a very definite conception of what he is living for. And if you ask, at random, a dozen men what is the end of their life, you will be surprised to find how few have formed to themselves more than the most dim idea. The question of the *summum bonum* has ever been the most difficult for the human mind to grasp. What shall a man do with his life? What is life for? Why is it given? These have been the one great puzzle for human books and human brains; ancient philosophy and mediaeval learning and modern culture alike have failed to tell us what these mean.

No man, no book save one, has ever told the world what it wants; so each has had to face the problem in his own uncertain light, and carry out, each for himself, the life that he thinks best.

Here is one who says literature is the great thing—he will be a literary man. He lays down for himself his ideal of a literary life. He surrounds himself with the best ideals of style; with his great ambition working towards great ends, after great models, he cuts out for himself what he thinks is his great life work. Another says the world is the great thing—he will be a man of the world. A third will be a business man; a fourth, a man of science. And each follows out his aim.

And the Christian must have a definite aim and model for his life. These aims are great aims, but not great enough for him. His one book has taught him a nobler life than all the libraries of the rich and immortal past. He may wish to be a man of business, or a man of science, and indeed he may be both. But he covets a nobler name than these. He will be the man after God's own heart. He has found out the secret philosophy never knew, that the ideal life is this—"A man after Mine own heart, who shall fulfill all My will." And just as the man of the world, or the literary man, lays down a program for the brief span of his working life, which he feels must vanish shortly in the unknown of the grave, so much more will the Christian for the great span of his life before it arches over into eternity.

He is a great man who has a great plan for his life—the greatest who has the greatest plan and keeps it. And the Christian should have the greatest plan, as his life is the greatest, as his work is the greatest, as his life and his work will follow him when all this world's is done.

Now we are going to ask today, "What is the true plan of the Christian life?" We shall need a definition that we may know it, a description that we may follow it. And if you look, you will see that both, in a sense, lie on the surface of our text. "A man after Mine own heart,"—here is the definition of what we are to be. "Who shall fulfill all My will,"—here is the description of how we are to be it. These words are the definition and the description of the model human life. They describe the man after God's own heart. They give us the key to the ideal life.

The general truth of these words is simply this: that the end of life is to do God's will. Now that is a great and surprising revelation. No man ever found that out. It has been before the world these eighteen hundred years, yet few have even found it out today. One man will tell you the end of life is to be true. Another will tell you it is to deny self. Another will say it is to keep the Ten Commandments. A fourth will point you to the Beatitudes. One will tell you it is to *do* good, another that it is to *get* good, another that it is to *be* good. But the end of life is in none of these things. It is more than all, and it includes them all. The end of life is not to deny self, nor to be true, nor to keep the Ten Commandments—it is simply to do God's will. It is not to get good nor be good, nor even to do good—it is just what God wills, whether that be working or waiting, winning or losing, suffering or recovering, or living or dying.

But this conception is too great for us. It is not practical enough. It is the greatest conception of man that has ever been given to the world. The great philosophers, from Socrates and Plato to Immanuel Kant and Mill, have given us their conception of an ideal human life. But none of them is at all so great as this. Each of them has constructed an ideal human life, a universal life they call it, a life for all other lives, a life for all men and all time to copy. None of them is half so deep, so wonderful, so far-reaching, as this: "A man after Mine own heart, who shall fulfill all My will."

But exactly for this very reason it is at first sight impracticable. We feel helpless beside a truth so great and eternal. God must teach us these things. Like little children, we must sit at His feet and learn. And as we come to Him with our difficulty, we find He has prepared two practical helps for us, that He may humanize the lesson and bring it near to us, so that by studying these helps, and following them with willing and humble hearts, we shall learn to copy into our lives the great ideal of God.

The two helps which God has given us are these:

I. The model life realized in Christ, the living Word.
II. The model life analyzed in the Bible, the written Word.

The usual method is to deal almost exclusively with the first of these. Today, for certain reasons, we mean to consider the second. As regards the first, of course, if a man could follow Christ he would lead the model life. But what is meant by telling a man to follow Christ? How is it to be done? It is like putting a young artist before a Murillo or a Raphael, and telling him to copy it. But even as the artist in following his ideal has colors put into his hand, and brush and canvas, and a hint here from this master, and a touch there from another, so with the pupil in the school of Christ. The great Master Himself is there to help him. The Holy Spirit is there to help him. But the model life is not to be mystically attained. There is spirituality about it, but no unreality. So God has provided another great help, our second help: the model life analyzed in the Word of God. Without the one, the ideal life would be incredible; without the other, it would be unintelligible. Hence God has given us two sides of this model life: realized in the Living Word; analyzed in the written Word.

Let us search our Bibles then to find this ideal life, so that copying it in our lives, reproducing it day by day and point by point, we may learn to make the most of our life, and have it said of us, as it was of David, "A man after mine own heart, who shall fulfill all My will."

(1) The first thing our ideal man wants is a reason for his being alive at all. He must account for his existence. What is he here for? And the Bible answer is this: "I come to do Thy will, O God." (Heb. x. 7.)

That is what we are here for—to do God's will. "I come to do Thy will, O God." That is the object of your life and mine—to do God's will. It is not to be happy or to be successful, or famous, or to do the best we can, and get on honestly in the world. It is something far higher than this—to do God's will. There, at the very outset, is the great key to life. Any one of us can tell in a moment whether our lives are right or not. Are we doing God's will? We do not mean are we doing God's work—preaching or teaching, or collecting money—but God's *will*. A man may think he is doing God's work, when he is not even doing

God's will. And a man may be doing God's work and God's will quite as much by hewing stones or sweeping streets, as by preaching or praying. So the question just means this—Are we working out our common everyday life on the great lines of God's will? This is different from the world's model life. "I come to push my way." This is the world's idea of it. "Not my way, not my will, but Thine be done"—this is the Christian's. This is what the man after God's own heart says: "I seek not mine own will, but the will of Him that sent me."

(2) The second thing the ideal man needs is *Sustenance*. After he has gotten life, you must give him food. Now, what food shall you give him? Shall you feed him with knowledge, or with riches, or with honor, or with beauty, or with power, or truth? No; there is a rarer luxury than these—so rare, that few have ever more than tasted it; so rich, that they who have will never live on other fare again. It is this: "My meat is to do the will of Him that sent Me" (John iv. 34).

Again, to do God's will. That is what a man lives for; it is also what he lives on. *Meat*. Meat is strength, support, nourishment. The strength of the model life is drawn from the divine will. Man has a strong will. But God's will is everlasting strength—Almighty strength. Such strength the ideal man gets. He grows by it, he assimilates it—it is his life. "Man shall not live by bread alone, but by every word that cometh out of God." Nothing can satisfy his appetite but this. He hungers to do God's will. Nothing else will fill him. Everyone knows that the world is hungry. But the hungry world is starving. It has many meats and many drinks, but there is no nourishment in them. It has pleasures, and gaiety, and excitement; but there is no food there for the immortal craving of the soul. It has the theater and worldly society, and worldly books, and worldly lusts. But these things merely intoxicate. There is no sustenance in them. So our ideal life turns its eye from them all with unutterable loathing. "*My* meat is to do God's will." To do God's will! No possibility of starving on such wonderful fare as this. God's will is eternal. It is eternal food the Christian lives upon. In springtime it is not sown, and in summer drought it cannot fail. In harvest it is not reaped, yet the storehouse is ever full. Oh, what possibilities of life it opens up! What possibilities of growth! What possibilities of work! How a soul develops on God's will!

(3) The next thing the ideal man needs is *society*. Man is not made to be alone. He needs friendships. Without society, the ideal man would be a monster, a contradiction. You must give him friendship. Now,

whom will you give him? Will you compliment him by calling upon the great men of the earth to come and minister to him? No. The ideal man does not want compliments, He has better food. Will you invite the ministers and the elders of the Church to meet him? Will you offer him the companionship of saint or angel, or seraphim of cherubim as he treads his path through the wilderness of life? No; for none of these will satisfy him. He has a better friendship than saint or angel or seraphim or cherubim. The answer trembles on the lip of everyone who is trying to follow the ideal life: *"Whosoever shall do the will of My Father which is in Heaven, the same is My brother, and sister, and mother"* (Matt. xii. 50; Mark iii. 35).

Yes. *My* brother, and *My* sister, and *My* mother. Mother! The path of life is dark and cheerless to you. There is a smoother path just by the side of it—a forbidden path. You have been tempted many a time to take it. But you knew it was wrong, and you paused. Then, with a sigh, you struck along the old weary path again. It was the will of God, you said. Brave mother! Oh, if you knew it, there was a voice at your ear just then, as Jesus saw the brave thing you had done, *"My* mother!" "He that doeth the will of My Father, the same is *My* mother." Yes; this is the consolation of Christ—"My mother." What society to be in! What about the darkness of the path, if we have the brightness of His smile? Oh! it is better, as the hymnist says,

> "It is better to walk in the dark with God,
> Than walk alone in the light;
> It is better to walk with Him by faith,
> Than walk alone by sight."

Some young man here is suffering fierce temptation. Today he feels strong; but tomorrow his Sabbath resolutions will desert him. What will his companions say if he does not join them? He cannot face them if he is to play the Christian. Companions! What are all the companions in the world to this? What are all the friendships, the truest and the best, to this dear and sacred brotherhood of Christ? "He that doeth the will of My Father, the same is *My* brother."

My mother, my brother, and my sister. He has a sister—some sister here. Sister! Your life is a quiet and even round of common and homely things. You dream, perhaps, of a wider sphere, and sigh for a great and useful life, like some women whose names you know. You question whether it is right that life should be such a little bundle of very little things. But nothing is little that is done for God, and it must be right if it be His will. And if this common life, with its homely things, is God's discipline for you, be assured that in your small corner, your unobserved, unambitious, simple woman's lot is very near and very dear to Him who said, "Whosoever doeth the will of My Father, the same is My sister."

(4) Now we have found the ideal man a Friend. But he wants something more. He wants *Language*. He must speak to his Friend. He cannot be silent in such company. And speaking to such a Friend is not mere conversation. It has a higher name. It is communion. It is prayer. Well, we listen to hear the ideal man's prayer. Something about God's will it must be; for that is what he is sure to talk about. That is the object of his life. That is his meat. In that he finds his society. So he will be sure to talk about it. Everyone knows what his prayer will be. Everyone remembers the words of the ideal prayer: *"Thy will be done."* (Matt. vi. 10).

Now mark the emphasis on *done*. He prays that God's will may be done. It is not that God's will may be borne, endured, put up with. There is activity in his prayer. It is not mere resignation. How often is this prayer toned off into mere endurance, sufferance, passivity. "Thy will be done," people say resignedly. "There is no help for it. We may just as well submit. God evidently means to have His way. Better to give in at once and make the best of it." Well, this is far from the ideal prayer. It may be nobler to suffer God's will than to do it, perhaps it is. But there is nothing noble in resignation of this sort—this resignation under protest as it were. And it disguises the meaning of the prayer. "Thy will be done." It is intensely active. It is not an acquiescence simply in God's dealing. It is a cry for more of God's dealing—God's dealing with me, with everything, with everybody, with the whole world. It is an appeal to the mightiest energy in heaven or earth to work, to make more room for itself, to energize. It is a prayer that the Almighty energies of the Divine will may be universally known, and felt, and worshipped.

Now the ideal man has no deeper prayer than that. He wants to get into the great current of will, which flows silently out of eternity, and swiftly back to eternity again. His only chance of happiness, of usefulness, of work, is to join the living rill of his will to that. Other Christians miss it, or settle on the banks of the great stream; but he will be among the forces and energies and powers, that he may link his weakness with God's greatness, and his simplicity with God's majesty, that he may become a force, an energy, a power for duty and God.

Perhaps God may do something with him. Certainly God will do something in him—for it is God who works in him both to will and to do of His good pleasure. So his one concern is to be kept in the will of God.

The ideal man has no deeper prayer than that. It is the truest language of his heart. He does not want a bed of roses, or his pathway strewn with flowers. He wants to do God's will. He does not want health or wealth, nor does he covet sickness or poverty,—just what God sends. He does not want success—even success in winning souls—or want of success. What God wills for him, that is all. He does not want to prosper in business, or to keep barely struggling on. God knows what is best. He does not want his friends to live, himself to live or die. God's will be done. The currents of his life flow far below the circumstances of things. There is a deeper principle in it than to live to gratify himself. And so he simply asks, that in the ordinary round of his daily life there may be no desire of his heart more deep, more vivid, more absorbingly present than this, "Thy will be done." He who makes this the prayer of his life will know that of all prayer it is the most truly blessed, the most nearly in the spirit of Him who sought not His own will, but the will of Him that sent Him.

> "Lord Jesus, as Thou wilt! if among thorns I go
> Still sometimes here and there let a few roses blow.
> No! Thou on earth along the thorny path hast gone,
> Then lead me after Thee, my Lord; Thy will be done."
> [Schmolk.]

(5) But the ideal man does not always pray. There is such perfect blessedness in praying the ideal prayer that language fails him sometimes. The peace of God passes all understanding, much more all expression. It comes down upon the soul, and makes it ring with the unutterable joy. And language stops. The ideal man can no longer pray to his Friend. So his prayer changes into *praise*. He is too full to speak, so his heart bursts into song. Therefore we must find in the Bible the praise of his lips. And who does not remember in the Psalms the song of the ideal man? The huntsmen would gather at night to sing of their prowess in the chase, and the shepherd would chant the story of the lion or the bear which he killed as he watched his flocks. But David takes down his harp and sings a sweeter psalm than all: *"Thy statutes have been my songs in the*

house of my pilgrimage" (Ps. cxix. 54). He knows no sweeter strain. How different from those who think God's law is a stern, cold thing! God's law is His written will. It has no terrors to the ideal man. He is not afraid to think of its sternness and majesty. "I will meditate on Thy laws day and night," he says. He tells us the subject of his thoughts. Ask him what he is thinking about at any time. "Thy laws," he says. How he can please his Master, what more he can bear for Him, what next he can do for Him—he has no other pleasure in life than this. You need not speak to him of the delights of life. "I will delight myself in Thy statutes," he says. You see what amusements the ideal man has. You see where the sources of his enjoyment are. Praise is the overflow of a full heart. When it is full of enjoyment it overflows; and you can tell the kind of enjoyment from the kind of praise that runs over. The ideal man's praise is of the will of God. He has no other sources of enjoyment. The cup of the world's pleasure has no attraction for him. The delights of life are bitter. Here is his only joy, his only delight: "I delight to do Thy will, O my God" (Ps. xl. 8).

(6) The next thing the ideal man wants is *education.* He needs teaching. He must take his place with the other disciples at his Master's feet. What does he want from the great Teacher? Teach me wisdom? No. Wisdom is not enough. Teach me what is truth? No, not even that. Teach me how to do good, how to love, how to trust? No, there is a deeper want than all. *"Teach me to do Thy will"* (Ps. cxliii. 10). This is the true education. Teach me to do Thy will. This was the education of Christ. Wisdom is a great study, and truth, and good works, and love, and trust, but there is an earlier lesson—obedience. So the ideal pupil prays, "Teach me to do Thy will."

And now we have almost gone far enough. These are really all the things the ideal man can need. But in case he should want anything else, God has given the man after his own heart a promise. God never leaves anything unprovided for. An emergency might arise in the ideal man's life; or he might make a mistake or lose heart, or be afraid to ask his Friend for some very great thing he needed, thinking it was too much, or for some very little thing, thinking it unworthy of notice. So God has given:

(7) The ideal *promise:* "If we ask anything according to His will, He heareth us . . . and we know that we have the petitions that we desired from Him" (I John v. 14). If he ask anything—no exception—no limit to God's confidence in him. He trusts him to ask right things. He is

guiding him, even in what he asks, if he is the man after God's own heart; so God sets no limit to his power. If anyone is doing God's will let him ask anything. It is God's will that he ask anything. Let him put His promise to the test.

Notice here what the true basis of prayer is. The prayer that is answered is the prayer after God's will. And the reason for this is plain. What is God's will is God's wish. And when a man does what God wills, he does what God wishes done. Therefore God will have that done at any cost, at any sacrifice. Thousands of prayers are never answered, simply because God does not wish them. If we pray for any one thing, or any number of things we are sure God wishes, we may be sure our wishes will be gratified. For our wishes are only the reflection of God's. And the wish in us is almost equivalent to the answer. It is the answer casting its shadow backwards. Already the thing is done in the mind of God. It casts two shadows—one backward, one forward. The backward shadow—that is the wish before the thing is done, which sheds itself in prayer. The forward shadow—that is the joy after the thing is done, which sheds itself in praise. Oh, what a rich and wonderful life this ideal life must be! Asking anything, getting everything, willing with God, praying with God, praising with God. Surely it is too much, this last promise. How can God trust us with a power so deep and terrible? Ah, He can trust the ideal life with anything. "If he ask anything." Well, if he does, he will ask nothing amiss. It will be God's will if it is asked. It will be God's will if it is not asked. For he is come, this man, "to do God's will."

(8) There is only one thing more which the model man may ever wish to have. We can imagine him wondering, as he thinks of the unspeakable beauty of this life—of its angelic purity, of its divine glory, of its Christ-like unselfishness, of its heavenly peace—how long this life can last. It may seem too bright and beautiful, for all things fair have soon to come to an end. And if any cloud could cross the true Christian's sky it would be when he thought that this ideal life might cease. But God, in the riches of His forethought, has rounded off this corner of his life with a great far-reaching text, which looks above the circumstance of time, and projects his life into the vast eternity beyond. *"He that doeth the will of God abideth forever"* (1 John ii. 17).

May God grant that you and I may learn to live this great and holy life, remembering the solemn words of Him who lived it first, who only lived it all: "Not everyone that saith unto me, Lord, Lord, shall enter into the kingdom of heaven; but he that doeth the will of My Father which is in heaven."

Chapter Twelve
"WHAT IS YOUR LIFE?"
AN OLD-YEAR SERMON

"Whereas ye know not what shall be on the morrow. For what is your life? It is even as a vapor, that appeareth for a little time, and then vanisheth away."—Jas. iv. 14.

Tomorrow, the first day of a new year, is a day of *wishes*. Today, the last day of an old year, is a day of *questions*. Tomorrow is a time of anticipation; today a time of reflection. Tomorrow our thoughts will go away out to the coming opportunities, and the larger vistas which the future is opening up to even the most commonplace of us. Today our minds wander among buried memories, and our hearts are full of self-questioning thoughts of what our past has been.

But if tomorrow is to be a day of hope, today must be a day of thought. If tomorrow is to be a time of resolution, today must be a day of investigation. And if we were to search the Bible through for a basis for this investigation, we should nowhere find a better than this question, *"What is your life?"*

We must notice, however, that life is used here in a peculiar sense— a narrow sense, some would say. The question does not mean, what quality is your life? What are you making of life? How are you getting on with it? How much higher is the tone of it this year than last? It has a more limited reference than this. It does not refer so much to quality of life as to quantity of life. It means how much life have you got? What value do you set upon your life? How long do you think your life will last? How does it compare with eternity?

And there are reasons which make this form of the question particularly appropriate, not only to this last day of the year, but, apart altogether from that, to the state of much religious thought upon the subject at the present moment. These reasons are mainly two. There is a large school just now who utterly ignore this question. There is a large school who utterly spoil it. There may be said to be two ways of looking at life, each of which finds favor just now with a wide circle of people.

1. The theory that life is everything.
2. The theory that life is nothing.

Or, adding the converse to these:

1. The theory that life is everything and eternity nothing.
2. The theory that life is nothing and eternity everything.

Now, those who hold the first of these, object to the time-view of life altogether. And there can be no doubt that this is the favorite of the two. For one thing, it is decidedly the fashionable view. It is the view culture takes, and many thinking men, and many thoughtful and modern books. Life, these say, is the great thing. We know something about life. We are in it—it is pulsating all around us. We feel its greatness and reality. But the other does not press upon us in the same way. It is far off and mystical. It takes a kind of effort even to believe it. Therefore let us keep to what we know, what we are in, what we are sure of.

The strength of this school is in their great view of life; their weakness and error, in their little view of time. Their enthusiasm for the quality of life makes them rush to the opposite extreme and ignore its quantity. The thought that life is short has little influence with them. They simply refuse to let it weigh with them, and when pressed with thoughts of immortality, or time-views of life, they affirm, with a kind of superiority, that they have too much to do with the present to trouble themselves with sentimentalisms about the future.

The second view is the more antiquated, perhaps the more illiterate. Life, with it, is nothing at all. It is a bubble, a vapor, a shadow. Eternity is the great thing. Eternity is the significant thing. Eternity is the only thing. Life is a kind of unfortunate preliminary—a sort of dismal antechamber, where man must wait, and be content for a little with the view of eternity from the windows. His turn to go is coming; meantime let him fret through the unpleasant interval as resignedly as he can, and pray God to speed its close.

The strength of this school is that it recognizes eternity, its weakness, and its great error, that it refuses to think of life and spoils the thought of eternity for those who do. The first school requires to be told that life is short; this, so far from having to be told that it is short, has to be told that life is long—for life to it is nothing.

It is clear, of course, that each of these views is the natural recoil from the other. The mistake is that each has recoiled too far. The life-something theory cannot help recoiling from the life-nothing theory; but it need not recoil into life-everything. So the eternity-something theory cannot help recoiling from the eternity-nothing theory; but it need not recoil into eternity-everything.

It is plain, then, that both these theories are wrong, and yet not altogether wrong. There is a great deal of truth in each—so much, indeed, that if the parts of truth which each contains were joined into one, they would form a whole—*the truth*. And if the sides were nearly equal,—as many who think life nothing as think life everything—there could be no attempt more useful than to find a harmony between. But the sides are not equal, and hence the better exercise will be to deal with the side which has the truth the furthest in arrear.

This, undoubtedly, is the life-school—the life-everything school. The other is, comparatively, a minority. At least, those who hold the extreme form of it are a minority. It is a more obvious and striking truth that life is something; it is not difficult to convince the man who makes eternity everything to allow something to life. But to get the man who makes life everything to grant a little to eternity is harder; for the power of the world to come may be yet unfelt and unproved, and the race of life be so swift that the rival flight of time remains unseen.

There are mainly two great classes who swell the ranks of the majority, who refuse to think of the flight of time.

1. The great busy working and thinking class, who are *too careful* of time to ever think of eternity as its successor. These have too little time to think of time.

2. The great lazy worldly class, who are *too careless* of time ever to think that it will cease. These have too much time to think of time—so much of it that they think there will be always much of it.

Now it is to these two classes that this old year's question comes home with special power, "What is your life?" And it is no reason why the majority should decline to face the question, that a fanatical minority have made the subject nauseous by the exaggeration of eternity. For if these men suffer in their lives by treating life as a thing of no importance, the others certainly suffer more by exaggerating life at the tremendous expense of eternity.

The great objection to thinking about eternity, or, to take the other side, about the brevity of life, is that it is not practical. The life-school professes to be eminently utilitarian. It will have nothing to do with abstractions, nothing that does not directly concern life. Anything that is outside the sphere of action is of little consequence to practical men. The members of this school feel themselves to be in the rush of the world's work, and it is something to think of that. It is something to live in the thick of it, to yield to the necessities of it, to share its hopes, and calmly endure its discipline of care. But when you leave life, they protest, you are away from the present and the real. You are off into poetry and sentiment, and the meditations you produce may be interesting for philosophers and dreamers, but they are not for men who take their stand on the greatness of life and crave to be allowed to leave the mystical alone.

Now the answer to that,—and it may be thoroughly answered,—may be given in a word. First of all, who told you eternity was nothing? Who told you it was an unpractical, unprofitable dream? Who told you to go on with your work and let time and other abstractions alone? It was certainly not God. God takes exactly the opposite view. He is never done insisting on the importance of the question. "O that they were wise . . . that they would consider their latter end"—that is what God says. "Make me to know mine end, and the measure of my days what it is"—that is what David, the man after God's own heart, says. "Teach me to number my days"—that is what Moses, the friend of God, says.

And you will notice the reason God gives for thinking about these things. It was enough, indeed, for Him to say it, without any reason; but He has chosen to give us one. Why are we to number our days? "That we may apply our hearts unto wisdom." That is the reason for thinking about time. It is to make us wise. Perhaps you have thought this is merely a piece of sentiment, a flower of rhetoric for the poet, a harmless, popular imagination for ignorant people who cannot discourse upon life, a dramatic truth to impress the weak to prepare their narrow minds for death? But no; it is not that. God never uses sentiment. And if you think a moment you will see that it is not the narrow mind which needs this truth, but his who discourses on life. The man who discourses most on life should discourse the most on time. When you discourse on life, you plead that it is in the interests of life. You despise the time—view as unpractical in the interests of the new life—school who care too much for life to spend their strength upon the sentiment of time. Ah, but if you really cared for life, this sentiment would only make you love it the more. For time is the measurement of life. And all in life must be profoundly affected by its poor, scant quantity. Your life on earth *is* a great thing, a rich and precious possession. It is true that it is full of meaning and issues which no man can reckon. But it is ten thousand times greater for the thought that it must cease. One of the chief reasons why life is so great is just that life is so short. If we had a thousand years of it, it would not be so great as if we had only a thousand hours. It is great because it is little. A man is to be executed, and the judge has given him a month to prepare for death—one short month. How rich every hour of it becomes, how precious the very moments are! But suppose he has only five minutes. Then how unspeakably solemn! How much greater is the five minutes life than the month life! Make eternity a month and life five minutes—if such a tremendous exaggeration of life could be conceived. How much greater does it become for being so very small!

How precious time is to a short-lived man! I am to die at thirty, you at sixty; a minute is twice as dear to me, for each minute is twice as short. So a day to me is more than a day to Methuselah, for he had many days, and I have but few. Oh! if we really felt the dignity of life, we should wonder no less at its brevity than at its dignity. If we felt the greatness of life at this moment, how much keenness would this further thought add to it—that we might be dead before this sermon was done! How many things we permit ourselves on the theory that life is great, would be most emphatically wrong on the theory that time was also great! How many frivolous things,—yes, how many great things even,— should we have to turn out this moment from our lives for just this thought, if we believed it, that time is short! For there is no room among the crowded moments of our life for things which will not live when life and time are past. So no one who does not feel the keen sense of time flying away at every moment with the work he has done and the opportunities he has lost, can know the true greatness of life and the inexpressible value of the self-selected things with which he fills its brief and narrow span. The thought of death must change at every point the values of the significant things of earth not less than the thought of life, and we must ever feel the solemn relations given to our life and work from the overwhelming thought that the working-life is brief.

A modern poet has described, in strangely suggestive words, the time when first the idea of time and death began to dawn upon this earth. The scene is laid in some eastern land, where a great colony had risen from the offspring of Cain, the murderer of his brother. Cain knew what death was—he had seen it—but he alone, of all his scattered family, for he kept his burning secret to himself. Cain's family grew and spread throughout the land, but no thought of death came in to check the joyous exuberance of life; till one day, in boyish pastime a hurled stone strikes Lamech's son, and the lad falls to the earth. Friends gather round him as he lies, and bring him toys and playthings to wake him from his sleep. But no sleep like this had ever come to Lamech's son before, and soft entreating words bring no responsive sound to the cold lips, or light to the closed eyes. Then Cain comes forward, whispering, "The boy is dead," and tells the awe-struck family of this mystery of death. And then the poet describes the magic of this word, how "a new spirit, from that hour, came o'er the house of Cain." How time, once vague as air, began to stir strange terrors in the soul, and lend to life a moment which it had not known before. How even the sunshine had a different look. How "work grew eager, and device was born." How

> It seemed the light was never loved before,
> Now each man said, "Twill go, and come no more."
> No budding branch, no pebble from the brook,
> No form, no shadow, but new dearness took
> From the one thought that Life must have an end.

So the thought that life will be no more, that each day lived is hastening on the day when life itself must stop, makes every hour of ours a million times more great, and tinges every thought, and word, and act, with the shadow of what must be.

From all this, it will now be clear that the man who is really concerned to live well must possess himself continually of the thought that he is not to live long. And it is in the highest interests of great living, to stimulate life, not to paralyze it, that God asks us all today, "What is your life?"

But the Bible has done more than ask this question. It has answered it. And when the Bible answers a question, it always gives the best answer. We could do no better, therefore, than consult it a little further now, for it so happens that there are few subjects which the Bible goes into so thoroughly as this one—few thoughts which rise more often or more urgently to the surface of the great Bible lives than "What is your life?"

And, besides, there is a peculiarity in Bible answers which makes them particularly valuable, and which has tended, more than anything else, to impress them profoundly upon the deeper spirit of every age. And that peculiarity is this, that the answer is never given in hard, bare words, but is presented, wrapped up in some figure of such exquisite beauty, that no mind could refuse to give it a place, were it only for the fineness of its metaphor. Take, as an example, the answer which follows the question in the text, "What is your life?" "It is even a vapor, that appeareth for a little time, and then vanisheth away." Who could afford to forget a thought like that, when once its beauty had struck root within the mind? And if God did not rather choose a few hard solid sentences of truth to perpetuate an answer to one of the most solid thoughts of life, is it not just because He wanted it to be remembered evermore— because He wanted the thought of the shortness and uncertainty of life to live in every living soul, and haunt the heart in times when other thoughts were passionless and dull? In childhood, before deeper thoughts had come, He would paint this truth, in delicate tints, on every opening soul; and in riper years, when trouble and sickness came and weaned the broken mind from sterner thoughts, He would have the man still furnished with these ever-preaching pictures of the frailty of his life.

Why is it that there is such strange attractiveness to many hearts in the Bible—thoughts of time, and why the peculiar charm with which the least religious minds will linger over the texts which speak of human life? It is because God has thrown an intensely living interest around these truths, by carrying His images of the thoughts He most wanted remembered into the great galleries of the imagination, where the soul can never tire. Had such thoughts been left to reason, it would have stifled them with its cold touch; had they been sunk in the heart, it would have consumed itself and them in hot and burning passion. But in the broad region of the imagination there is expansiveness enough for even such vast truths to wander at their will, and power and mystery enough to draw both heart and reason after them in wondering, trembling homage. And if no day almost passes over our heads without some silent visitation to remind us what we are, it is because the Bible has utilized all the most common things of life to bring home these lessons to the soul, so that no shadow on the wall, nor blade of withered grass, is void of meanings which every open heart can read.

Now, it is a remarkable fact, in this connection, that the Bible has used up almost every physical image that is in any way appropriate to the case. And if we were to go over the conceptions of life which have been held by great men in succeeding ages of the world, we should find scarce anything new, scarce anything which the Bible had not used before.

There lie scattered throughout this Book no fewer than *eighteen* of these answers, and all in metaphor, to the question, "What is your life?"

And anyone who has not before gathered them together, cannot but be surprised at the singular beauty and appropriateness of the collection. To begin with, let us run over their names. "What is your life?" It is:

A tale that is told. A sleep.
A pilgrimage. A vapor.
A swift post. A shadow.
A swift ship. A flower.
A handbreath. A weaver's shuttle.
A shepherd's tent removed. Water spilt on the ground.
A thread cut by the weaver. Grass.
A dream. Wind. Nothing.

Generally speaking, the first thing to strike one about these images is that they are all quick things—there is a suggestion of brevity and evanescence about them, and this feeling is so strong that we might fancy there was only one answer to the question, what is your life; namely, your life is *short*. But if we look closer at them for a moment, shades of difference will begin to appear, and we shall find the hints of other meanings as great and striking, and quite as necessary to complete the conception of "your life."

First of all, then, and most in detail, three of these metaphors give this answer:—

I. *Your life is a very little thing.* We have admitted that life is a very great thing. It is also a very little thing. Measure it by its bearing on eternity; there is no image in God's universe to compare with it for majesty and dignity. It is a sublime thing—life. But measure it by its bearings upon time, by its results on the world, on other lives; there is no image too small to speak of its meanness and narrowness, for it is a little thing, "your life." It is "a shadow," it is "a shepherd's tent removed," it is "a tale that is told."

A shadow. It is unreal; it is illusory. It falls across the world without affecting it; perhaps it only darkens it. Then it rises suddenly, and is gone. It leaves few impressions; and if it could, shadow cannot act much on other shadows. So life at the best is a poor, resultless, shadowy thing.

A shepherd's tent removed. Just before sunset the slopes of the Eastern hills would be dotted with Arab tents. And when night fell, the traveller in these lands, as he lay down to rest would see the glimmering of their fires and hear the noisy bleating of their flocks. But in the morning, when he looked out, both herds and herdsmen would be gone. Hours ago, perhaps, the tents had been struck, and the hills would be silent and lonely as if no foot had ever stirred the dew on their slopes before. So man, the Bible says, traces out his trackless path through life. He is here today, in the noise of the world's labor; tomorrow, when you look for him, he is gone. Through the night sometime his frail tent has been struck, and his place is empty and still. His life has left no track to tell that it was there—except a burnt-out fire to show that there a shepherd's tent had been removed.

But the best of these images is the third—*A tale that is told.* Some think this means a thought or meditation. "Your life is a meditation," as the margin has it. But as the psalm in which the words occur was written by Moses, it is probable that the obvious meaning of the words is the correct one. In their journeyings the children of Israel would have many weary, unoccupied hours. There would be no books to relieve the monotony, and no doubt the people would attempt to beguile the tedious marches and the long hours by the camp fires at night, with the familiar Oriental custom of narrating personal adventures in the form of stories or tales. Night after night, as this went on, the different tales of the storytellers would begin to get mixed, then to confuse their audience, then even to weary them. The first tale, which made a great impression once, would lose its power, and the second, which was thought more wonderful still, would be distanced by the third. Then the third would be forgotten, and the fourth and the fifth; till *all* would be forgotten, and last night's tale would be the vivid picture in every mind today. But the story-teller would know that tonight another would have his turn, and sit in the place of honor, and tell a more vivid tale than he told the night before, and his would be forgotten and ignored.

So we do spend our years as a tale that is told. The dead have told their tales; they have said their say. They thought we would remember what they did and said. But, no; they are forgotten. They have become old stories now. And our turn will come—our turn to stop; our turn for the angel of death to close the chapter of our life, whether it be a novel or a psalm, and write the universal "Finis" at the end. What though a sentence here and there may linger for a few brief years to find a place—without quotation marks—in some tale better told, the tale itself must close and be forgotten, like the rest, an ill-told, ill-heard, and ill-remembered tale.

II. There is, next, and briefly, another set of metaphors which bring out the more common answer (which, therefore, it will only be necessary to name), *that life is a short thing.* Shortness, of course, is different from littleness. A lightning flash is short, but not little. But life is both short and little. And there are two ways in which life is short: (1) Measured by growth. (2) Measured by minutes. Those who are growing most feel time shortest. They have started with the wrecks of being to fashion themselves into men, and life is all too short to do it in. Therefore they work out their salvation with fear and trembling—fearful lest death should come, trembling lest life should stop before it is worked out. But they who measure life by its minutes have nothing to say of its brevity; for their purpose it is long enough. It is not more time they want, but "the more capacious soul," as someone says, "to flow through every pore of the little that they have." But there is no distinction in the Bible treatment of the two. Time is the same to all. It is a *handbreadth; a weaver's shuttle; nothing; an eagle hasting to the prey; a swift post; a swift ship.* David used to pray to God to give him a measure for his days. Well, he got it. It was the breadth of his hand. We carry about with us continually the measure of our days. "My days are as an handbreadth."

The others are familiar symbols enough. The weaver's shuttle—is it the monotony, the sameness, the constant repetition of life? Rather the quickness, the rapid flight through the thin web of time; the shuttle being then, perhaps, the quickest image men had.

Then those in the country in early times could know nothing more rapid or sudden than the swoop of an eagle on its prey; then, by the seaside, nothing more fleeting than the swift sailing away of a ship driven by the unseen wind, or the hasty arrival of the "swift post" or messenger with tidings from afar. And it was not for want of opportunity if they did not learn their lessons well in those simple days, when the few changes life had were each thus stamped with the thought of the great change into eternity.

III. The next thought is so closely allied to this that one can scarcely separate it but for convenience. It suggests the idea of *transitoriness.* Your life is a transitory thing. It is a thing of change. There is no endurance in it, no settling down in it, no real home to it here. Therefore God calls it a *pilgrimage*—a passing on to a something that is to be. Still closely allied to this, too, is the simile of the text—that life is a *vapor.* It means there is no real substance in it. It is a going and coming for a moment, then a passing away forever. And then there are two or three metaphors which advance this idea still further. In their hands life passes from transitoriness into mystery. This life of ours, they show us, is a *mysterious thing*. And, it is true, life is a mysterious thing. We do not understand life—why it should begin, why it should end. There is some meaning in it somewhere that has baffled every search; some meaning beyond, some more real state than itself. So the Bible calls it a *sleep*, a *dream*, the *wind*. No book but the Bible could have called our life a sleep. The great book of the Greeks has called death a sleep:

"Death's twin-brother, sleep."

But the Bible has the profounder thought. Life is the sleep. Death is but the waking. And the great poets and philosophers of the world since have found no deeper thought of life than this; and the greatest of them all has used the very word—our little life is rounded with a sleep. It seems to have been a soothing thought to them, and it may be a sanctifying thought to us, that this life is not the end; and therefore it is a wise thing to turn round sometimes in our sleep, and think how there is more beyond than dreams.

There are but two thoughts more to bring our questions to a close, and they will add a practical interest to what has gone before.

IV. What is your life? *Life is an irrevocable thing.* We have just finished an irrevocable year. As we look back upon it, every thought and word and act of it is there in its place, just as we left it. There are all the Sabbaths in their places, and all the well-spent days or ill-spent days between. There is every sin and every wish and every look still in its own exact surroundings, each under its own day of the month, at the precise moment of the day it happened. We are leaving it all at twelve o'clock tonight; but, remember, we leave it exactly as it stands. No single hour of it can be changed now, no smallest wish can be recalled, no angry word taken back. It is fixed, steadfast, irrevocable—stereotyped forever on the past plates of eternity. Our book has a wonderful metaphor of this—"*water spilt upon the ground,* which cannot be gathered up again." No; we cannot gather up these days and put them back into time's breaking urn, and live them over again. They are spilt upon the ground, and the great stream of time has sucked them up, and cast them already on the eternal shores among all bygone years, and there they bide till God's time comes, and they come back, one by one, in order as they went, to again meet us and Him before the judgment bar.

Tomorrow is to be a time of resolution, is it? Well, let this resolution take the foremost place of all, that, when this day of next year comes, and we look once more at the irrevocable past, there shall be fewer things to wish undone, or words to wish unsaid, and more spots where memory shall love to linger still, more steps which, when retraced in thought, will fill the heart with praise.

V. Lastly: life is more than an irrevocable thing, it is *an uncertain thing*—so certainly uncertain, that it is certain we shall not all be here to see this next year close. What means the grim image in the Bible of the weaver's thread suspended in the air, and the blade of the lifted knife just touching it with its edge? It means that you must die. The thread of your life is to be cut. The knife may be lifted now, the keen blade just touching it; one pressure of the hand, and it is done. One half, left unfinished, still hanging to the past—the other, dropped noiselessly into eternity. Oh, life is an abruptly closing thing! Is it not as grass? In the morning, it groweth up and flourisheth, and in the evening, it is cut down and withereth. Is your life ready for the swiftly falling knife, for the Reaper who stands at your door? Have you heard that there is another life—a life which cannot die, a life which, linked to your life, will make the past still bright with pardon and the future rich with hope? *This life is in His Son.*

CHAPTER THIRTEEN
WHAT IS GOD'S WILL?

"The God of our fathers hath chosen thee, that thou shouldest know His will."—Acts xxii. 14.

We resume today a subject, the thread of which has been broken by the interval of a few Sabbaths—the subject of the will of God.

Already we have tried to learn two lessons:—

(1) That the end of our life is to do the will of God.

(2) That this was the end of Christ's life.

It will help to recall what has gone before if we compare this with another definition of the end of life with which we are all familiar.

Of course this is not the most complete statement of the end of our life; but it is the most practical, and it will recall the previous conclusions if we refer to this for a moment.

Our Shorter Catechism, for instance, puts the end of life in quite different words. "Man's chief end," it says, "is to glorify God and enjoy Him forever." But this answer is just too great for us. There is too much in it. It is really the same answer, but turned towards God. It is too great to understand. It is as true, but too profoundly true. It is wonderfully conceived and put together, but it goes past us. It expresses the end of life God-ward—determines the quality of all the things we do by the extent to which they make way in the world for the coming glory of God. But this is too wonderful for us. We want a principle life-ward as well as God-ward. We want something to tell us what to do with the things beneath us and around us and within us, as well as the things above us. Therefore there is a human side to the Shorter Catechism's answer.

What is the chief end of man?

Man's chief end is to do the will of God.

In one sense this is not such a divine answer. But we are not divine. We understand God's will: God's glory, only faintly—we are only human yet, and "glory" is a word for heaven.

Ask a schoolboy, learning the first question in the Catechism, to do a certain thing for the glory of God. The opportunity of doing the thing may be gone before the idea can be driven into the boy's head of what the glory of God means. But tell him to do the thing because it is God's will that he should do it—he understands that. He knows that God's will is just what God likes, and what he himself probably does *not* like. And the conception of it from this side is so clear that no schoolboy even need miss the end of life—for that is simply doing what God likes. If our souls are not great enough to think of God's glory as the practical rule of life, let them not be too small to think of God's will. If we look after the end of life from this side, God will look from the other. If we do the will of God, God will see that it glorifies God.

Let us suppose, then, that after casting about for an object in life, we have at last stopped at this—the end of my life is to do the will of God. Let us suppose also that we have got over the disappointment of finding that there is nothing higher for us to do in the world. Or, perhaps, taking the other side, suppose we are beginning to feel the splendid conviction that, after all, our obscure life is not to be wasted: that having this ideal principle within it, it may yet be as great in its homely surroundings as the greatest human life—seeing that no man can do more with his life than the will of God. Though we may never be famous or powerful, or called to heroic suffering or acts of self-denial which will vibrate through history, though we are neither intended to be apostles nor missionaries nor martyrs, but to be common people living in common houses, spending the day in common offices or common kitchens, yet doing the will of God there, we shall do as much as apostle or missionary or martyr. They can do no more than do God's will where they are, even as we can do as much where we are—and answer the end of our life as truly, faithfully, and triumphantly as they.

Suppose we feel all this, and desire, as we stand on the threshold of the truly ideal life, that, God helping us, we shall live it if we may, we are met at once with the question, "How are we ever to know what the will of God can be?" The chief end of life is to do the will of God. *Question:* How am I to know the will of God—to know it clearly and definitely? Is it possible? and if so, how?

Now, to begin with, we have probably an opinion on the matter already. And if you were to express it, it would be this: that it is not possible. You have thought about the will of God, and read and thought, and thought and read, and you have come to this conclusion that the will of God is a very mysterious thing—a very mysterious thing, which some people may have revealed to them, but does not seem in any way possible to you.

Your nature is different from other people's; though you have strained your eyes in prayer and thought, you have never seen the will of God yet. And if you ever have been in the same line with it, it has only been by chance, for you can see no principle in it, nor any certainty of ever being in the same line again. One or two special occasions, indeed, you can recall when you thought you were near the will of God, but they must have been special interpositions on God's part. He does not show His will every day like that: once or twice only in a lifetime is as much of this high experience as one ever dare expect.

Now, of course, it is no use going on to find out what God's will is if the thing is impossible. If this experience is correct—and we cannot know God's will for the mystery of it—we may as well give up the ideal life at once. But if you examined this experience, even cursorily, you would find at once how far away from the point it is.

1. In the first place, it is merely an experience; it is exclusively based on your own experience, not on God's thoughts regarding it, but on your own thoughts. The true name for this is presumption.

2. It assumes that, the end of life being to do God's will, and you not being able to know God's will, are therefore not responsible for fulfilling the end of life. This is self-deception.

3. It suggests the idea that God could teach you His will if He liked, seeing that He had done so once or twice by your own admission. Yet, though He wants you to do His will, and you want it too, He deliberately refuses to tell you what it is. This is an accusation against God.

It is something worse than unreasonable, therefore, to say that we think it hopeless for us ever to know God's will. On the contrary, indeed, there is a strong presumption that we should find it out. For if it is so important a thing that the very end of life is involved in it, it would be absurd to imagine that God should ever keep us the least in the dark as to what His will may mean.

And this presumption is changed into a certainty when we balance our minds for a moment on the terms of this text. "The God of our fathers hath chosen thee, that thou shouldest know His will." It is not simply a matter of presumption, it is a matter of election. Have you ever thought of this strange, deep calling of God? We are called to salvation, we have thought of that; we are called to holiness, we have thought of that; but as great as either is this, we are called to know God's will. We are answering our call in other ways; are we answering it in this? What is God's will? Are we knowing God's will? How much have we learned of that to which we have been called? And is it our prayer continually, as it was his to whom these words were said, that we may be "filled with the knowledge of His will"?

It is a reasonable object of search, then, to find out what God's will for us may be. And it is a reasonable expectation that we may find it out so fully as to know at any moment whether we are in the line of it or not; and when difficulty arises about the next step of our life, we may have absolute certainty which way God's will inclines. There are many kinds of assurance in religion; it is as important to have assurance of God's will as to have assurance of God's salvation. For just as the loss of assurance of salvation means absence of peace, faith, and usefulness, so absence of assurance of God's will means miserable Christian life, imperfect Christian character, and impaired Christian usefulness.

We start our investigation, therefore, in the belief that God *must* have light for all of us on the subject of His will, and with the desire to have assurance in the guidance of our life by God as clear and strong as of its redemption and salvation by Christ.

In one sense, of course, no man can know the will of God, even as in one sense no man can know God Himself. God's will is a great and infinite mystery—a thing of mighty mass and volume, which can no more be measured out to hungry souls in human sentences than the eternal knowledge of God or the boundless love of Christ. But even as there is a sense in which one poor human soul can hold enough of the eternal knowledge of God and the boundless love of Christ, so is there a sense in which God can put as much of His will into human words as human hearts can bear—as much as human wills can will or human lives perform.

When we come to put this will into words, we find that it divides itself into two great parts.

> I. There is a part of God's will which everyone may know—
> *a universal part.*
> II. A part of God's will which no one knows but you—*a particular part.*

A universal part—for everyone. A particular part—for the individual.

I. To begin with the first. There is a part of God's will which everyone may know. It is written in divine characters in two sacred books, which every man may read. The one of them is the Bible, the other is nature. The Bible is God's will in words, in formal thoughts, in grace. Nature is God's will in matter and tissue and force. Nature is not often considered a part of God's will. But it is a part, and a great part, and the first part. And perhaps one reason why some never know the second is because they yield no full obedience to the first. God's law of progress is from the lower to the higher; scant obedience at the beginning of His will means disobedience with the rest. The laws of nature are the will of God for our bodies. As there is a will of God for our higher nature—the moral laws—as emphatically is there a will of God for the lower—the natural laws. If you would know God's will in the higher, therefore, you must begin with God's will in the lower: which simply means that if you want to live the ideal life, you must begin with the ideal body. The law of moderation, the law of sleep, the law of regularity, the law of exercise, the law of cleanliness—this is the law or will of God for you. This is the first law, the beginning of His will for you. And if we are ambitious to get on to do God's will in the higher reaches, let us respect it as much in the lower; for there may be as much of God's will in minor things, as much of God's will in taking good bread and pure water, as in keeping a good conscience or living a pure life. Whoever heard of gluttony doing God's will, or laziness, or uncleanness, or the man who was careless and wanton of natural life? Let a man disobey God in these, and you have no certainty that he has any true principle for obeying God in anything else: for God's will does not only run into the church and the prayer-meeting and the higher chambers of the soul, but into the common rooms at home down to wardrobe and larder and cellar, and into the bodily frame down to blood and muscle and brain.

This, then, is the first contribution to the contents of the will of God. And, for distinction, they may be called the *physical contents.*

Next in order we come to the *moral contents,* both of these coming under the same head as parts of God's will which everyone may know.

These moral contents, as we have seen, are contained in the Word of God; and the Bible has a variety of names for them, such as testimonies, laws, precepts, statutes, commandments.

Now this is a much more formidable array than the physical contents. It is one thing to be in physical condition—a prizefighter may be that—but it is quite another to be in moral condition. It is a difficult matter to explain exactly what God's will in this great sense is; for, on the one hand, there is the danger of elevating it so high as to frighten the timid soul from ever attempting to reach it, and, on the other, the insensible tendency to lower it to human standards and aims.

It must be understood, however, to the full that, as far as its formidableness is concerned, that is absolutely unchangeable. God's moral law cannot be toned down into anything less binding, less absolutely moral, less infinitely significant. Whatever it means, it is meant for every man in its rigid truth as the definite and formal expression of God's will for him.

From the moral side there are three different departments of God's will. Foremost, and apparently most rigid of all, are the Ten Commandments. Now the Ten Commandments contain, in a few sentences, one of the largest-known portions of God's will. They form the most strict code of morality in the world: the basis of all others, the most venerable and universal expression of the will of God for man. Following upon this there come the Beatitudes of Christ. This is another large portion of God's will. This forms the most unique code of morality in the world, the most complete and lovely additional expression of the will of God for Christians. Passing through the human heart of Christ, the older commandment of the Creator becomes the soft and mellow beatitude of the Savior—passes from the colder domain of law with a penalty on failure, to the warm region of love with a benediction on success. These are the two chief elements in the moral part of the will of God for man. But there is a third set of laws and rules, which are not to be found exactly expressed in either of these. The Ten Commandments and the Beatitudes take up most of the room in God's will, but there are shades of precept still unexpressed which also have their place. Hence we must add to all this mass of law and beatitude many more laws and many more beatitudes which lie enclosed in other texts, and other words of Christ which have their place like the rest as portions of God's will.

Here, then, we already know a great part of what God's will is; although, perhaps, we have not often called it by this name. And it may be worthwhile, before going on to find out anymore, to pause for a moment and find out how to practice this.

For, perhaps, when we see how great a thing it is, this will of God, our impulse for the moment is to wish we had not known. We were building ourselves up with the idea that we were going to try this life, and that it was easy and smooth compared with the life we left. There was a better future opening to us, with visions of happiness and holiness and even of usefulness to God. But our hopes are dashed now. How can we do God's will—this complicated mass of rules and statutes, each bristling with the certainty of a thousand breakages? How can we keep these ten grave laws, with their unflinching scorn of compromise and exacting obligation, to the uttermost jot and tittle? How can our coarse spirits breathe the exquisite air of these beatitudes, or fit our wayward wills to the narrow mold of all these binding texts? Can God know how weak we are, and how blind and biased towards the breakages, before ever we thought of Him? Can He think how impossible it is to keep these laws, even for one close-watched experimental hour? Did Christ really mean it—not some lesser thing than this—when He taught in the ideal prayer that God's will was to be done on earth *even* as it is done in heaven?

There can be but one answer. "God hath chosen thee, that thou shouldest know His will." And God expects from each of us neither less nor more than this. He knows the frailty of our frame; He remembers we are dust, yet such dust that He has given each of us the divinest call to the vastest thing in heaven. There, by the side of our frailty, He lays down His holy will—lays it down confidingly, as if a child could take it in its grasp, and, as if He means the child to fondle it and bear it in its breast, He says, "If a man love Me, he will keep My words."

There must be something, therefore, to ease the apparent hopelessness of doing this will of God—something to give us heart to go on with it, to give strength to obey God's call. We were not prepared to find it running in to the roots of things like this; but there must be something brighter somewhere than the dark side we have seen. Well, then, let us think for a moment on these points:

1. In the first place, there *must* be such laws. God is a king—His kingdom the kingdom of heaven. His people are His subjects. Subjects must have laws. Therefore we start with a necessity. Laws must be.

2. But who are afraid of laws? Good subjects? Never. Criminals are afraid of laws. Who dread the laws of this country, cry out against them, and would abolish them if they could? Drunkards, thieves, murderers. Who love the laws of this country? The honest, the wise and the good. Then who are afraid of God's laws—would abolish them if they could? The wicked, the profligate, the licentious. But *you* would not. The just and holy, the pure in heart and life love them, respect them. More still, they demand them. It would be no kingdom without them—no kingdom worth belonging to. If it were not for its laws of truth and purity, and its promise of protection from unrighteousness and sin, it would have no charm for them. It is the inaccessible might and purity of will in the kingdom of God that draw all other wills as subjects to its sway. It is not only not hard, therefore, that there should be such elements in God's will as law; it is a privilege. And it is more than a privilege to have them.

3. It is a privilege to do them. And it is a peculiar privilege, this. It consists partly in forgetting that they are laws—in changing their names, commandment, precept, testimony, statute, into this—the will of God. No sternness then can enter with the thought, for God's name is in the name, and the help of God, and the power of God, and the constraining love of Christ. This takes away the hopelessness of trying to keep God's will. It makes it a personal thing, a relation to a living will, not to didactic law.

And there is, further, a wonderful provision near it. When God puts down His great will beside me telling me to do it, He puts down just beside it as great a thing, His love. And as my soul trembles at the fearfulness of will, love comes with its calm omnipotence, and draws it to Himself; then takes my timid will and twines it around His, till mine is fierce with passion to serve, and strong to do His will. Just as if some mighty task were laid to an infant's hand, and the engine-grasp of a giant strengthened it with his own. Where God's law is, God's love is. Look at law—it withers your very soul with its stern inexorable face. But look at love, or look at God's will, which means look at love's will, and you are reassured, and your heart grows strong. No martyr dies for abstract truth. For a person, for God, he will die a triple death. So no man will die for God's law. But for God he will do it. Where God's will, then, seems strong to command, God's love is strong to obey. Hence the profound texts, "Love is the fulfilling of the law." "And this is the love of God that we keep His commandments, and His commandments are not grievous."

God's will, then, is as great as God, as high as heaven, yet as easy as love. For love knows no hardness, and feels no yoke. It desires no yielding to its poverty in anything it loves. Let God be greater, and His will sterner, love will be stronger and obedience but more true. Let not God come down to me, slacken truth for me, make His will weaker for me: my interests, as subject, are safer with my King, are greater with the greatness of my King. Only give me love, pure, burning love and loyalty to Him, and I shall climb from law to law through grace and glory, to the place beside the throne where the angels do His will. There are two ways, therefore, of looking at God's will—one looking at the love side of it, the other at the law; the one ending in triumph, the other in despair; the one a liberty, the other a slavery. And you might illustrate this in a simple way, to make it finally clear,—for this is the hardest point to hold,—in some such way as this.

Suppose you go into a workshop occasionally, and watch the workmen at their task. The majority do their work in an uninterested, mechanical sort of way. Everything is done with the most proper exactness and precision—almost with slavish precision, a narrower watch would say. They come exactly at the hour in the morning, and throw down their work to a second exactly when the closing bell has rung. There is a certain punctiliousness about them, and a scrupulosity about their work; and as part cause of it, perhaps, you observe an uncomfortable turning of the head occasionally as if some eve were upon them, then a dogged going on of their work again, as if it were always done under some restraint.

But among the workmen you will notice one who seems to work on different principles. There is a buoyancy and cheerfulness about him as he goes about his work, which is foreign to all the rest. You will see him at his place sometimes even before the bell has rung, and if unfinished work be in his hands when closing time has come, he does not mind an extra five minutes when all the others are gone. What strikes you about him is the absence of that punctiliousness which marked the others' work. It does not seem at all a tyranny to him, but even a freedom and a pleasure; and though he is apparently not so mechanical in his movements as his mates, his work seems better done and greater, despite the ease and light-heartedness which mark him through its course. Now the difference between them is this: The first set of men are hired workmen. The man by himself is the master's son. Not that he is outwardly different; he is a common workman in a fustian jacket like the rest. But he is the master's son. The first set work for wages, come in at regulation hours lest aught be kept off their wages, keep the workshop laws in terror of losing their place. But the son keeps them, and keeps them better, not for wages, but for love.

So the Christian keeps the will or the laws of God because of the love of God. Not because they are workshop regulations framed and hung up before him at every moment of his life; but because they are his Master's will. They are as natural to him as air. He would never think of not keeping them. His meat is to do the will of his Father which is in heaven. There is no room for punctiliousness in this the true way of doing God's will. A scrupulous Christian is a hired servant and not the Master's son.

II. But now, very briefly, in the second and last place, there is an unknown part of God's will—at least, a part which is only known to *you*. There is God's will for the world, and God's will for the individual. There is God's will written on tables of stone for all the world to read. There is God's will carved in sacred hieroglyphic which no one reads but you. There is God's will rolling in thunder over the life of universal man. There is God's will dropped softly on the believer's ear in angel whispers or spoken by the still small voice within. This final element in God's will, to distinguish it from the moral and physical contents which go before, one might call the more strictly *spiritual* content.

This is a distinct addition to the other parts—an addition, too, which many men ignore, and other men deny. But there is such a region in God's will—a region unmapped in human charts, unknown to human books, a region for the pure in heart, for the upright, for the true. It is a land of mystery to those who know it not, a land of foolishness, and

weaknesses, and delusive sights and sounds. But there is a land where
the Spirit moves, a luminous land, a walking in God's light. There is a
region where God's own people have their breathing from above, where
each saint's steps are ordered of the Lord.

Now this region may be distinguished from the other regions by its
secrecy. It is a private thing; between God and you. You want to know
what to do next—your calling in life, for instance. You want to know
what action to take in a certain matter. You want to know what to do
with your money. You want to know whether to go into a certain scheme
or not. Then you enter into this private chamber of God's will, and ask
the private question, "Lord, what wouldest Thou have me to do?"

Then it is distinguished by its action. It concerns a different depart-
ment of our life. The first part of God's will, all that has gone before,
affects our *character*. But this affects something more. It affects our *career*.
And this is an important distinction. A man's career in life is almost as
important as his character in life; that is to say, it is almost as important
to God, which is the real question. If character is the end of life, then
the ideal career is just where character can best be established and developed. A man is to live for his character. But if God's will is the end of
life, God may have a will for my career as well as for my character,
which does not mean that a man is to live for his career, but for God's
will *in* his character *through* his career.

I may want to put all my work upon my character. But God may
want my work for something else. He may want to use me, for instance;
I may not know why, or when, or how or for whom. But it is possible
He may need me, for something or other at some time or other. It may
be all through my life, or at some particular part of my life which may
be past now, or may be still to come. At all events, I must hold myself
in readiness and let Him trace my path. Though it does not look now
as if He had anything for me to do, the next turn of the road may bring
it; I must watch the turnings of the road for God. Even for the chance
of God needing me it is worthwhile doing this—the chance of Him
needing me even once. There is a man in Scripture whom God perhaps
used but once. He may have done many other things for God; still, there
was one thing God gave him to do so far overshadowing all other things
that he seems to have done but this. He seems, indeed, to have been
born, to have lived and died for this. It is the only one thing we know
about him. But it is a great thing. His name was Ananias. He was the
instrument in the conversion of Paul. What was he doing in Damascus

that day, when Paul arrived under conviction of sin? Why was he living in Damascus at all? Because he was born there, and his father before him perhaps you will say. Let it be so. A few will be glad to cherish a higher thought. He was a good man, and his steps were ordered—by ordinary means, if you like—by the Lord. Could Ananias not have been as good a man in Jericho or Antioch or Ephesus? Quite as good. His character might almost have been the same. But his career would have been different. And, possibly, his character might have been different from the touch of God upon his career. For when God comes into a man's career, it sometimes makes a mighty difference on his character—teaches him to live less for character and for himself, and more for his career and for God, rather more for both—more for his character by living more for his career. Gold is gold wherever it is, but it is some difference to the world whether it make a communion cup or gild the proscenium of a theatre.

There is a difference, then, between God in character and God in career. You may have God in your character without having God in your career. Perhaps you should have been in London today, perhaps in China. Perhaps you should have been a missionary; perhaps you should be one yet. Perhaps you should have been in poorer circumstances, or in a different business altogether. Perhaps you have chosen a broader path than God would have willed for you. Your character may not seem to have suffered; but your career has. You may be doing God's will with one hand consecrated to Christ, and making your own autobiography with the other consecrated to self.

Would you know the will of God, then? Consult God about your career. It does not follow because He has done nothing with you last week or last year, He may have nothing for you now. God's will in career is mostly an unexpected thing—it comes as a surprise. God's servants work on short notices. Paul used to have to go off to what was the end of the world in those days, on a few hours' warning. And so may you and I. It is not a thing to startle us, to alarm us, to make us say, "If this might be the upshot we would let God's will alone." It would be a wonderful privilege to come to you or me; yes, a wonderful privilege that He should count us worthy to suffer this or anything more for Him.

But you are old, you say. Ananias was old. Or steeped in a profession. Paul was steeped in a profession. Or you are inexperienced and young. A lad came to Jesus once with five loaves and two small fishes, but they fed five thousand men. So bring your lad's experience, your young offer of service, and God may use you to twice five thousand souls. That does not mean that you are to do it. But be in God's counsels, and He will teach you yes or no.

How are you to know this secret will of God? It is a great question. We cannot touch it now. Let this suffice. It can be known. It can be known to you. The steps of a good man are ordered by the Lord. "I will guide thee with Mine eye." Unto the upright in heart He shall cause light to arise in darkness. This is no mysticism, no visionary's dream. It is not to drown the reason with enthusiasm's airy hope or supercede the word of God with fanaticism's blind caprice. No, it is not that. It is what Christ said, "The sheep hear His voice, and He calleth His own sheep by name, and leadeth them."

CHAPTER FOURTEEN

THE RELATION OF THE WILL
OF GOD TO SANCTIFICATION

"This is the will of God, even your sanctification."—I Thess. iv. 3

"As He which hath called you is holy, so be ye holy in all manner of conversation; because it is written, 'Be ye holy, for I am holy.'"—I Pet. i. 15, 16.

"Lo, I come to do Thy will, O God. . . . By the which will we are sanctified through the offering of the body of Jesus Christ once for all."—Heb. x. 9, 10.

Our discussion of the will of God landed us—perhaps in rather an unforeseen way—in the great subject of sanctification. You may remember that we made this discovery, that the end of sanctification, in the sense of consecration, is to do the will of God, and that the proof was based on these words: "Present your bodies a living sacrifice, holy, acceptable unto God, and be not conformed to this world." Why? "That ye may prove what is that good and acceptable and perfect will of God." We are to present ourselves to God, not because it is a pleasant and luxurious thing to live in the state of consecration, but to do the will of God. Or, to sum this up in a single sentence, it might read: "This is sanctification, even to prove the will of God."

But our text today is apparently the very opposite of this. "This is the will of God, even your sanctification." Then it looked as if sanctification was in order to the will of God; now it looks as if the will of God was in order to sanctification.

It is evident, therefore, that there is still something in this part of the subject which demands a clearance. And in order to gain this it will be necessary to present the other side of the same question, and complete the view of the subject of holiness itself.

There are in the Bible two great meanings to the word sanctification. The first may be roughly called the Old Testament word. The second is identified, but not exclusively, with the New. The Old Testament meaning had this peculiarity, that it did not necessarily imply any inward change in the heart sanctified. In fact, it was not even necessarily applied to hearts at all, but to things. A field could be sanctified, a house could be sanctified, an altar, a tabernacle, gold and silver vessels, the garments of the priest, the cities of refuge. Anything, in short, that was set apart for sacred use was said to be *sanctified*. But the New Testament word had a deeper meaning. It meant not only outward consecration, but inward holiness. It meant an internal purification of the heart from all uncleanness, and an enduing it with the mind of Christ. It was not a mere separation like the first, but a visitation—a separation from the lower world, and a visitation from the higher, the coming in of God's Spirit from above with a principle of holiness that was to work an inward likeness to the character of God.

The practical object of the first process is mainly to put the thing in position where God can use it. A golden candlestick was sanctified, so that it might be of some use to God. A house was sanctified, so that it might be exclusively His—to do what He liked with it. In like manner a man is consecrated—that God may use him. It is the process by which he is put into position for God. And all that sanctification does for him, in the first sense of the word, is so to put him in position that he shall always be within reach of God—that he shall do what God likes, do, that is to say, what God wills.

But there is something more in sanctification than man's merely being a tool in the hands of God. If there were not, automatons could do the work far better than men. They would never oppose God's will, and they would always be in position. But God's will has a reaction upon the instruments whom He employs. God's will does not stop with His will, as it were. It recoils back upon the person using it, and benefits him. If the instrument is a sanctified cup, or a sanctified house, it does not recoil back, and make an internal change in them; but if it is a person who does God's will, God's will is not only done, but the person or doer is affected. God never keeps anything all to Himself. He who so loved the world that He gave His only begotten Son, does He not with Him also freely give us all things? His Son is for us, His love is for us, His will is for us. How do we know that it is for us? Because this is the will of God, even your sanctification.

Whatever else may be involved in it, this is in it; whatever else He may get from it, this is something which you get, your sanctification. "By the which will," as Hebrews says, "we are sanctified." "This is My will, not My gain, but yours; not My eternal advantage, but yours; not My holiness, but 'your sanctification.'" Do you think God wants your body when He asks you to present it to Him? Do you think it is for His sake that He asks it, that He might be enriched by it? God could make a thousand better with a breath. It is for your sake He asks it. He wants your gift to give you His gift—your gift which was just in the way of His gift. He wants your will out of the way, to make room for His will. You give everything to God. God gives it all back again, and more. You present your body a living sacrifice that you may prove God's will. You shall prove it by getting back your body—a glorified body. You lose the world that you may prove God's will. God's will is that you shall gain heaven. This is the will of God, therefore, that you should gain heaven. Or this is the will of God that you should gain holiness, for holiness is heaven. Or this is the will of God, even your sanctification.

To sum up these facts, then, we find that they shape themselves into these two propositions:—

1. Our sanctification, or, more strictly, our consecration, is in order to the will of God, "to prove what is that good and acceptable and perfect will of God."

2. This reacts upon ourselves—a conspicuous part of God's will being that we should be personally holy. "This is the will of God, even your sanctification."

The first of these has already been discussed, and now the question comes to be how we can best fulfill this conspicuous part of the will of God and become holy ourselves. It is God's will for all of us that we should become holy. How are we to become holy?

We have probably asked this question many times already in our life. We have thought, and read, and prayed about it, and perhaps we have never reached the conclusion how indeed we are to become holy. Perhaps the question has long ago assumed another and evasive form with us,

"When are we going to become holy?" or perhaps a hopeless form, "How *ever* are we to become holy?"

Now the real way out of the difficulty is to ask a deeper question still: "Why do I want to be holy?" All the great difficulties of religion are centered round our motives. Impurities in a spiritual stream generally mean impurities at the spiritual source. All fertility or barrenness of soul depends upon which source supplies the streams of the desires. Our difficulties about becoming holy, therefore, most likely lie in our reasons for wanting to become holy. For if you grant the true motive to holiness, you need no definition of holiness. True holiness lies in touching the true motive. We shall get nearer the true roots of holiness, therefore, if we spend a little time over the root question: "Why do I want to be holy?"

1. The first thing which started some of us to search for a better life, perhaps, was *infection*. We caught an infection for a better life from someone we knew. We were idling our own way through life, when someone crossed our path—some one with high aims and great enthusiasms. We were taken with the principles on which that life was lived. Its noble purpose charmed us: its disregard of the petty troubles and cares of life astonished us. We felt unaccountably interested in it. There was a romance in its earnestness and self-denial that captivated us, and we thought we should like to take down our own life, and put it together again on this new plan. So we got our first motive to holiness.

Now this was not a wrong motive—it was only an imperfect one. It answered its purpose—so far. For God takes strange ways to start a man's religion. There is nothing more remarkable in the history of conversion, for instance, than the infinite diversity of answers to this question: "What made you first think about your soul?" God does take strange ways to start a man for heaven. The way home is sometimes shown him by an unexpected finger-post; and from a motive so unworthy that he dare not tell it in afterlife, there comes to many a man his first impulse toward God. And long after he has begun to run the Christian race, God may try to hasten his lagging steps by the spur of a motive as far beneath an heir of heaven as his spiritual life is beneath what it ought to be.

But the principle to be noted through it all is this, that the motives which God allows us to start on are not the ones we are to live on. It may be adversity in business that gives us a fresh start. It may be affliction, or ambition, or church-pride, or a thousand things. But such an impulse cannot last, and it cannot carry us far. And there must come a time to exchange it for a higher one if we would grow in grace, or move onward into a holier life. A man's motive must grow, if grace would grow. And many a man has to live on old grace, because he lives on an old motive. God let us begin with a lower one, and then when He gave us more grace, it was that we might get a higher one; but we spent the grace on something else, and our motive is no higher than before. So, although we got a start in religion, we were little the better for it, and our whole life has stood still for want of a strong enough motive to go on.

2. It was not necessary that we should have caught our infection from a friend. There is another great source of infection, and some of us are breathing its atmosphere every day—*books*. We may have got our motives to be good from a book. We found in works on ethics, and in all great poets, and even perhaps in some novels, that the highest aim of life was to be true and pure and good. We found modern literature ringing with the praises of virtue. By-and-by we began to respect it, then to admire it, then to wish for it. Thus we caught the enthusiasm for purity which has changed our whole lives, in a way, and given us a chief motive to religion.

Well, we must thank God for having given us a start, anyhow. It is something to have begun. It is a great thing to have an enthusiasm to be true and pure and good. Nor will the Bible ever be jealous of any lesser book which God may use to stir men up to a better life. But all lesser books sin and come short. And the greatest motives of the greatest of the lesser books fall as far short of the glory of God just as those who live only by the enthusiasms which are kindled on the altar of modern literature fall short of the life and mind of Christ. God may give these motives to a man to start with. If he will not look into God's Book for them, God may see fit to put something remotely like them into men's books. Jesus Christ used to come to men just where they were. There is no place on earth so dark that the light of heaven will not come to it; there is no spot of earth where God may not choose to raise a monument of His love. There is always room anywhere in the world for a holy thought. It may come to a man on the roadside, as to Paul; or in the fork of a sycamore tree, as to Zaccheus. It may come to him at his boats, as to Peter; or at his Bible, as to the Eunuch. But, whether it come at the boats, or whether it come at the Bible, whatever is good is God's; and men may be thankful that the Giver of all good has peopled the whole earth and air and sky with thoughts of His glory, and filled the world with voices which call men near to Him. At the same time, it must be understood again that the initial motives are never meant to continue us far on the road to God. As a matter of fact, they never can continue us, and if a man does not get higher ones, his religion must, and his morality may, come to a bitter end. The melancholy proof occurs to everyone in a moment, that those who inspire us with these almost Divine enthusiasms are, and many of them have been, degraded men and women themselves. For if a man's motives to goodness are not higher than the enthusiasms of his own higher nature, the chances are that the appeals of his lower nature, in time, will either curb or degrade them.

The true motive to holiness, then, is not to be caught from books.

3. In the next place, some of us, perhaps, were induced to aim at a better life from *prudential* motives, or from *fear.*

We had read in the Bible a very startling sentence—"Without holiness no man shall see the Lord." Now we wished to see God. And we found the Bible full of commands to keep God's law. So, with fear and trembling, we began to try. Its strictness was a continual stimulus to us. We were kept watching and praying. We lived in an atmosphere of fear, lest we should break it. No doubt this has done good—great good. Like the others, it was not a bad motive—only an imperfect one. But, like the others, it will have to be exchanged for a higher one, if true progress in holy living is to be made.

4. Then some of us found another motive in *gratitude.* The great love of God in Christ had come home to us with a peculiar power. We felt the greatness of His sacrifice for us, of His forgiveness of us. And we would try to return His love. So we set our hearts with a gracious purpose towards God. Our life and conversation should be becoming the gospel of Christ. We would do for His sake what we would never do for our own sake. But even a noble impulse like this has failed to fulfill our heart's desire, and even our generosity has left us little nearer God.

5. And lastly, there is this other thought which has sometimes helped us onward for a time—a feeling which comes over us at communion times, at revival times, which Christian workers feel at all times: "Here are we surrounded by great privileges—singled out from the world for God's peculiar care. God comes very close to us; the very ground is holy oftentimes. What manner of persons ought we to be in all holy conversation and godliness? How different we ought to be from

all the people around! How much more separate from every appearance of evil! How softly we should walk, who bear the vessels of the Lord!"

Now some of these motives are very beautiful. They are the gifts of God. Doubtless many have attained to a certain measure of holiness by employing them. And they have at least awakened in us some longings after God. But they are all deficient, and hopelessly inadequate to carry on what sometimes they so hopefully begin.

And they are deficient in these three ways:—

1. They are unscriptural—rather, they do not convey the full scriptural truth.

2. They are inadequate to produce more than a small degree of holiness.

3. They never produce the true quality of holiness.

If we have not yet had higher motives than these, then it follows that our spiritual life is being laid down upon principles which can never in the nature of things yield the results we had hoped and waited for.

We have been wondering why our growth in grace has been so small—so small, indeed, that sometimes it has almost seemed to cease. And as we look into our hearts, we find this one reason, at least—perhaps the great one—that our *motive* is incomplete.

Now, the weakness of the old motive, apart from the error of it, consisted in this: in the first place it wanted authority; in the second, it proposed no standard. As regards the first, there was no reason why one should strive to be better. It was left to one's own discretion. Our friend said it, or our favorite author, and the obligation rose or fell with the nearness or remoteness of their influence. And as regards the standard, our friend or our favorite author's favorite hero was but a poor model at the best, for only a most imperfect spiritual beauty can ever be copied from anything made of clay.

Well, then, what is the right motive to holiness of life? We have been dealing with ordinary motives hitherto; now we must come to extraordinary ones. Holiness is one of the most extraordinary things in life, and it demands the noblest motives, the noblest impulses, or none. Now we shall see how God has satisfied this demand of our nature for an extraordinary motive to this extraordinary thing, holiness—satisfied it so completely, that the soul, when it finds it out, need never feel unsatisfied again. God's motive to holiness is, *"Be ye holy, for I am holy."*

It is a startling thing when the voice of God comes close to us and whispers, "Be ye holy"; but when the question returns from our lips, "Why should we be holy?" it is a more solemn thing to get this answer, "For I am holy." This is God's motive to holiness—"For I am holy." *Be ye holy:* here is its authority—its divine obligation. *For I am holy*—here is its divine motive.

Be ye holy. Think of the greatness of the obligation. Long ago, when we began the Christian life, we heard a voice, "Be ye holy." Perhaps, as we have seen, it was an infectious voice, the voice of a friend. Perhaps it was an inspiring voice, the voice of poetry and literature. Perhaps it was a warning voice, the voice of the law. But it was not a commanding voice—the voice of God. And the reason was, perhaps, that we were not thinking of the voice: we were thinking of the "holy." We had caught sight of a new and beautiful object—something which seemed full of promise, which was to consecrate even the common hours of our life. The religious world seemed bright to us then, and the books and the men were dear that would help us to reach out our hands to this. It was something new that had come into our life—this fascination of holiness. Had we been asked about the voice which said, "Be ye holy," we should indeed have said it was God's. But, in truth, it was only our own voice, which had caught some far-off echoes from our reading, or our thinking, or our friends. There was no authority in the voice, therefore, and it rested with our own poor wills whether we should grow in holiness or not. Sometimes our will was strong, and we were better men and women then than ever in our lives before; but there were intervals when we listened to another voice, "Be ye prosperous," or "Be ye happy," and then we lost all we had gained.

But with the divine obligation before us, it is no longer optional that we should be holy. We must be holy. And then see how the motive to holiness is attached to the obligation to holiness—the motive for holiness: *"For I am holy."* The motive accounts for the obligation. God's one desire for the whole earth is that it should be holy—just because He is holy. And the best He can do with men is to make them like Himself. The whole earth is His and He would have it all in harmony with Him. God has a right to demand that we should be holy—that every one should be holy, and everything, just because He is holy Himself. To take even the lowest ground, we allow no ornaments in our house that are not lovely and pleasant to the eye. We have no business to cumber God's earth with ourselves if we are not holy—no business to live in the same world with Him. We are an offense to God—discordant notes in the music of the universe.

But God lays this high obligation upon us for our own sake. For this we were made. For this we were born in a Christian land. For this, strange things have happened in our lives—strange pieces of discipline have disturbed their quiet flow, strange troubles, strange providences, strange chastenings. There is no other explanation of the mystery of our life than this, that God would have us holy. At any cost God will have us holy. Whatever else we may be, this one thing we *must* be. This is the will of God, even our sanctification. It is not necessary that we should be prosperous or famous, or happy. But it is necessary that we should be holy; and the deepest moments of our lives give us glimpses sometimes of a more tender reason still why God says, "Be ye holy." It is for our own sakes, because it would be hell to be unholy.

There is now only one thing wanting in our new motive to holiness. We have discovered the sources of its obligation far up in the counsels of God, and deep down in the weakness of our own nature. We have found holiness to be an absolutely necessary virtue—to live without which is to contradict our Maker. But we have not yet looked at its *quality*. The thing we are to pursue so ardently—what is it? How are we to shape it to ourselves when we think of it? Is there any plain definition of it—any form which could be easily stated and easily followed. It may be very easily stated. It is for those who have tried it to say whether it be easily followed. Be ye holy, *as* He is holy. *As* He is holy, as He who hath called you is holy, *so* be ye holy. This is the form of holiness we are asked to aim at. This is the standard, God's commentary on the motive, "As He . . . so ye." Ponder for a moment the difference between these pronouns. *He—Ye. He* who hath called you—Jesus Christ. *He* who did no sin, neither was guile found in his mouth. *He* who when He was reviled, reviled not again. When He suffered, He threatened not. *He* who was without spot or blemish, in whom even His enemies found no fault.

Ye the fallen children of a fallen race. *Ye* with hearts deceitful above all things, and desperately wicked. *Ye* are to become as *He.* The two pronouns are to approach one another. The crucifiers are to work their way up to the crucified. *Ye* are to become as *He.* Here is a motive as high as the holiness of God. It makes us feel as if we had our life-work before us still. We have scarcely even begun to be like God—for we began perhaps with no higher motive than to be like some one else—not like God at all. But the little betterness that we get from books, the chance impulses that come from other lives, have never fulfilled in us the will of God—could never sanctify such hearts as ours and make *ye* become as *He.*

No doubt a great deal of human good is possible to man before he touches the character of Christ. High human motives and human aims may make a noble human life. But they never make a holy life. A holy life is a life like Christ's. And whatever may be gained from the lower motives to a better life, one thing must necessarily be absent from them all—the life like Christ's, or rather, the spirit like Christ's. For the life like Christ's can only come from Christ; and the spirit of Christ can only be caught from Christ.

Hence, therefore, we come at last to the profound meaning of another text which stands alone in the Word of God and forms the only true climax to such a subject as this.

"Lo I come to do Thy will, O God," the author of the Hebrews quotes from David, and goes on to add, *"By the which will we are sanctified."* Christ came to do God's will, by the which will we are sanctified. This is the will of God, even your sanctification. But the writer of the Hebrews adds another lesson: "By the which will we are sanctified." How? "Through the offering of the body of Jesus Christ once for all." Our sanctification is not in books, or in noble enthusiasm, or in personal struggles after a better life. It is in the offering of the body of Jesus Christ once for all. Justification is through the blood of Jesus Christ once for all. Sanctification is through the body of Jesus Christ once for all. It is not a thing to be generated, but to be received. It is not to be generated in fragments of experience at one time and another—it is already complete in Christ. We have only to put on Christ. And though it may take a lifetime of experience to make it ours, the sanctification, whenever it come, can only come from Christ. If we ever are sanctified, it will only be because, and inasmuch as we have Christ. Our sanctification is not what morality gives, not even what the Bible gives, not even what Christ gives, it is what Christ *lives.* It is Christ Himself.

The reason why we resort so much to lower impulses to a Christian life is imperfect union with Christ. We take our doctrines from the Bible and our assurance from Christ. But for want of the living bright reality of His presence in our hearts we search the world all round for impulses. We search religious books for impulses, and tracts and sermons, but in vain. They are not there. "I am Alpha and Omega, the beginning and the end." "Christ is all and in all." The beginning of all things is in the will of God. The end of all things is in sanctification through faith in Jesus Christ. "By the which will ye are sanctified." Between these two poles all spiritual life and Christian experience run. And no motive outside Christ can lead a man to Christ. If your motive to holiness is not as high as Christ, it cannot make you rise to Christ. For water cannot rise above its level. "Beware, therefore, lest any man spoil you through philosophy and vain deceit, after the tradition of men, after the rudiments of the world, and not after Christ. For in Him dwelleth all the fullness of the Godhead bodily. And ye are complete in Him which is the head of all principality and power" (2 Col. viii. 10). "Who of God is made unto us wisdom and righteousness, and sanctification, and redemption" (1 Cor. i. 30). "*As* ye have therefore received the Lord Jesus, *so* walk ye *in Him.*"

Chapter Fifteen
HOW TO KNOW THE WILL OF GOD

"If any man will do His will, he shall know of the doctrine, whether it be of God."—John vii. 17.

There is an experience which becomes more and more familiar to everyone who is trying to follow Christ—a feeling of the growing loneliness of his Christian life. It comes from a sense of the peculiarly personal interest which Christ takes in him, which sometimes seems so strong as almost to make him feel that his life is being detached from all the other lives around him, that it is being drawn out of the crowd of humanity, as if an unseen arm linked in his were taking him aside for a nearer intimacy and a deeper and more private fellowship. It is not, indeed, that the great family of God is to be left in the shade for him, or that he is in any way the favorite of heaven; but it is the sanctifying and, in the truest sense, humbling realization that God makes Himself as real to each poor unit as if he were the whole; so that even as in coming to Christ at first he felt himself the only lost, so now in staying with Christ he feels himself the only found. And it is, perhaps, true that without any loss in the feeling of saintly communion with all those throughout the world who say "Our Father" with him in their prayers, the more he feels that Christ has all of him to Himself, the more he feels that he has Christ all to himself. Christ has died for other men, but in a peculiar sense for him. God has a love for all the world, but a peculiar love for him. God has an interest in all the world, but a peculiar interest in him. This is always the instinct of a near fellowship, and it is true of the universal fellowship of God with His own people.

But if there is one thing more than another which is more personal to the Christian—more singularly his than God's love or God's interest—one thing which is a finer symbol of God's love and interest, it is the knowledge of God's will—the private knowledge of God's will. And this is more personal, just as it is more private. My private portion of God's love is only a private *share* in God's love—only a part—the same in quality and kind as all the rest of God's love, which all the others get from God. But God's will is a thing for myself. There is a will of God for me which is willed for no one else besides. It is not a share in the universal will, in the same sense as I have a share in the universal love. It is a particular will for me, different from the will He has for anyone else—a private will—a will which no one else knows about, and which no one can know about, but me.

To be sure, as we have seen before, God had likewise a universal will for me and every man. In the Ten Commandments, in conscience, in the Beatitudes of Christ, God tells all the world His will. There is no secret about this part, it is as universal as His love. It is the will on which the character of every man is to be formed and conformed to God's.

But there is a will for career as well as for character. There is a will for *where*—in what place, viz., in this town or another town—I am to become like God as well as *that* I am to become like God. There is a will for where I am to be, and what I am to be, and what I am to do tomorrow. There is a will for what scheme I am to take up, and what work I am to do for Christ, and what business arrangements to make, and what money to give away. This is God's private will for me, for every step I take, for the path of life along which He points my way: God's will for my *career*.

If I have God's will in my character, my life may become great and good. It may be useful and honorable, and even a monument of the sanctifying power of God. But it will only be a life. However great and pure it be, it can be no more than a life. And it ought to be a mission. There should be no such thing as a Christian life. Each life should be a mission.

God has a life-plan for every human life. In the eternal counsels of His will, when He arranged the destiny of every star, and every sand-grain and grassblade, and each of those tiny insects which live but for an hour, the Creator had a thought for you and me. Our life was to be the slow unfolding of this thought, as the cornstalk from the grain of corn, or the flower from the gradually opening bud. It was a thought of what we were to be, of what we might become, of what He would have us do with our days and years, our influence and our lives. But we all had the terrible power to evade this thought, and shape our lives from another thought, from another will, if we chose. The bud could only become a flower, and the star revolve in the orbit God had fixed. But it was man's prerogative to choose his path, his duty to choose it in God. But the divine right to choose at all has always seemed more to him than his duty to choose in God, so, for the most part, he has taken his life from God, and cut his career for himself.

It comes to pass, therefore, that there are two great classes of people in the world of Christians today:

(1) Those who have God's will in their character;

(2) Those who have God's will likewise in their career.

The first are in the world to live. They have a *life*. The second are in the world to minister. They have a *mission*.

Now those who belong to the first class, those who are simply living in the world and growing character, however finely they may be developing their character, cannot understand too plainly that they are not fulfilling God's will. They are really outside a great part of God's will altogether. They understand the universal part, they are molded by it, and their lives are in some sense noble and true. But they miss the private part, the secret whispering of God in the ear, the constant message from earth to heaven. "Lord, what wilt Thou have me to do?" They never have the secret joy of asking a question like this, the wonderful sense in asking it, of being in the counsels of God, the overpowering thought that God has taken notice of you, and your question—that He will let you do something, something peculiar, personal, private, which no one else has been given to do. This thought gives life for God its true sublimity, and makes a perpetual sacrament of all its common things. Life to them is at the best a bare and selfish thing, for the truest springs of action are never moved at all; and the strangest thing in human history, the bounding of the career from step to step, from circumstance to circumstance, from tragedy to tragedy, is unexplained and unrelated, and hangs, a perpetual mystery, over life.

The great reason possibly why so few have thought of taking God into their career is that so few have really taken God into their life. No one ever thinks of having God in his career, or need think, until his life is fully molded into God's. And no one will succeed in knowing even what God in his career can mean till he know what it is to have God in the secret chambers of his heart. It requires a well-kept life to know the will of God, and none but the Christ-like in character can know the Christ-like in career.

It has happened, therefore, that the very fact of God's guidance in the individual life has been denied. It is said to give life an importance quite foreign to the Divine intention in making man. One life, it is argued, is of no more importance than any other life, and to talk of special providences happening every hour of every day is to detract from the majesty and dignity of God; in fact, it reduces a religious life to a mere religious caprice, and the thought that God's will is being done to a hallucination of the mind.

And there is another side to the objection, which though less pronounced and definite, is subtly dangerous still—that there does indeed seem to be some warrant in Scripture for getting to know the will of God, but that, in the first place, that probably means only on great occasions which come once or twice in a lifetime; and, in the second, that the whole subject is so obscure that, all things considered, a man had better walk by his own common sense, and leave such mysteries alone.

But the Christian cannot allow the question to be put off with poor evasions like these. Every day, indeed, and many times a day, the question rises in a hundred practical forms. "What is the will of God for me? What is the will of God for me today, just now, for the next step, for this arrangement and for that, and this amusement, and this projected work for Christ?" For all these he feels he must consult the will of God; and that God has a will for him in all such things, and that it must be possible somehow to know what that will is, is not only a matter of hope, but a point in his doctrine and creed.

Now without stopping to vindicate the reasonableness of such expectations as these, it may simply be affirmed as a matter of fact that there are a number of instruments for finding out the will of God. One of them is a very great instrument, so far surpassing all the rest in accuracy that there may be said to be but one which has never been known to fail. The others are smaller and clumsier, much less delicate, indeed, and they often fail. They often fail to come within sight of the will of God at all, and are so far astray at other times as to mistake some other thing for it. Still they are instruments, and notwithstanding their defects, have a value by themselves. When the greater instrument employs their humbler powers to second its attempts, they immediately become as keen and as unerring as itself.

The most important of these minor instruments is reason, and although it is a minor instrument, it is great enough in many a case to reveal the secret will of God. God is taking your life and character through a certain process, for example. He is running your career along a certain chain of events. And sometimes the light which He is showing you stops, and you have to pick your way for a few steps by the dimmer light of thought. But it is God's will for you then to use this thought, and to elevate it through regions of consecration, into faith, and to walk by this light till the clearer beam from His will comes back again.

Another of these instruments is experience. There are many paths in life which we all tread more than once. God's light was by us when we walked them first, and lit a beacon here and there along the way. But the next time He sent our feet along that path He knew the sidelights should be burning still, and let us walk alone.

And then there is circumstance. God closes things in around us till our alternatives are all reduced to one. That one, if we must act, is probably the will of God just then.

And then there is the advice of others—an important element at least—and the welfare of others, and the example to others, and the many other facts and principles which make up the moral man, which, if not strong enough always to discover what God's will is, are not too feeble oftentimes to determine what it is *not*.

Even the best of these instruments, however, has but little power in its own hands. The ultimate appeal is always to the one great instrument, which uses them in turn as it requires, and which supplements their discoveries, or even supplants them if it choose by its own superior light, and might, and right. It is like some great glass that can sweep the skies in the darkest night and trace the motions of the furthest stars, while all the rest can but see a faint uncertain light piercing for a moment here and there the clouds which lie between.

And this great instrument for finding out God's will, this instrument which can penetrate where reason cannot go, where observation has not been before, and memory is helpless, and the guiding hand of circumstance has failed, has a name which is seldom associated with any end so great. It is a name which every child may understand, even as the stupendous instrument itself with all its mighty powers is sometimes moved by infant hands when others have tried in vain.

The name of the instrument is obedience. Obedience, as it is sometimes expressed, is the organ of spiritual knowledge. As the eye is the organ of physical sight; the mind, of intellectual sight; so the organ of spiritual vision is this strange power, obedience.

This is one of the great discoveries the Bible has made to the world. It is purely a Bible thought. Philosophy never conceived a truth so simple and yet so sublime. And, although it was known in Old Testament times and expressed in Old Testament books, it was reserved for Jesus Christ to make the full discovery to the world, and add to His teaching another of the profoundest truths which have come from heaven to earth—that the mysteries of the Father's will are hid in this word "obey."

The circumstances in which Christ made the great discovery to the world are known to everyone.

The Feast of Tabernacles was in progress in Jerusalem when Jesus entered the temple to teach. A circle of Jews was gathered round Him who seem to have been spellbound with the extraordinary wisdom of His words. He made no pretension to be a scholar. He was no graduate of the Rabbinical schools. He had no access to the sacred literature of the people. Yet here was this stranger from Nazareth confounding the wisest heads in Jerusalem, and unfolding with calm and effortless skill such truths as even these temple walls had never heard before. Then "the Jews marveled, saying, 'How knoweth this man letters, never having learned?'" What organ of spiritual knowledge can He have, never having learned? *Never having learned*—they did not know that Christ *had* learned. They did not know the school at Nazareth whose Teacher was in heaven—whose schoolroom was a carpenter's shop—the lesson, the Father's will. They knew not that hidden truths could come from God, or wisdom from above.

What came to them was gathered from human books, or caught from human lips. They knew no organ save the mind; no instrument of knowing the things of heaven but that by which they learned in the schools. But Jesus points to a spiritual world which lay still far beyond, and tells them of the spiritual eye which reads its profounder secrets and reveals the mysteries of God. "My doctrine is not Mine," He says, "but His that sent Me"; and "My judgment is just," as He taught before, "because I seek not Mine own will, but the will of the Father which hath sent Me." And then, lest men should think this great experience was never meant for them, He applies His principles to every human mind which seeks to know God's will. "If any man will do His will, he shall know of the doctrine, whether it be of God."

The word doctrine here is not to be taken in our sense of the word doctrine. It is not the doctrine of theology. "Any man" is to know if he will do His will. But it is God's teaching—God's mind. If any man will do His will, he shall know God's mind; he shall know God's teaching and God's will.

In this sense, or indeed in the literal sense, from the first look at these words it appears almost as if a contradiction were involved. To *know* God's will is *to do* God's will. But how are we to *do* God's will *until* we know it? To *know* it; that is the very dilemma we are in. And it seems no way out of it to say, "*Do* it and you shall *know* it." We want to know it, in order to do it; now we are told to do it, in order to know it! If any man *do*, he shall *know*.

But that is not the meaning of the words. That is not even the words themselves. It is not, if any man *do*, he shall know; but if any man *will* do. And the whole sense of the passage turns upon that word *will*. It means, "If any man *is willing* to do, he shall know." He does not need to do His will in order to know—he only need be willing to do it. For "will" is not at all the sign of the future tense as it looks. It is not connected with the word "do" at all, but a separate verb altogether, meaning "is willing," or "wills." If any man wills, or if any man is willing, to do, he shall know.

Now notice the difference this makes in the problem. Before, it looked as if the doing were to come first and then the knowing His will; but now another element is thrown in at the very beginning. Being willing comes first and then the knowing; and thereafter the doing may follow—the doing, that is to say, if the will has been sufficiently clear to proceed.

The whole stress of the passage therefore turns on this word "will." And Christ's answer to the question, "How to know the will of God?" may be simply stated thus: "If any man is willing to do God's will he shall know," or, in plainer language still, "If any man is sincerely trying to do God's will, he shall know."

The connection of all this with obedience is just that being willing is the highest form of obedience. It is the spirit and essence of obedience. There is an obedience in the world which is no obedience, because the act of obedience is there, but the spirit of submission is not.

"A certain man," we read in the Bible, "had two sons; and he came to the first, and said, 'Son, go work today in my vineyard.' He answered, 'I will not': but afterward he repented and went. And he came to the second, and said likewise. And he answered, 'I go, sir': and went not. Whether of them twain did the will of his father?" Obedience here comes out in its true colors as a thing in the will. And if any man have an obeying will, a truly single and submissive will, he shall know of the teaching, or of the leading, whether it be of God.

If we were to carry out this principle into a practical case, it might be found to work in some such way as this: Tomorrow, let us say, there is some difficulty before us in our path. It lies across the very threshold of our life, and we cannot begin the working week without, at least, some notice that it is there. It may be some trifling item of business life, over which unaccountable suspicions have begun to gather of late, and to force themselves in spite of everything into thought and conscience, and even into prayer. Or, it may be, some change of circumstance is opening up, and alternatives are appearing, and demanding choice of one. Perhaps it is some practice in our life which the clearing of the spiritual atmosphere and increasing light from God are hinting to be wrong, while reason cannot coincide exactly and condemn. At all events there is something on the mind—something to do, to suffer, to renounce—and there are alternatives on the mind to distinguish, to choose from, to reject. Suppose, indeed, we made this case a personal as well as an illustrative thing, and the question rises, How are we to separate God's light on the point from our own, disentangle our thoughts on the point from His, and be sure we are following His will, not the reflected image of ours?"

The first process towards this discovery naturally would be one of outlook. Naturally we would set to work by collecting all the possible materials for decision from every point of the compass, balancing the one consequence against the other, then summing up the points in favor of each by itself, until we chose the one which emerged at last with most of reason on its side. But this would only be the natural man's way out of the dilemma. The spiritual man would go about it in another way. This way, he would argue, has no religion in it at all, except perhaps the acknowledgment that reason is divine; and though it might be quite possible and even probable that the light should come to him through the medium of reason, yet he would reach his conclusion, and likely a different conclusion, quite from another side.

And his conclusion would likewise be a better and sounder conclusion. For the insight of the non-religious method may be impaired, and the real organ of knowing God's will so out of order from disuse, that even reason would be biased in its choice. A heart not quite subdued to God is an imperfect element, in which His will can never live; and the intellect which belongs to such a heart is an imperfect instrument and cannot find God's will unerringly—for God's will is found in regions which obedience only can explore.

Accordingly, he would go to work from the opposite side from the first. He would begin not in out-look, but in in-look. He would not give his mind to observation. He would devote his soul to self-examination, to self-examination of the most solemn and searching kind. For this principle of Christ is no concession to an easy life, or a careless method of rounding a difficult point. It is a summons rather to learn the highest and most sacred thing in heaven, by bracing the heart to the loftiest and severest sacrifice on earth—the bending of an unwilling human will till it blends in the will of God. It means that the heart must be watched with a jealous care, and most solemnly kept for God. It means that the hidden desires must be taken out one by one and regenerated by Christ— that the faintest inclination of the soul, when touched by the spirit of God, must be prepared to assume the strength of will and act at any cost. It means that nothing in life should be dreaded so much as that the soul should ever lose its sensitiveness to God; that God should ever speak and find the ear just dull enough to miss what He has said; that God should have some active will for so be ready to make it our daily prayer, that we may know God's will; and when the heart is prepared like this, and the wayward will is drilled in sacrifice and patience to surrender all for the human will to perform, our hearts will not be the first in the world to be ready to obey.

When we have attained this by meditation, by self-examination, by consecration, and by the Holy Spirit's power, God's will may come out in our career at every turning of our life, and be ours not only in sacramental aspiration but in act.

To search for God's will with such an instrument is scarce to search at all. God's will lies transparently in view at every winding of the path. If perplexity sometimes comes, in such way as has been supposed, the mind will gather the phenomena into the field of vision, as carefully, as fully, as laboriously, as if no light would come at all, and then stand still and wait till the wonderful discerning faculty of the soul, that eye which beams in the undivided heart and looks right out to God from every willing mind, fixes its gaze on one far distant spot, one spot perhaps which is dark to all the world besides, where all the lights are focused in God's will.

How this finite and this infinite are brought to touch, how this invisible will of God is brought to the temporal heart must ever remain unknown. The mysterious meeting-place in the prepared and willing heart between the human and divine—where, precisely, the will is finally moved into line with God's—of these things knoweth no man save only the Spirit of God.

The wind bloweth where it listeth. "We hear the sound thereof, but cannot tell whence it cometh or whither it goeth." When every passion is annihilated, and no thought moves in the mind, and all the faculties are still waiting for God, the spiritual eye may trace perhaps some delicate motion in the soul, some thought which stirs like a leaf in the unseen air and tells that God is there. It is not the stillness, nor the unseen breath, nor the thought that only stirred, but these three mysteries in one which reveal God's will to me. God's light, it is true, does not supersede, but illuminates our thoughts. When God sends an angel to trouble the pool let us have faith for the angel's hand, and believe that some power of heaven has stirred the waters in our soul.

Let us but get our hearts in position for knowing the will of God— only let us be willing to know God's will in our hearts that we may do God's will in our lives, and we shall raise no questions as to how this will may come, and feel no fears in case the heavenly light should go.

But let it be remembered, as already said, that it requires a well-kept life to will to do this will. It requires a well-kept life to *do* the will of God, and even a better-kept life to *will* to do His will. To be willing is a rarer grace than to be doing the will of God. For he who is willing may sometimes have nothing to do, and must only be willing to wait; it is far easier to be doing God's will than to be willing to have nothing to do—it is far easier to be working for Christ than it is to be willing to cease. No, there is nothing rarer in the world today than the truly willing soul, and there is nothing more worth coveting than the will to will God's will. There is no grander possession for any Christian life than the transparently simple mechanism of a sincerely obeying heart. And if we could keep the machinery clear, there would be lives in thousands doing God's will on earth even as it is done in heaven. There would be God in many a man's career whose soul is allowed to drift—

a useless thing to God and the world—with every changing wind of life, and many a noble Christian character rescued from wasting all its virtues on itself and saved for work for Christ.

And when the time of trial comes, and all in earth and heaven is dark and even God's love seems dim: what is there left to cling to but this will of the willing heart, a God-given, Godward bending will, which says amidst the most solemn and perplexing vicissitudes of life:

> "Father, I know that all my life
> Is portioned out for me;
> The changes that are sure to come
> I do not fear to see;
> I ask Thee for a present mind,
> Intent on pleasing Thee."